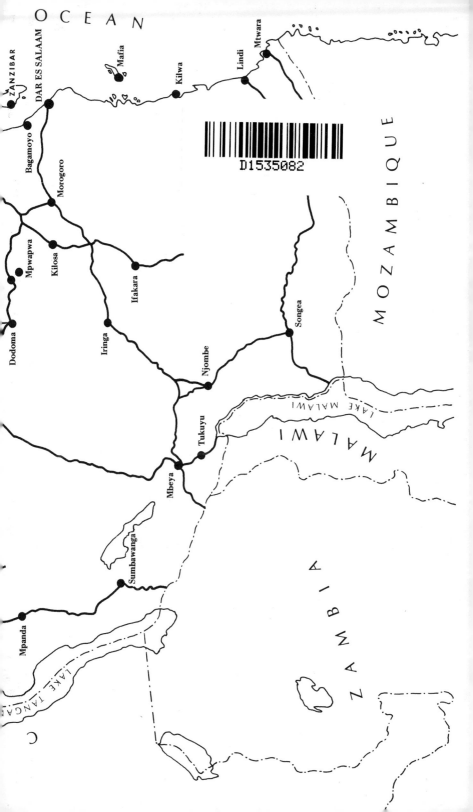

Hoover Institution Publications

VUTA KAMBA*

*"Hit the bricks"—a strike slogan

VUTA KAMBA
THE DEVELOPMENT OF TRADE UNIONS IN TANGANYIKA

William H. Friedland

Hoover Institution Press

Stanford University • Stanford, California

The Hoover Institution on War, Revolution and Peace, founded at Stanford
University in 1919 by the late President Herbert Hoover, is a center for advanced study and research on public and international affairs in the twentieth
century. The views expressed in its publications are entirely those of the
authors and do not necessarily reflect the views of the Hoover Institution.

Hoover Institution Publications 84
Standard Book Number 8179-1841-8 (hard); 8179-1842-6 (paper)
© 1969 by the Board of Trustees of the Leland Stanford Junior University
Library of Congress Catalog Card Number: 74-81689
Printed in the United States of America

For Joan

Contents

Tables

Charts

Preface

This study deals with the kinds of change that develop within organizations that are transferred from a cultural context in which they have developed "organically" over long periods of time to one in which development occurs with breathtaking speed. While the study concerns a single type of organization in a single country—the trade unions in Tanganyika—the process is widely applicable. The search by the political, social, and economic elite in developing countries for effective developmental models has led to the introduction of a variety of organizational forms.

The book has been a long time in preparation and I must apologize to the many Tanganyikans who have asked again and again when it would be available. Literally hundreds of Tanganyikans have contributed their experience and knowledge toward the gathering of material for the book. I am grateful to them and would like to express my appreciation here. A number of key Tanganyikan unionists contributed unusually to the collection of data. I am especially indebted to Rashidi M. Kawawa, Maynard M. Mpangala, Michael Kamaliza, Patrick Mandawa, Victor Mkello, C. S. Kasanga Tumbo, Alfred Tandau, and Michael Juma for their time and support. Mathew Kashindye, himself an experienced unionist, worked with me as a translator-interpreter and contributed a great deal of substantive material as well.

Field work for the study was initially conducted in Tanganyika between June 1959 and August 1960. A brief return visit in the summer of 1963 permitted an updating of materials on the scene and a number of repeat interviews of union leaders at various levels. The original field work was supported by a Foreign Area Training Fellowship of the Ford Foundation; the return visit was supported by the New York State School of Industrial and Labor Relations and the Center for International Studies of Cornell University. Nor would this work have achieved final publication without the support of the Hoover Institution on War, Revolution and Peace, of Stanford University. I am indebted to all these organizations for their support. The manuscript has benefitted from critical comments by Robert Alford, Gayl Ness, Jay Schulman and John Windmuller. In the preparation of the manuscript I must acknowledge the editorial assistance of Dorothy Nelkin, Dora Flash, Michael Rotkin, and Christine Tapley who edited the manuscript for the Hoover Institution. Ann Albertsmen, Alice Moore, Eileen Baker, and Janet Johnson have typed extensive portions of manuscript.

Note should be made of the continual use of "Tanganyika" rather than "Tanzania" in the manuscript. Although the United Republic of Tanzania has existed since 1964, the fusion of the component parts of Tanganyika and Zanzibar is far from complete. The lack of fusion has been very noticeable to the student of trade unions, since no significant attempts have yet been undertaken to merge the unions in the constituent parts of the Republic. Thus, the present trade union organization, the National Union of Tanganyika Workers, continues to refer only to the mainland portion of the country. Since no part of the manuscript is concerned with Zanzibar, I have used the name Tanganyika throughout.

Abbreviations

AFL-CIO	American Federation of Labor-Congress of Industrial Organizations
ARLD	Annual Report of the Labour Department
ARPC	Annual Reports of the Provincial Commissioners
CJC	Central Joint Council of the Sisal Industry
DGB	Deutscher Gewerkschaftsbund (German Trade Union Federation)
GTUC	Ghana Trades Union Congress
ICFTU	International Confederation of Free Trade Unions
ITF	International Transport Workers Federation
ITS	International trades secretariats
JSAC	All Line Joint Staff Advisory Council of the East Africa Railways and Harbours Administration
JSC	Joint Staff Council
NUTA	National Union of Tanganyika Workers
PWD	Public Works Department
RAU	Railway African Union
TALGWU	Tanganyika African Local Government Workers Union
TANU	Tanganyika African National Union
TFL	Tanganyika Federation of Labour
TGWU	Transport and General Workers Union
TRAU	Tanganyika Railway African Union
TUC	Trades Union Congress (Great Britain)
WFTU	World Federation of Trade Unions

I Institutional Transfer

VUTA KAMBA—"shut 'er down," "hit the bricks," or just plain "strike"—
constituted a key slogan for Tanganyikan workers as they began to develop
their trade unions. Introduced only after the second world war, Tanganyika's
workers took to unionism with vigor. Not unsurprisingly, they focused on the
dramatic component of unionism and militant industrial action soon characterized their approach to industrial relationships. Until January 1964 when,
by government action, the unions were suddenly restructured, VUTA
KAMBA represented the spirit of Tanganyikan unionism. This was a spirit of
militancy, independence, and conflict, and fitted with the ethos of political
self-development that developed concurrently; after independence, this spirit
clashed increasingly with the orientations of the new African government.

In examining the case of African unionism in Tanganyika, this study is
concerned with general questions of social change. Most modern social
theorists have had a continuing interest in the shift from pre-industrial and
industrial society; this study follows in this genre. The shift in social structure
from pre-industrial to industrial generated much of the interest of early sociologists. It was the focus of Saint-Simon's interest in formal organization,
Spencer's discussion of the evolution of society from homogeneity to heterogeneity, Weber's traditional and legal-bureaucratic systems of authority,
Durkheim's mechanical and organic solidarity, Toennies' *Gemeinschaft* and
Gesellschaft, and a great many other typologies too numerous to mention.[1]
In recent years, the focus has changed somewhat to a concern with industrialization and modernization, as sociologists such as Moore, Smelser, Hoselitz,
Parsons,[2] and others have sought to understand the social forces both facili-
tating and impeding change in underdeveloped areas of the world. Nor is the
concern limited to sociologists: political scientists have discovered that the
rapid evolution in underdeveloped areas is providing unusual opportunities
for the examination of the modernization of political systems.[3] Similarly,
anthropologists, finding that traditional tribal communities have largely abandoned their accustomed ways under the onslaught of Western expansion, have
turned increasingly to a consideration of the dynamics of change.

1

In general, studies in social change in all of these areas can be said to be grounded in one of two kinds of theoretical orientations. On the one hand, there are the grand theories which date from the early days of the development of the social sciences and which continue to be generated to a considerable degree. The "cosmic" theories such as those of Toynbee, Teggart, Sorokin, MacIver and, more recently in this area, Parsons,[4] have been so grandiose as to render them almost impossible of empirical verification. On the other hand, there has been a veritable avalanche of descriptive writing which has attempted some small scale generalization. Although several attempts have been made,[5] no success has yet been registered in devising an overreaching and verifiable theory to encompass and interrelate all of these many contributions to the study of society and social change.

The long-standing suggestion of Merton that, given the present state of sociology, there is substantial value in attacking problems in terms of "middle-range theory"[6] underlies the approach of the present study. The purpose of the study is twofold: one, to propose a methodology which may be useful in studying certain limited and well-defined aspects of social change; and two, to formulate some propositions about change which derive from the case study but which may be given other applications in the future by other social scientists. Accordingly, the present study sets out to examine change that takes place in what has been called "institutional transfer."[7] It seeks to delineate the character of transfer in rather specific terms so that transfer can be distinguished from other forms of cultural diffusion. Thus, as a specific case study it serves as the vehicle for examining both what happens during the process and those propositions that can be tested in future studies of institutional transfer.

INSTITUTIONAL TRANSFER: A SPECIAL CASE OF ACCULTURATION

The present study represents an attempt to bring together some concepts of social change from a variety of intellectual disciplines. The anthropologists' interest has focused on cultural evolution and, more important, on change as a result of contact between cultures. The concept of culture contact had its origins in a lengthy dispute among anthropologists over the relative merits of evolution and diffusion.[8] The evolutionists held that human cultures underwent a process of evolution in which each cultural group passed through the same stages. The diffusionists held that cultural products were diffused through cultural contact and that evolutionary stages might be passed by as a result. The sterile controversy over diffusionism versus evolutionism was settled, to the extent that such controversies are settled, largely in favor of the diffusionist approach, although evolutionary theory continues to have some significance.[9] One of the main theories formulated by the diffusionists is that differing cultures passed to each other

2

products of material culture (e.g., tools, technology); institutional patterns (e.g., patrilineal systems of descent); or values and ethical systems (e.g., religious beliefs).

Much of the analysis of culture contact focused on studies of contact between preliterate peoples. Thus, Malinowski showed the passage of cultural items through the *kula* ring in the South Pacific.[10] Similarly, a number of American anthropologists studied the diffusion of the sun dance through American Indian cultures, showing how each utilized the same cultural item in a different way.[11] Anthropologists also studied the spread of European culture to the nonliterate societies in Asia, Africa, South America, and Oceania, as European culture was taken over by indigenous peoples. It was soon noted that this contact, although often through missionaries concerned only with religious and ethical systems, produced extensive change in material and nonmaterial culture.[12] Indigenous social institutions began to lose their "purity," as European culture became incorporated into preliterate society.

Not only were elements of Western culture borrowed extensively but entirely new cultural forms began to appear. Culture contact had widespread ramifications in disorganizing traditional systems, giving rise to protest, messianic, and other kinds of movements, some of which were syncretic.[13]

Attempts were begun in the 1930's by anthropological theorists to encompass the phenomenon of acculturation in a less descriptive and more theoretical manner.[14] The necessity for a theoretical approach became obvious, as increased variety in contact situations emerged from the growing body of descriptive studies of culture contact. Although cultures with superior technologies normally donated many cultural items to those with inferior technologies, in some cases less developed cultures either stubbornly refused to accept superior technologies or became selective. Obviously when contact occurred between cultures, all aspects of culture could not be transmitted nor were all transmitted aspects accepted.

Part of the difficulty with the acculturation theory is that in attempting to handle a broad variety of phenomena—types of cultures, types of contact, the types of cultural items that are exchanged—it has not been very predictive. Therefore, its usefulness in guiding the analysis of acculturative change has been limited. In all likelihood, the attempt to develop a general theory of acculturation has failed because the elements involved in culture contact are still too complex to be manageable. This should not mean, however, that some level of predictiveness cannot be developed and, indeed, the present study represents such an attempt.

Sociologists have generally been less concerned with intercultural contact than have anthropologists. Recently, the development of organizational studies has given rise to a new genre of sociological studies, one aspect of which is concerned with change.[15] Largely, however, organizational change has been examined as a product of the dynamics within a single social system.[16] The present study, though an organizational analysis, seeks to examine a variety of factors producing change when an organization is transferred from one culture context in which it has developed gradually to another where it is introduced at once as a fairly detailed unit. The institution studied is the trade union which was introduced or transferred by a colonial power to fill distinct needs felt to exist in a colony.

THE CONCEPTUAL BASIS FOR THE STUDY OF INSTITUTIONAL TRANSFER

The concept of *institution* is basic to sociology and has had a wide discussion in sociological literature.[17] For our purposes it will suffice to define social institutions as consisting of well-established, understood, and organized patterns of behavior that fulfill certain functions for groups in society as a whole.[18] This study is particularly concerned with the formal organizations that serve as a major embodiment of institutions in modern society. Formal organizations are consciously constituted on the basis of written charters for the purpose of attaining relatively limited goals. Although formal organizations act as the embodiment of institutions, they never encompass all institutional behavior; a great deal of institutional behavior takes place outside the context of formal organization. In the case of institutional transfer, it is the formal organization that is the unit of transfer rather than the more vaguely defined and amorphous institution.

Institutional transfer occurs when institutions—that is, organizations—are diffused as total complexes from one sociocultural context to another. This type of diffusion occurs in relatively short periods of time; e.g., a few years. Institutional transfer thus constitutes a special and limited case of cultural diffusion. The main difference between transfer and diffusion lies in the fact that transfer is a premeditated and purposeful act by individuals who introduce the institution as a unit rather than the institution being gradually assimilated by the receiving culture in some piecemeal and eclectic fashion. This particular study examines a situation in which congeries of cultural products, bound together in the original culture, were transferred as a matter of government policy in an attempt to resolve specific social and administrative problems.

Institutions, in their organized form, have physical possessions which carry, in many cases, much symbolism: i.e., buildings, mimeograph machines, personnel. Institutions also exist in a social sense; that is, as patterns of behavior (roles), independent of material phenomena, which can be analyzed in their own right. In this respect, it is not the institution that is transferred but the idea that actors have of the institution. Thus, unions were not brought from England to Africa; instead a set of ideas about a constellation of roles organized to carry on particular activities and solve certain problems was transferred.

4

Defined in this manner, a considerable number of transfer institutions can be found in Africa and Asia. Cooperatives, political parties, trade unions, universities, and voluntary associations are but a few examples of institutional transfer which have concrete organizational form. Nonorganizational institutional transfer can also exist as, for example, when a legal code is introduced into one cultural context after having developed in a different one.[19] Cases can also be found where institutions are transferred not simply as ideas but as complete units including all personnel required to carry on the work of the institutions.[20]

The difference between the process of transfer when the idea alone is transferred and when idea and personnel are transferred can be seen by comparing trade unions in most of sub-Saharan Africa with those of the Republic of South Africa. In most of sub-Saharan Africa, the idea of trade unionism was taken over directly by Africans without the cultural background or socialization appropriate to modern social institutions. In contrast, European workmen with long experience as trade unionists in the United Kingdom and elsewhere carried the idea of unionism with them to South Africa as well as to Southern Rhodesia and Katanga. Studies of organizational change of this type must concentrate on adaptation to new environments of almost literally transferred organizations. This study, on the other hand, is not concerned with this type of total transfer but considers instead environmental differences and cultural interpretations.

Rose has stated that an institution may be functional to one social group and dysfunctional to another.

> The "function" of an institution depends upon the role one plays in relation to the institution. . . . The British anthropologist Firth provides an example: The trade union has the function of providing security and a proportionate share of the productive wealth to its members, but it is also disruptive from the standpoint of industrial organization. If these are regarded as different orders of functions, can a single functionalist explanation account for the whole institution?[21]

If an institution can have functions and dysfunctions for different groups, it is necessary to specify each affected unit that will be analyzed, so that functions can be considered in relation to each one. This identification is necessary for an understanding of the process of transfer since, as will be shown, donors stress particular institutional elements that are functional from their point of view. Whether these elements are received depends on their functional character for receivers.

Because institutional elements have different meanings to different groups, it is useful to designate functions or institutional elements that are associated with functions as being core or subsidiary to these groups. One social group may see a particular function as core to an institution while another may regard the same function as subsidiary, nonfunctional or possibly even dysfunctional. Thus, to trade unionists, the function of the union as a means for the expression of dissatisfaction can be considered to be core; from the point of view of an employer the expression of dissatisfaction may be dysfunctional because it is disruptive to the enterprise or it may be a subsidiary function. In contrast to the unionists' viewpoint, management might regard the union's core function to be that of social control; that is, to provide an orderly and systematic means for the expression of dissatisfaction that serves to dampen discontent.

The distinction between core and subsidiary functions is not identical to the distinction made by Merton between latent and manifest functions. Merton defines manifest functions as "referring to those objective consequences for the specified unit . . . which contribute to its adjustment or adaptation and were so intended . . . "; latent functions are "unintended and unrecognized consequences of the same order."[22] Merton's delineation is made from the viewpoint of an objective observer. The distinction between core and subsidiary functions refers instead to the views of function in terms of members of the social unit for which the cultural product is relevant.

The concept of core and subsidiary functions relates to another concept: certain functions or institutional elements can be said to partake of a dimension of visibility-invisibility. The functions of an institution will be more visible to a group that defines them as core than will subsidiary functions. Similarly, institutional elements related to core functions will be visible.

Transfer takes place from one sociocultural system, the donors, to another, the receivers.[23] The donors, however, are not always the agents of transfer. The agents of transfer can be actors from the receiving society who may have formulated models for their own purposes as a result of extensive contact with the donor society. Two important factors will influence the process of transfer: the purpose of transfer and the structure of power within which transfer takes place.

It is useful to relate the conceptual approach to this particular case study—the transfer of trade unionism to Tanganyika. No institution such as trade unionism existed in indigenous African society until relatively recently.[24] Indeed, in most of Africa it has only been since the turn of the century that the economic basis for unionism was created by the development of wage labor. The introduction of wage labor gave rise both to the gradual growth of a working class and to considerable economic dissatisfaction. This led, in turn, to the beginnings of worker protest and, in Tanganyika and a number of other countries,[25] to the wholesale introduction of trade unionism as a channel believed to be efficient for managing the dissatisfaction.

Thus, the donors, in this case the British administration, introduced trade unionism when worker protest began to raise serious problems of social and administrative control. It was believed that unions, introduced in the "proper" way in Africa, might provide a peaceful and orderly means for channeling discontent that might otherwise accumulate and be expressed eventually in some violent form.[26] Thus the model of transfer developed by the British donors emphasized institutional aspects that focused on the social control functions of trade unions. For Africans, however, the function of social control was initially meaningless, for the core function of unions from their viewpoint was the expression of dissatisfaction, of protest. This meant that some aspects of the transfer model developed by the donors were invisible to Africans while other aspects, those associated with the expression of dissatisfaction, were eminently visible. The strike threat and the strike weapon, for example, were better understood than were institutional elements related to other activities such as arbitration and mediation. There were some institutional elements that became visible by virtue of the heavy emphasis placed on them by the agents of transfer but were meaningless to many receivers, since they did not appear to serve any functions for them.

A MODEL FOR THE ANALYSIS OF INSTITUTIONAL TRANSFER

Underlying the model to be developed is the premise that when institutions, or their organizational embodiment, are transferred from one cultural context to another, a process of change will occur in which the particular form of the institution in the receiving society will differ from that existing in the donor society. The changes that will occur, it is contended, are systematic and patterned. Although random elements may enter, much of the transfer of institutional patterns takes place within social contexts capable of examination. The present model seeks to clarify the method of analysis that will be used to elucidate the changes and the factors producing change.

Four stages exist in the analysis of institutional transfer. These stages are, essentially, logical units created by the analyst to facilitate his work. Empirically, it is often difficult to delineate clearly each stage. Nevertheless, approaching the analysis of transfer through stages simplifies the process of elucidating the action of different social groups involved in transfer.

The four stages are:

1. The original reality that exists in the donor culture.
2. The particular model extracted from this reality for purposes of transfer.
3. The model received by actors in the receiving sociocultural system.
4. The immediate and subsequent adaptation of the received model.

7

The Original Reality

When institutions develop organically in a society, they do not follow any single model. Development is gradual and occurs through processes such as accretion and differentiation. The resultant social forms are rarely neat and clear-cut; invariably social institutions are found to be only vaguely delineated. Even when institutions are embodied in and bounded by formal organizations, the reality is found to have a complexity that defies simple categorization.

Although there is a good deal of variation among institutions that develop within a society, when compared with identical institutions in other societies, characteristic overall patterns for each society can be seen.[27] In the present study, the approach is to consider the complex institutional realities of technologically advanced Western societies, since they form the basis of transfer models.

There are two aspects of the realities from which transfer models will be selected, both of which must be examined. First, there are formal instrumentalities that embody much of the institution: laws, constitutions, by-laws, directives, administrative procedures, and handbooks. Second, there is a great deal of nonformal institutional behavior that has not been reduced to writing but which is patterned and normative.[28] Nonformal aspects of institutions are usually less visible to model-makers than are formal. They exist as the "conventions" cited by Ashby,[29] and are extremely important in influencing the development of the model in the receiving sociocultural system because many of these nonformal institutional elements that serve as linkage between formal aspects of the organization will not be transferred. Their absence creates serious organizational problems.

The Formulation of the Transfer Model

Primary considerations in the formulation of the transfer model are whether the agents of transfer come from the donor society or from the receiving society and what their goals are. In modern times, one group of these agents has represented colonial powers and governments and has, with varying degrees of consciousness, sought to introduce institutional forms into colonial territories that would mirror those found in the "mother" country. The second group has consisted primarily of agents originating in the colonial country who have occupied some marginal position involving both their indigenous society and the mother country.

It is probable that formal rather than nonformal elements will be selected to be incorporated into the transfer model and that these elements will be presented in a formal way, e.g., in written form as policy statements and in model constitutions. If the goals of the agents of transfer are concerned with the maintenance of social control (as happens frequently when representatives of colonial governments undertake transfer), the model will stress roles, mechanisms, and structures concerned with control and will underemphasize those dealing with dissatisfaction and protest. If the goals of the agents of transfer are concerned with a transference of power (as happens when indigenous elements undertake transfer), the model will emphasize structures that mobilize discontent. These are broad generalizations concerning the motives involved in transfer. Before any systematic treatment of the selection mechanisms involved in the preparation of the transfer model can be elucidated, a number of studies will be needed to provide an empirical basis for the formulation of a typology.

The Reception of the Transfer Model

Whoever the agents of transfer may be, the character of what is received by actors in the receiving sociocultural system differs from that which is transmitted by the agents of transfer. Although transfer may be more complete or accurate if the agents of transfer originate in the receiving society, it is nevertheless likely that models will shift as their elements are diffused to receivers because of the variety of factors influencing reception.

These factors are based on the cultural, social, economic, and historical circumstances of receivers. Certain institutional elements in the model may prove to be almost invisible to receivers because they have no related cultural experience by which to understand specific elements of the transferred institution. Obviously, there can be little understanding of a complex piece of technological equipment if the receivers have few tools beyond digging sticks and stone hammers. Similarly, the roles involving these technical components which are meaningless in the receiving society can be expected to be reproduced only in part or in a different form if at all.[30]

Unique historical experiences and the character of the indigenous social structure will also affect the nature of reception. Actors in receiving societies with relatively undifferentiated social structures find it difficult to receive institutional elements that emphasize levels of social differentiation that do not exist indigenously. Where few ideas have developed that permit individuals to extricate themselves from kinship or other traditional attachments, they may be unaware of the nonformal aspects of roles from the donor society.

In general, the kinds of institutional elements most easily transferred are:

1. *Formal aspects.* These are institutional elements that are embodied in written form; they can include formal roles (offices), codes, written directives, legal systems, constitutions.
2. *Distinctive symbolic equipment.* These can include unusual forms of clothing such as Western dress or academic gowns, symbols of office (mayoral chains, gavels), bureaucratic appurtenances (desks, office arrangements, files).
3. *Institutional elements that are formally and legally stressed.* Transfer takes place within a structure of power. Where the agents of transfer occupy positions of power in the social structure, they may

emphasize selected institutional elements with considerable vigor. In such a case, these aspects may be received although not understood by the recipients.

Adaptation of the Transfer Model

The fact that a model is received does not mean that it will be entirely adapted by receivers. A model is a simplified version of reality: it cannot convey all aspects of the institution as it exists in the donor sociocultural system. Thus, receivers will have to "flesh-out" the model in day-to-day interaction according to their possibly inadequate understanding of the formal as well as nonformal elements. Aspects of the model as it is in fact received may prove to be inappropriate to the conditions of the new situation. The receivers may either begin a process of local innovation or seek new models which may be available either indigenously or from other nonindigenous sources.

This final stage of adaptation of the transferred model is a gradual process which continues over a long period of time. In the previous three stages cited, although the time lag involved may be considerable, it is frequently possible to delimit time periods during which each stage takes place. In the final stage, there is continuous adaptation of institutional elements to make the transfer institution more appropriate to the receiving society.

THE MODEL AND THE PRESENT STUDY

The model for the analysis of institutional transfer represents a suggestion for the micro-analysis of institutional change. In the present study, Chapter II is intended to provide the reader with some background information on Tanganyika. Chapters III and IV deal with the first two stages of the transfer model. In Chapter III, a model of British trade unionism is briefly developed. Chapter IV illustrates how Tanganyika's Labour Department formulated its original transfer model. In the remainder of the book, the character of reception of the transfer model and its subsequent revision are analyzed. The concluding chapter formulates several propositions concerning the sources of organizational change in institutional transfer. The main burden of the study concludes with the complete transformation of the unions in the early months of 1964. An epilogue has therefore been included to indicate some of the changes that have occurred since that time.

II Tanganyika: The Background

Tanganyika, situated on the eastern shore of Africa, lies just south of the Equator and is bordered on the east by the Indian Ocean and by Africa's great lakes on the west and northwest. Its coastal area is a low-lying and relatively humid plain. Much of the rest of the country consists of an arid and high plateau (3000-5000 feet). The northern, northwestern, and south-western borders of the country are more mountainous, and rainfall occurs more frequently and is better distributed throughout the year. It is in these latter areas, as well as in the coastal belt, that the bulk of the population lives. Rainfall in much of the country, except in the mountainous areas, is concentrated into one or two short seasons during which 20 to 24 inches fall, leaving the countryside relatively isolated and many of the roads impassable.[1]

Tanganyika's population, estimated at approximately ten million persons, consists mainly of Africans. There are, however, a small number of Europeans and Asians who have in the past constituted an extremely important stratum for political, economic, and social reasons. The importance of the immigrant communities has declined considerably although not entirely since 1961 when independence was achieved.

The economy of Tanganyika is less developed than that of many other countries in Africa because of certain aspects of its political history. It has long lagged behind that of Britain's other dependencies in East Africa, Kenya and Uganda—a situation which has not changed substantially since independence was obtained. Despite the backwardness of the economy, Tanganyika's unions developed with greater strength than did those elsewhere in East Africa.

THE HISTORICAL BACKGROUND[2]

The coastal areas of eastern Africa were explored by Persians and small settlements established by them around the 10th century. Later, Arabs, moving south, established settlements along the coast and fought the Portuguese—moving north—for their control. When the Omani Arabs settled permanently in Zanzibar around 1700, a nominal suzerainty was established over most of the coast and at some inland places. Control, even at the coast, remained tenuous until after the capital was moved from Muscat to Zanzibar in 1832. The Arabs used the hinterland of the continent as a slave-recruiting area.

Tanganyika, as such, did not exist until the "scramble for Africa" by the European powers in the 1870s and 1880s. Although Great Britain had extensive interests in the area and exercised considerable influence over the Sultan of Zanzibar, the Germans established a base on the coast directly opposite Zanzibar and won recognition of their claims to the inland areas when Carl Peters obtained a series of treaties on behalf of the German East Africa Company in 1884. German control was first exercised by this private company, but by 1888 the area became a formal German colony—German East Africa.

The first few years of German hegemony were devoted to the creation of a central administration of government. This entailed subduing the tribes that would not acknowledge German authority. A series of rebellions marked the reaction to German hegemony, the most dramatic of which was the Maji Maji rebellion of 1905-1906, which claimed some 120,000 lives. By 1910, order and security had been established, and significant German immigration had taken place, but still there were somewhat less than 3000 Germans resident in the territory. Some land was appropriated in upland areas where the Germans settled and created plantations. To work the plantations, the Germans periodically instituted forced labor to ensure an adequate labor supply.

The Germans also initiated the process of modernization or westernization. Many Christian missions were established by them to proselytize Africans, and schools were usually part of mission responsibilities. A report issued by the German Colonial Institute in 1911 indicates that there were over one thousand schools and 66,647 pupils. Thus, by the time Tanganyika was occupied by the British in 1919 there were already some German-educated Africans.

During World War I the German army in Tanganyika fought a mobile, rolling fight covering the entire country and only surrendered two weeks after the collapse of Germany on November 25, 1918. The destruction of life and property in Tanganyika was considerable and the developing modern economy was brought to a standstill.

From 1919 the British ruled Tanganyika under a mandate from the League of Nations. Two basic British policies took form during the governorship of Sir Donald Cameron. These were: (1) Tanganyika was to be an African country and was to be developed for Africans; (2) the indigenous population was to be governed under the policy of indirect rule; that is, government by Europeans through indigenous rulers. The designation of Tanganyika as an African country precluded large scale immigration of Europeans such as had occurred and was to continue in Kenya. This policy, although it saved

Tanganyika from the serious race problems that developed in Kenya and Northern and Southern Rhodesia, had less happy economic ramifications since it considerably slowed the pace of economic development.

Indirect rule was imported by Cameron from Nigeria where he had served under Sir Frederick Lugard, the formulator of this policy of colonial administration. Lugard formulated the policy when he was sent by an economy-minded Colonial Office to rule Northern Nigeria with only a handful of Europeans. What was originally a question of expediency was elevated to a principle of administration and, indeed, became a mystique among colonial administrators.

Calculated to insulate indigenous societies from serious external shock, the principle of indirect rule was intended to produce gradual change through established traditional authorities. While a creditable goal, this was not achieved in Tanganyika for many reasons, among which was the peculiar fact that many of the indigenous societies either had acephalous political systems—tribes without rulers—or had few differentiated political roles. While there were some tribes with centralized political systems, many more were either chiefless or they dispersed power very broadly. It became difficult for the British, in such circumstances, to find chiefs, let alone to buttress their ostensibly traditional authority.

British control of the country continued during the period between the first and second world wars, but little development took place. Following World War II, British administration was continued under a trusteeship agreement with the United Nations until December 7, 1961, when Tanganyika obtained full sovereignty.

THE POPULATION

Tanganyika's population is scattered over 362,000 square miles and the country is therefore mainly underpopulated, although there are mountain areas in the north, northwest, and southwest where population densities are high—in some places exceeding 500 persons per square mile. Less than 5 percent of the population lives in towns.[3] Most of the people live on the land, continuing, albeit with some significant changes, traditional life patterns. The rural pattern of social organization stresses ethnic attachments, and there have been estimates that Tanganyika's tribes range variously from 100 to hundreds.[4] Traditional society places great emphasis on kinship organization and, while varying considerably between patrilineal and matrilineal descent systems, most rural Tanganyikans continue to be enmeshed in a kinship structure whose ramifications are felt in economic, social, and political experience. This has meant a strong emphasis on the kinship group as a collectivity; general resistance to change, although in some cultural areas some ethnic groups have moved ahead very rapidly; and the integration of sacred and secular controls to

13

sustain and maintain the social system. Traditional orientations continue to be expressed by many Tanganyikans—even the most modern—in the form of a sense of attachment to home and kin. For many, as will be seen (in Chapters VII and VIII, for example) traditional attitudes become manifest within certain contexts of the modern world.

Economically, most Tanganyikans depend on subsistence agriculture or pastoral activities for their sustenance. The bulk of the tribes and 95 percent of the people speak Bantu languages, so that the basic structure of most of the languages is similar. People from adjoining tribes can frequently understand each other's language, although as a person gets farther away from home, he experiences difficulties and must use Swahili as a means of communication. Swahili, which is based on Bantu grammar, is widely spoken in East Africa and has emerged as a genuine national language. It has, therefore, been used by political and trade union leaders as the primary language of communication.

Most Africans in Tanganyika, until recent times, were animistic in their religion, the clan head being responsible, in effect, to the ancestors. In Arab times, the Islamic faith took root and has continued to grow. Christianity, which was introduced by the missions, has been of prime significance in creating a new elite of literate and westernized Africans who formed the nationalist movement and the trade unions; it is significant that most modern Tanganyikan leaders are Christians.

By the standards of most developed societies, Tanganyika's towns are small, but their importance to the country cannot be overrated. The capital city, Dar es Salaam, had about 125,000 residents in 1960, while Tanga, the second largest town, had a population of about 60,000. The population in most of the remaining towns is less than 15,000, and many of the towns are only large hamlets. Africans in the towns live in houses built with local materials (mud, coconut thatch) although there is increased use of permanent materials for house construction. The larger towns have regular electricity supplies, but in some of the smaller towns, electricity may be available only for certain hours during the day, and the small towns have none. The situation with respect to a public water supply is similar: none in the smaller towns. Small and limited though the towns were, it was largely there that the political and the trade union movements began to develop and found social power, although the growth of marketing cooperatives in the rural areas was also to contribute to political development.

THE SOCIETY AND THE COLONIAL SITUATION[5]

> One day in 1951, when one of my European colleagues was away on leave . . . I was busy in the laboratory with some tests when a European woman came in with a sample bottle of milk. She looked around for a few moments and did not say anything.

14

"Good morning, madam," I said.

When I spoke she turned around and asked, "Is there anybody here?"[6]

Tom Mboya's experience in Nairobi, Kenya, was not unique. The colonial situation was one in which Africans were treated by many Europeans (and frequently by Asians as well) as nonpersons,[7] that is, as if no one were present, or in some strongly negative fashion. The colonial situation was also compounded by the paternalistic tone of British administration, which tended to regard Africans very much as helpless children requiring care and protection on the one hand, but careful supervision on the other.

The treatment that Africans received from the European population as a whole was duplicated, except in rare cases, in industrial relations. In one case witnessed by the writer, a high-level official of a large government organization treated an African trade unionist as a very young child; in another case, a labor officer generally sympathetic to the unionists talked about "kicking --- downstairs" because he became obnoxious. Such attitudes contaminated the atmosphere in which negotiations between the unionists, management, and government took place. Although these represented the normal patterns of social relationships in the colonial situation, the situation was changing rapidly because of the growth of power of the nationalist movement and of the unions. And, although the British government and the upper echelons of the administration recognized that the movement toward independence was well under way, the bulk of the Europeans as individuals had not acknowledged the fact either in terms of general political attitudes or, more importantly, in terms of social relationships between themselves and Africans.

The towns during the colonial period were divided into racial communes.[8] The Europeans lived in the best part of town, and at the top of this group were the British. In the middle rank were the Asians (Hindus, Muslims, Sikhs) who also lived in physically separate sections of the town but in circumstances not equal to those of the Europeans. The Africans were crowded into the least developed part of town where few amenities could be found.

Social interaction followed racial and ethnic lines, and interracial social contacts were until recent times very rare. The communes were best exemplified in the European community by "the club." In smaller towns, the club was the gathering place for all Europeans, although some — e.g., Italians and Greeks — were not particularly welcome. In the larger towns, the greater European population permitted the proliferation of a variety of clubs which distinguished between the ethnicity and income of Europeans. Thus, the Dar es Salaam Club was primarily for the upperclass British and the European Railway Club was for British artisans. Similarly, there was a Greek Club and an Italian Club. The club syndrome also was manifested among the Asians, although to a lesser extent.

15

Until the drive for independence was well advanced, intercommunal social activities were rare. When it was realized that Africans would obtain their independence, social activities involving the three communities became more frequent at formal occasions.

Racial and ethnic distinctions correlated generally with the division of labor and with economic distinctions. While the British were the top administrators of government and of the major commercial enterprises, other Europeans were plantation owners (mainly Greeks) and artisans (mainly Italians). The Asians constituted a middle class of petty merchants, storekeepers, contractors, and artisans. The lowest economic and social group, until the development of the political movement, consisted of the Africans who were the workers and laborers in the towns.[9]

The Africans come from a large number of Tanganyikan tribes and, indeed, from other African countries (Zambia, Rhodesia, South Africa, Malawi, the Congo, Rwanda, and Burundi). In the towns, the traditional tribal patterns have less meaning than in the outlying districts, and considerable social disorganization has been experienced.[10]

The growth of urbanism and the increased commitment of Africans to urban living has given rise to new forms of social organization hitherto unknown in Eastern Africa. A considerable number of modern voluntary associations such as trade unions, sports organizations, welfare groups, countrymen or tribal associations, have developed.

THE ECONOMY

Prior to the arrival of the Europeans, the Africans sustained themselves by subsistence agriculture, pastoral activities, or both. Some trade had been developed by the Arabs in slaves and ivory but this had little significance to the economies of the indigenous societies except in areas near Arab centers on the coast and inland at such places as Tabora and Ujiji. A few Arab markets existed that were necessary for the sustenance of the slave and ivory trade but these did not carry any substantial volume of imports into the area.

It was not until the Germans established control over what became German East Africa (and later Tanganyika) that the groundwork for a modern economy was created. The Germans began many plantations and initiated an export and import trade of some significance. In 1900, exports were valued at £ 214,682 and by 1912 their value was £ 1,000,000.[11]

The British designation of Tanganyika as an African country meant that settlement (and therefore development) by Europeans was not generally encouraged. In addition, the possibility that Tanganyika might be turned back to Germany precluded serious investment of British capital. Much of the 1920s was devoted to reestablishing some semblance of a modern economy after the devastation of World War I. Concerted efforts were made in sisal and coffee production. No sooner had this been accomplished than the depression of the 1930s wrought additional damage. Indeed, it was not until after World War II that the economy began to grow in any systematic fashion.

The modern economy of the country rests to a considerable degree on a fluke of economic history. In the immediate postwar period, the British Labour government, anticipating a serious world shortage in edible oils and fats, initiated a plan for the utilization of hundreds of square miles in Tanganyika, Kenya, and Northern Rhodesia for the mechanized production of groundnuts (peanuts). The Tanganyikan project became the pilot operation of the so-called "groundnut scheme," which was doomed from the outset. Ignorance of weather and soil conditions, mismanagement, the importation of trained technicians without tools and heavy equipment without replacement parts, and other factors produced almost complete wastage of resources.[12] The groundnut scheme, combined with the general awakening of the world economy in the postwar period, however, did help to develop the existing economic infrastructure in Tanganyika and brought the country more directly into the world's economy.

Tanganyika's economy is mainly based on agriculture and extractive industries. Typical of most underdeveloped economies, the country produces basic raw materials for export, and imports much of its manufactured goods. Table II.1 shows the principal exports valued in 1960 at over one million pounds. As shown in Table II.2, sisal, the primary export crop in 1960 was produced almost entirely by non-African growers — a situation that has remained constant. All of the minerals shown in Table II.1 are extracted in expatriate-owned or -directed enterprises. The Tanganyika government owns a half interest in Williamson Diamond Mines, the major diamond producer, but the mine is managed by the DeBeers interests, which own the other half.

Table II.1   Exports Valued at over £ 1,000,000, Tanganyika, 1960

Product	Value in £
Sisal	15,441,631
Cotton, raw	8,827,131
Coffee (unroasted)	7,325,669
Diamonds	4,652,800
Cashew Nuts	2,125,788
Meat and meat preparations	1,942,181
Hides, skins and fur skins, undressed	1,836,026
Gold	1,231,408
Tea	1,150,671
Lead ore and concentrates	1,076,787
Groundnuts	1,052,733

Source: Tanganyika Ministry of Commerce and Industry, *Commerce and Industry in Tanganyika, 1961, Appendix B, p. 84.*

Table II.2 Distribution of Ownership of Sisal Production, 1956, by Race and Ethnicity

Race	Percent of Production	Total
European		
Greek	32.0%	
British	31.3	
Swiss	8.7	
Dutch	2.1	
Italian	0.8	
German	0.4	
Total European		75.3%
Asian	24.1	24.1
African	0.6	0.6
Total	100.0%	100.0%

Source: C.W. Guillebaud, Economic Survey of the Sisal Industry of Tanganyika, 1959, Table V, p. 129.

In contrast to sisal and the extractive industries, cotton and coffee are grown in small quantities largely by Africans, and are handled through an extensive network of cooperatives initiated by the British following the establishment of the Kilimanjaro Native Cooperative Union in 1932. These cooperatives have grown in significance and size particularly since World War II and, in the 1950s, became one important base for the development of the nationalist movement.

Many other African-based crops such as cashew nuts were handled by Asian middlemen who provided the economic sinews for a distribution system in the preindependence period and who still act as bulking agents, buyers, and transporters. Since Africans took over political power, a policy has been followed of both expanding the network of cooperatives throughout the country and of opening up a substantial segment of the system of distribution to the consumer cooperatives.

Tanganyika's employed labor force has remained relatively stable since World War II.[13] Of its population of almost ten million, approximately 400,000 Africans are employed. As Table II.3 shows, about half of this group is employed by the government and the sisal plantations. The remaining workers are employed in plantations that are growing crops other than sisal, in commercial undertakings, and a small but growing number in industries or service trades. Some 40,000 Africans are estimated to be employed in domestic service. The economy like that in many underdeveloped countries is highly centralized, and a small number of employers hire the bulk of the labor force.

Until World War II, much of the employed population consisted of "target workers" who migrated to centers of employment to work for a limited time so that they could pay taxes or purchase cloth or other manufactured commodities. Once the target was achieved, most workers returned to

1. Mboya's visit to Dar es Salaam, June 1955. *Left to right*: Maynard M. Mpangala, Arthur Ohanga, Tom Mboya, Rashidi Kawawa (partially obscured by Mboya), Ali Selemani Kindamba, John Rupia. Mboya and Gaya represented the International Confederation of Free Trade Unions on this visit from Kenya and were instrumental in the formation of the Tanganyika Federation of Labour. John Rupia was then Vice President of TANU.

2. First Congress of the Tanganyika Federation of Labour, October 1955. *Seated*: Mabwana A. Odoro (Assistant Treasurer), M. M. Kamaliza (Treasurer), J. E. Shaba (Junior Vice President), J. B. Ohanga (President), F. B. Jumbe (Senior Vice President), R. M. Kawawa (General Secretary), P. H. Kilala. *Second row*: Juma Kombo, G. Isomba, Ali Hassani, S. Abdala, A. E. Sijeny, I. H. Athumani, Sheikh Mselem, M. M. Mpangala (Assistant General Secretary), A. S. Kindamba, Ali Mohammed. *Third row*: L. Athethe, L. W. Otieno, J. R. Mwakyemba, A. E. Singini, A. H. Abubakar, E. N. N. Kanyama, A. K. Feruzi, Hassani Selemani, D. Lumolumo, J. O. Odigo.

3. The 1957 annual conference of the Tanganyika Federation of Labour held in Dar es Salaam. *Left to right*: N.T.C. Msumba (secretary of the conference); Essau Akena, TFL Assistant General Treasurer (also General Secretary of the Dockworkers and Stevedores Union); J. Mpina (of the Tanganyika Railway African Union), TFL General Treasurer; E.N.N. Kanyama, TFL Junior Vice President (also General Secretary of the Tanganyika Railway African Union); Michael M. Kamaliza, TFL President (also General Secretary of the Commercial and Industrial Workers Union); Rashidi M. Kawawa, TFL General Secretary; F. E. Mngodo, TFL Senior Vice President (also General Secretary of the Public Works Department Workers Union).

4. A 1960 union meeting under a mango tree. Members of the Plantation Workers Union on the Dewji sisal estate near Dar es Salaam hear a report on the internal problems of the union.

5. Sheha Amiri and Victor M. Mkello of the Plantation Workers Union. Mkello was General Secretary of the Plantation Workers Union from its founding until 1964; he was also President of the Tanganyika Federation of Labour at the time of its demise. Sheha Amiri was one-time Organizing Secretary of the Plantation Workers Union and became Acting Assistant General Secretary of the union in 1963. Both were rusticated for two months early in 1963 by President Julius Nyerere.

6. C. S. Kasanga Tumbo, General Secretary of the Tanganyika Railway African Union, 1959-61. He served briefly as Tanganyika's High Commissioner to the United Kingdom until he went into political opposition.

7. Mwalimu J. K. Nyerere addressing a trade union meeting in the early sixties at the Jangwani Grounds, Dar es Salaam.*

8. Members of the trade union applaud Nyerere's speech at the Jangwani Grounds.*

9. A recent trade union procession through Dar es Salaam to mark May Day (Workers Day).*

10. M. Kamaliza, present Secretary General of NUTA (National Union of Tanzania Workers), addresses a recent public meeting of trade union members to mark May Day.*

11. President Nyerere and M. Kamaliza, the present Secretary General of NUTA (*second from right*), at a 1965 meeting of NUTA in Dar es Salaam.*

*Source: Tanganyika Information Services

1.
2.

3.
4.

5.
6.

9.

Table II.3   Percent of African Labor Force Employed by Government
Institutions and the Sisal Industry 1953-1958

Year	Percent Employed in Sisal Industry	Percent Employed by Government	Total
1953	34%	18%	52%
1954	32	17	49
1955	31	19	50
1956	31	18	49
1957	31	17	48
1958	31	17	48

Source: Tanganyika, Annual Report of the Labour Department, 1953-1958.

their homes and to their subsistence way of life. Following World War II, an increasing number of workers became stabilized in wage employment. The growth of this committed labor force has been of considerable significance in the development of trade unionism.

Although there has been a great increase in the number of literate and educated Africans in the labor force since the 1950s, the bulk of the employed labor force consists of unskilled manual workers. Table II.4 shows the distribution of occupational groups in Tanganyika in 1958 when trade unions were growing rapidly. The table is somewhat deceptive since many of the categories classified by the Labour Department as skilled and semiskilled would be considered semiskilled and unskilled in a more developed economy. Many headmen, for example, at that time were illiterate, as were many craftsmen such as masons and carpenters whose workmanship often left much to be desired. To a considerable degree, therefore, the employed labor force was homogeneous, except for the school teachers and the clerical staffs of government organizations, plantations, mines, industries, and commercial establishments, who were westernized and educated. This factor of homogeneity has considerable significance in the development of trade unionism.

POLITICS AND POLITICAL ORGANIZATION

Just as Tanganyika's economy was controlled by foreigners until 1959, so also was its political life. Although a mandate and a trusteeship territory, Tanganyika was administered by a British governor in much the same manner as any colony. The Governor-in-Council formulated legislation which was implemented by a civil service of British officials. There was no involvement of the African population in this process until after World War II. Even with the application of the principle of indirect rule, Africans were not significantly involved in political activities.

Table II.4   Distribution by Occupational Groups of Employed
Male Africans in Tanganyika
July 1958

Occupational Group	Number	Percent of Labor Force
Educated (Westernized)		
Clerical	11,031	3
School teachers	5,783	2
Total	16,814	5
Skilled, Semiskilled, Supervisory		
Office and store	8,750	2
Mechanics and fitters	6,319	2
Carpenters and joiners	5,986	2
Masons and bricklayers	7,078	2
Drivers	9,203	3
Domestics	4,443	1
Headmen	14,388	4
Other skilled	39,551	12
Total	95,718	28
Unskilled	226,656	67
Total	339,188	100

Source: Tanganyika, Annual Report of the Labour Department, 1958, Appendix II,
Table 1 (6), p. 46. (Note: Figures rounded off to nearest full percentage point.)

The development of local political institutions began with the creation, in December 1926, of the Legislative Council, which consisted of the governor, thirteen senior government officials, and seven appointed "unofficials" (five Europeans and two Asians). No Africans could be found, according to the governor, who could speak English with sufficient ease to become members of the council. The Legislative Council was the primary instrumentality utilized by the British to accommodate various groups within Tanganyika. Thus Africans were given representation in 1945 when two African chiefs were appointed. Later, other Africans were named to the council who were more representative of the population than were the two chiefs. As the nationalist movement and the unions began to develop, Julius Nyerere, the leader of the Tanganyika African National Union (TANU) and Rashidi Kawawa of the Tanganyika Federation of Labour (TFL) were appointed.

Politics in the modern sense of the term did not begin until 1954 when Julius Nyerere, who had recently returned from graduate studies at the University of Edinburgh, converted the Tanganyika African Association, a cultural association of westernized Africans, into a political party, renaming it TANU.

The TANU experienced an almost immediate dramatic growth. What began as a small group of westernized Africans soon took root among the illiterate urban masses and later spread to the rural populace. The growth of the TANU and that of the trade unions was almost parallel, and although organizational autonomy was retained, each group provided considerable support to the other. The unions, of course, concentrated their energies on economic rather than on political questions.

The TANU captured all the seats in the first elections for the Legislative Council in 1958, establishing that the party had almost unchallenged political support in all elements of the African population. Self-government under a TANU ministry was achieved in September 1960. Independence was obtained on December 7, 1961, and one year later Tanganyika became a republic.

A SHORT HISTORY OF TANGANYIKAN UNIONISM[14]

The first specific references to discontent and protest by workers in Tanganyika occurred in 1931. Thurnwald notes that various tribes reacted differently to wage employment and that the Wasukuma were clannish, so that when one of the tribe was aggrieved, fellow tribesmen joined in a strike.[15] A more modern manifestation of labor discontent occurred in a strike of dockworkers at the port of Tanga in 1938. The strike was spontaneous, however, and no organization of workers emerged from it.[16] The basis for trade unionism was laid in a major strike of dockworkers in Dar es Salaam in September 1947. The strike, lasting a full week and supported by most segments of the African population, spread up the rail line in a series of short strikes in the major towns between Dar es Salaam and Mwanza on Lake Victoria, 765 miles away. This strike was not spontaneous, and the group of dockworkers that organized it were advised by the Labour Department on how to form and register a union. The union was registered in December 1947 and survived through two rather unsettled years, when a violent strike in February 1950 forced its dissolution.

The Dockworkers Union, however, provided a lesson to the Labour Department in the development and growth of unionism. As a result of this experience the department instituted joint consultation as a mechanism for the handling of grievances in order to avoid the hasty creation of trade unions.

When unions began to develop again in 1952, the main leadership, unlike that of the Dockworkers Union, came from westernized and educated clerks rather than from illiterate manual workers. Small unions began to appear which, under the guidance of the Labour Department, were localized and craft-based. These unions developed at a slow pace and their membership was very small until 1954. The main growth of the unions took place after 1955.

The suggestion to create a central federation of labor and to regroup the unions came as a result of a three-day visit to Dar es Salaam by Tom Mboya, then leader of the Kenya Federation of Labour. Following Mboya's advice, a conference was held in October 1955 at which the Tanganyika

21

Federation of Labour (TFL) was formed. One of the main decisions made at this conference was to amalgamate the localized craft unions into a small number of national industrial organizations. The remainder of 1955 and much of 1956 were devoted to this task, during which time union membership increased slowly.

By mid-1956, some of the problems of internal organization had been resolved and the unions turned to industrial action. A series of localized disputes led to increased hostility between the inexperienced trade unionists and the Labour Department. In one case, a strike was threatened by the Local Government Workers Union to coincide with the visit of Princess Margaret to Dar es Salaam. A small incident that occurred during the visit soon accelerated into a threatened general strike of domestic and hotel workers. When the Labour Department intervened in a manner regarded as unfair by the TFL, two-day sympathy strikes were called by a number of unions. The strike of domestic workers and of a considerable number of sympathy strikers took place on December 6-8, 1956. The widespread response in these strikes showed that the unions had built up considerable support among workers in Dar es Salaam.

As a result of the sympathy strikes, a substantial number of strikers employed by automobile agencies were discharged. Throughout December and January 1957, the atmosphere in Dar es Salaam remained tense and at one point the TFL threatened to call a national general strike if the workers were not reinstated. The general strike was averted by two European trade unionists who, on a special visit to Tanganyika, helped to obtain a settlement. As a result of the settlement, a minimum wage was established in Dar es Salaam for which achievement the unions were able to claim credit.

The period following the general strike was marked by continual growth of the unions. In 1957 the first organization of plantation workers was undertaken by the TFL. By 1958, a number of collective agreements began to be written, and the unions had clearly emerged as a potent force influencing industrial relations. The TFL and its unions, in spite of significant strength in dealing with employers, showed considerable internal weakness. Financial problems were preponderant. The unions were unable to collect dues regularly from the members. When money was collected, it was handled in an irresponsible manner and substantial quantities disappeared. In addition, extremely rapid growth placed serious organizational strains upon the unions. The leadership felt it necessary to add many full-time officials and, since very few people had any relevant experience, the overwhelming bulk of the leadership had to learn their trade unionism while actually working as full-time officials.

As will be discussed in Chapter X, the close relationship that had existed between the unions and TANU began to break down after TANU took over the government in 1960.[17] The quarrel between the unions on the one side and TANU and the government on the other was ostensibly resolved in January 1964 when most of the full-time leaders of the unions were arrested following a mutiny of the Tanganyika army. In February 1964, as a result of legislation adopted by the National Assembly, the Tanganyika Federation of Labour and its constituent unions were abolished. In their stead a single national union was created, whose two top officials were to be appointed by the President of the Republic and whose subsidiary officials were to be appointed by the top union officer. The creation of the new organization, the National Union of Tanganyika Workers (NUTA), marked the end of autonomous trade unionism in Tanganyika.

III The Complexities of British Trade Unionism

Because the British provided the model for Tanganyika's trade unions, it is useful to examine briefly the salient characteristics of British unionism and of its industrial relations system. Great Britain's trade unions trace their development back through almost two hundred years. As the earliest industrializing nation in history, Britain's experience with unionism has been complex. In addition, because British industry has been a primary component of its national economy, trade union experience has necessarily been rich and varied. Any review of key aspects of British unionism—of structure, leadership, industrial and political relations—cannot encompass the fullness of trade union realities which manifest complexities that defy generalization.[1] Of necessity, this review selects only some of the most significant developments which were also those that provided models for Tanganyikan developments.

Despite restrictions of early legislation, unions had become significant social entities in Great Britain by the middle of the nineteenth century. As industrialization gave rise to a variety of categories of skilled workers, organizations of craftsmen became established. One of these, the Amalgamated Society of Engineers, formed in 1851, proved to be financially and organizationally stable and was emulated with some success by other unions.

The salient fact in British trade union history is that unions were never centrally organized nor did their evolution follow any preconceived theory or plan. Growing out of many experiments of small groups of workers organizing with little focus or direction other than that necessary to improve a specific problem at a given moment, union development was "a spontaneous healthy process arising out of the needs of the common people."[2]

STRUCTURE AND INTERNAL ORGANIZATION OF UNIONS

Because of its diverse background, British trade unionism is complex and difficult to characterize simply. Three general types of unions, however, can be delineated:[3]

24

1. *Craft unions.* The oldest form of unionism, these organizations group workers of similar skills.
2. *Industrial unions.* Workers in a particular industry are grouped into one union with no regard for differences between skills.
3. *General unions.* These are "blanket" organizations which group workers from many industries and skills.

Of the three types, the general unions stand out as the most significant in post-World War II Great Britain because of the size of their membership and their presence in so many industries. No single type of unionism can be said to dominate British unionism, however, since all are significant in some degree.

Although most unions can be classified into one of the three types, there are a considerable number of deviant organizations. There are, for example, unions of nonmanual workers formed on the basis of occupational groups such as civil servants and teachers. Moreover, several professional associations such as the Association of Local Government Officers and the National Federation of Insurance Workers have gradually become trade unions.[4] There are also many localized unions in all industries having territorial monopolies. Many of these deviant organizations are not affiliated with the British Trade Union Congress (TUC).

There has been, and continues to be, wide diversity in the size of unions, but the tendency toward amalgamation has been marked. The number of unions has decreased although the total union membership has increased; thus, the average size of unions has grown considerably. Further indication of this concentration is that in 1951, 66.5 percent of the total membership was concentrated in 17 out of a total of 704 unions, and 90 percent was found in 93 unions.[5]

The internal organization of the unions also reflects the complexities arising out of gradual and diversified development. The main structural unit upon which each union is built is the branch, a locally based organization.[6] Branches are frequently grouped in district organizations, which deal with broader matters and act as intermediaries between the branch and the central organization. The district bodies vary in importance in different unions according to their size, the size of the branches, and other factors. The central organization, consisting of the officers who operate at the union's headquarters, has tended to become increasingly important in British trade union life although, again, the degree of importance varies from union to union.

The problem of reconciling the efficiencies of centralization with democratic participation of the branches has become increasingly urgent, as the size of unions has grown through amalgamations. In most unions this problem is handled by dividing the decision-making powers in various ways between three groups: the executive council, the delegate conference, and the full-time officials.[7]

1. *Executive councils.* The trend in most unions has been for control to become centralized in executive councils whose members are elected by the branches. This centralization of power has occurred by slow stages, as pragmatic considerations required changes in practices that were ultimately formalized constitutionally. The present-day activities of the executive councils give them their unusual powers. Among these are the handling of national negotiations, determination of national employment policies, regulation of strike action, and the direction and control over the administration of the unions, which frequently and in varying degrees includes control and maintenance of finances.

2. *Delegate conferences.* The most important checks on the power of the executive councils are the conferences of rank and file delegates, which form the second group in the triarchy. Although the delegate conferences differ in their power, size, and frequency, all "pass judgment on the stewardship of the union's executive council and officers and . . . sanction the initiation of fresh policy. In either case the main duty of the conference is to give or withhold its assent . . . Without it a union either disintegrates or becomes a rigid dictatorship."[8] These conferences also serve to inspire the loyalty and unity of the membership. Usually all permanent officials and the members of the executive councils attend the delegate conferences as ex-officio delegates, but care is taken that they do not dominate the conferences which are intended as a means of expression both of the opinions of lay members and of the spirit of the union as a whole. Debate in conferences is often expressed raucously, and the ability of delegates to persuade the conference through convincing rhetoric is more important than the technical, factual knowledge needed by the union leaders.

3. *Officials.* The third group in the triarchy of the unions comprises the full-time officials who, particularly at the upper levels, are involved with negotiations and dealings with employers. Middle-level leaders are, in addition, frequently involved in political activities in their local communities. Full-time employment as an officer is the reward for a relatively small number of activists. Future leaders prove their devotion to the cause of trade unionism by voluntary unpaid activities in a lengthy apprenticeship which also serves as a socializing experience.

In the early days of the unions, the leadership had charismatic qualities and was inspired by a strong sense of social purpose. More recently, the ability to articulate clearly complex statistical data has become more crucial than demagogic skill to the union leadership. "A trade union leader must be a combination of spokesman, statesman, lawyer, financier, negotiator, and supervisor. He must of all things be an exceptionally able advocate. He must have international associations and master a crop of intricate problems arising

26

from contacts with foreign workers."[9] At all levels, the primary criterion for the selection of trade union leaders is their specialized knowledge drawn from long personal experience within the union structure.

The key administrative position in every union is usually that of general secretary. From union to union, his duties and the interpretation of his role vary significantly. In some cases, the general secretary is conceived of largely as a high-level clerical assistant to the policy-making executive council. In others, he is the key officer influencing policy formation of the union. Although the general secretary usually must conform to policies laid down by the executive council, there have been some instances of successful dissent.[10] Except in large unions, such as the Transport and General Workers Union, the duties of the general secretary are specifically defined in union constitutions.

Theoretically democratic, British unions were originally based on direct membership participation. Ideally, the membership role involves participation and thorough familiarity with the details of trade union matters. In practice, membership involves only acceptance and adherence to a set of rules and policy and payment of dues. Most union activities are sustained, in fact, by a small number of volunteers who contribute their time after working hours. The high level of voluntary activity is indicated by the low ratio of full-time officers to members. In 1952, for example, in the 18 largest unions, this ratio averaged 1:3700; ranging from 1:300 at one end of the scale to 1:19,000 at the other.[11] Voluntary workers, many of them shop stewards, handle problems such as dues collection and grievance settlement.

The extent of voluntarism in British trade unionism is very unusual, and it has contributed significantly to the nature of the structure of the British unions. For example, on the principle that only lay members should make policy decisions, some large unions, including the Transport and General Workers Union and the National Union of Public Employees, specifically exclude full-time officials from being candidates for election to the executive councils.

British trade union leaders, characteristic of union leaders generally in Europe, are politically conscious and most are socialists. There is a strong moral commitment to the working class, to working class solidarity, and to the institutions of that class. Leaders are expected to adhere to an appropriate code of morality: ostentation is eschewed; wages are low (although rising substantially in some categories of employment and in certain unions). Similarly, although trade unions concentrate on winning economic benefits for workers and solving on-the-job problems, there is still a strong sense of social movement, although this is less integral to the trade unions today than it was in the early days.[12]

THE TRADES UNION CONGRESS[13]

Although trade unions have remained largely autonomous, in that each controls its own funds and determines its own policies, the central trade union confederation—the Trades Union Congress (TUC)—has become increasingly significant over the years. The TUC was formed in 1868 but became the coordinating center of British unionism only in 1921 in response to a desire for unity originating in the post-World War I slump. Composed of individual unions affiliated on a voluntary basis, the TUC is relatively weak in terms of the power exercised over its affiliates. The congress, consisting of delegates designated by the affiliated unions, meets annually to determine general policy questions and to elect a general council of 35 members representing 18 trade groups. The main policy-making group between congresses—the general council—is structurally weak since its members owe primary loyalty to their own unions rather than to the TUC.

The TUC is responsible for coordinating the industrial action of its affiliates, using its influence to settle disputes when negotiations fail, watching and promoting legislation, adjusting interunion conflict, promoting common action and generally assisting in the organization of workers. The general council cannot intervene in a trade dispute unless it is requested to do so by the parties involved. Thus, the autonomy of the affiliates is maintained and the general council has power only insofar as the unions demand it.

The TUC reaches the local level through trades councils. These are voluntary and not very significant units of the TUC. Most are concerned with coordinating local branch activity on the basis of TUC policy.

The main basis of TUC authority with the trade unions themselves lies in its informal connections with them, through which it suggests policy and leaves the unions to implement it. The TUC can most often be influential in its role as trade unionism's representative in external political relationships. During World War II, the TUC developed a structure of committees and national consultative bodies to advise on industrial policy. Many of these were perpetuated after the war. Even in this matter, however, the TUC has no control over the articulation of individual unions with the government. The TUC has also been responsible for the international affiliations of British unionism and is one of the three largest members of the International Confederation of Free Trade Unions.

INDUSTRIAL RELATIONS

The fundamental elements of British industrial relations are rooted in (1) voluntary negotiations between employers and unions; (2) the resulting collective agreements that regulate most conditions of employment; and (3) the shop stewards who function at the shop level to enforce agreements or present grievances on behalf of workers.

The strike in a variety of forms and sizes is only one among many forms of industrial action that have been used in Great Britain to bring direct pressure to bear on employers regarding inequalities and the restrictions of freedom intrinsic to the industrial structure. Sabotage in various forms, sometimes involving damage to machinery or public exposure of fraudulent practices connected with an industry, has been used both as an independent strategy and as an accompaniment to strikes. Public demonstrations have been used alone or with strikes to develop public sympathy; and boycotts, of which fair lists, blacklists, and union labels are extensions, have been widely used as political and economic weapons. As a form of sympathetic strike, boycotts have usually accompanied major strikes, often contrary to the official policy of the union leadership. *Ca'canny*, or slow-down tactics, used most often at times when the prevailing political sentiments are unsympathetic to overt strikes, is a method that often precedes a full strike. The British government in 1927 made illegal those sympathetic strikes designed to coerce the government. This legislation assumes that economic and political motives are clearly definable and separable —a fact which, though open to some question in the light of British history, has formed the basis of the attitude toward strikes.

When normal bargaining between unions and employers is unsuccessful, arbitration as a means of settlement of disputes has been of some significance. The voluntary nature of arbitration has been an explicit principle, except during World War II when emergency legislation making arbitration compulsory in order to end work stoppages was enacted. Prior to 1940, it was necessary that both sides consent to bringing an industrial dispute to arbitration. Under the Industrial Disputes Order of 1951, a party was given the right to take the dispute to the Minister of Labour for arbitration without the consent of the other party. The decision of the Tribunal formed by the minister, in such a case, was made binding upon both parties.[14]

Another significant element in the British industrial relations system is the process known as joint consultation although there is substantial disagreement as to its importance. Joint consultation has come to mean many things and has been given varying definitions by different groups. There is general agreement, however, that consultation is a narrowly defined auxiliary to collective bargaining:

> Many employers, managers, trade unionists and workers look on joint consultation as a narrowly limited process, which serves a useful purpose in that it enables the participants to act after having been made aware of the intentions, attitudes and difficulties of those who will be most affected by their actions, but does not involve agreement, or joint action, nor the obligations and responsibilities which could go with them. In their view, joint consultation is to be sharply distinguished from collective bargaining and collective agreement by the difference in *responsibility* attached to the two processes. In practice, however, this distinction may become blurred . . . The distinction between consultation and bargaining then remains clear only in instances of disagreement. In collective

29

bargaining disagreements are frequently referred to arbitration, but there can be no resort to arbitration in the consultative process.[15]

In Great Britain during World War I, various forms of consultation were initiated on an ad hoc basis, as managers sought greater cooperation for essential production. It was later felt that steps should be taken to make permanent those ad hoc arrangements. Under the chairmanship of J. H. Whitley, the Deputy of the House of Commons, a Committee on Relations between Employers and Employed was organized which recommended that joint industrial councils representative of employers and workers be permanently established. In the interwar period, the joint industrial councils and other committees of the Whitley type tended to disappear. Those councils that continued, concentrated on wages and conditions and rarely discussed more general subjects. At the beginning of World War II, the movement was again revived in the so-called joint production committees. Following the war, in the period of full employment, joint consultation continued to be of interest, and various bodies were created which were expected to work at the national, district, and workshop levels.

In spite of the variations found in Britain and the lack of definition of processes of joint consultation, the following generalizations can be made:

1. The idea of joint consultation is of some importance in British industrial relations even if the results of its application have been disappointing.
2. Joint consultation is regarded as an auxiliary to, rather than a substitute for, collective bargaining. Joint consultation is based on the premise that consensus between employers and workers can be achieved through discussion, whereas collective bargaining has as its underlying force the coercive mechanism of the strike and the lockout
3. The demand for joint consultation rather than collective bargaining has existed largely during periods of full employment, and it has been most successful during wartime when both parties to disputes were united by a common national purpose.

TRADE UNIONS AND POLITICS

British unions have always had a strong political orientation and, in their planning and activities, have emphasized their relations with political organizations. One of the two general political objectives that the unions have sought is as a pressure group to influence government policies and legislation in matters relating to workers and affecting their economic and social condition. The second objective has been to enhance the political, economic, and social status of the working class. Although the trade union movement as a result of this orientation has been increasingly involved in national affairs and maintains complex, though largely informal, ties with the British Labour Party and the government, it has retained its autonomy. This is due to the nature of the relationship with the Labour Party, which is one of mutual influence but "noncoercive intervention."[16]

Unions are free to choose whether to affiliate with political organizations. In 1950, for example, only 83 out of 704 unions were affiliated with the Labour Party, and membership of these unions comprised only about half of the total membership of the unions. The fact that union affiliation fees form a significant percentage of Party funds[17] augments the importance of the trade union vote at Labour Party conferences; however, since unions do not vote as a bloc, they are less influential than their substantial budgetary control would indicate. Moreover, members of the affiliated unions have the option of "contracting out" of paying the affiliation fee. A considerable variation in political interest between different unions is illustrated by the varying proportion of members who contract out.[18] A part of the political fee goes to supporting parliamentary candidates and to local political activity as well as to the Labour Party.

The only formal organizational links between the Labour Party and the unions are two committees, the Policy and Publicity Sub-Committee of the Labour Party Executive, which has two TUC representatives, and the TUC Economic Committee which has two Labour Party representatives. The National Council of Labour, a different but relatively inactive body, has eight representatives from each of three sectors of the labor movement: the Labour Party, the TUC, and the Cooperative Union. Although initially intended to make common policy decisions, it functions largely to settle differences of opinion between the three groups.

Unions, although supportive of, and supported by, Labour Party governments, have remained relatively self-sufficient and independent. One means by which they have maintained this autonomy has been to prevent overlapping leadership; most unions do not permit their officers to enter Parliament. Strongly conscious of their potential strength, unions are defensive of their autonomy and, by refraining from industrial action for direct political ends, expect in return that the government will refrain from intervening in industrial matters. That this relationship continues despite temporary lapses during times of national emergency, indicates a general attitude within British society. "Society has, as it were, given its approval to the principle of separating, as far as possible, industrial from political government."[19]

By virtue of its complexity resulting from a long history of unplanned, evolutionary development, British unionism offered a great variety of potential models that could be selected by colonial labor departments for institutional transfer.

IV The Labour Department and the Formulation of the Transfer Mod

In analyzing the role of the Tanganyikan Labour Department in formulating the transfer model, it is necessary to make explicit at the outset that no clear-cut and well-developed plan was created on an a priori basis. The Labour Department was an administrative agency of the Tanganyikan government; as such, it responded to demands as they arose. Since administrative policies are normally formulated in response to specific problems and pressures, Labour Department models were a combination of preconceived policies in certain areas and a response to the need for solving specific administrative dilemmas in others. Much of what the department did, both in its formal activities and in providing informal direction through personal contacts, focused upon those aspects that the department considered essential in order for it to maintain administrative control. In some areas, then, aspects of the transfer model were more clearly and consciously developed than in others.

Because contacts between department officers and the unionists were myr-iad and were marked by varying degrees of sympathy and identification, much information was transmitted that could have influenced the formulation of sub-models. Although it is possible to specify the more consciously planned aspects of the model, the influence of these informal contacts is more difficult to elucida

The Labour Department was only one of several sources for the transfer model. The contacts that the trade unionists had with the embryonic political system (especially the Legislative Council), with trade unionists and others from abroad, also affected developments. But these contacts were neither as coherent nor as systematic as those with the Labour Department; they will be discussed only as they bear on the formation of Labour Department policy.

THE LABOUR DEPARTMENT

The Labour Department of Tanganyika was the first such department in th British African colonies.[1] Created following an investigation of labor conditions in Tanganyika by Major Orde Browne, the job of the department, among other things, was:

to investigate all questions connected with labour economy, such as waste of labour, the method of reward, feeding, medical treatment, housing, etc.; and to inspect the labour conditions on public undertakings such as railway and road construction, and on private plantations, and to supervise the erection and control of camps for labour on its way from and to the place of recruitment.[2]

In its early years, the department focused much of its effort on alleviating the shortage of candidates available for employment.

During the economic crisis of the 1930s, the department ceased to exist, as the Tanganyika administration (like colonial administrations everywhere) sought to cut administrative costs. Recreated in 1938, the department picked up most of its previous activities although it moved increasingly into inspection activities.

The department on the whole was throughout its entire existence a rather conservative unit. At the time when worker protest began to take on organized forms in Tanganyika, few officers of the department had any experience or knowledge about labor matters or problems of unionism.[3] As noted by Roberts, in the period between 1942 and 1952, largely under the impetus of the British Labour Party, trade union advisers were sent out to various colonies. Their reception was apt to be cool because it was feared that they might encourage African trade unionism. Only in some cases were they successful.[4] In the case of Tanganyika, trade unionists, first sent in 1947, were relatively unsuccessful as officers of the department and, indeed, the ability of a few to survive over the years was accompanied by a decline in their personal orientation toward unionism.

Because of their background experiences, most labor officers tended to reflect typical administration attitudes toward Africans and, particularly, toward organized African protest. As late as 1960, several of those interviewed showed no understanding of the changing political climate and the fact that Africans would soon rule an independent Tanganyika.

Many labor officers had spent considerable time in upcountry stations where the European community, composed of Europeans in all walks of life, was very closely knit.[5] Thus, the personal background of the labor officers and the context of European life in a colonial situation tended to foster an essentially conservative viewpoint. In their work as representatives of the Labour Department, these officers had to come into regular contact with Africans for whom most Europeans had a deep contempt. Africans living in urban areas were generally regarded as "detribalized" and dishonest. Those Africans who were educated to some degree were regarded with special suspicion. They spoke English rather than Swahili— an action regarded as "cheeky" or "Bolshie." Thus the African trade unionists were never at the outset treated as equals, and only rarely so even in the final days of the colonial regime. They were considered by Europeans as children playing at games in which incendiary bombs were the toys.

Formally assigned to watch over the labor situation, the Labour Department constituted a ready-made administrative agency to take over the responsibilities of industrial relations once worker protest began to be manifest. Even more important, however, the Labour Department commanded what little available expertise there was in dealing with labor problems.

Although all levels of the Provincial Administration had experience in dealing with Africans, it was soon recognized that the problem was clearly different in an urban setting than in the rural environment.[6] The meetings of Labour Commissioners of the East and Central African territories, which began after World War II, served to increase the expertise and therefore the significance of the department as the local agency dealing with labor. The department, in fact was able to influence the development of events and to help provide specific guides to the organizational structures that were to develop. It could not alter, however, the specific manifestations of labor dissatisfaction.

The department's importance was further enhanced simply because of the central role government played in any colonial territory. The passage of the initial Trade Union Ordinance in 1932 made registration of unions with the government compulsory.[7] This colonial situation contrasted to that in England where registration was not only voluntary but also largely a formality. In Tanganyika, the authority to register unions—that is, to give them legal existence—has passed through various agencies of government, from the Registrar of Trade Unions to the Registrar-General and back to the Ministry of Health and Labour.[8] In 1956 following the upsurge in trade unionism, a new Trade Union Ordinance was adopted that required, among other things, the re-registration of all unions while passing the power of registration to the Labour Commissioner.[9] This gave the commissioner a compelling weapon whereby he could, for example, refuse to register a union if it did not adhere to the department's model constitution.

Even more significant, however, was the informal power possessed by the department's officers in the form of their monopoly of information and skills about labor matters. In a period in which small numbers of individuals were beginning to experiment with means of expressing dissatisfaction, the department was in a position to withhold informal advice if those who were expressing dissatisfaction did not pay attention to department officers.

The Labour Department did not begin to formulate policies with respect to trade unionism and industrial relations until outside pressures were brought to bear. Three sources of these pressures are most significant.

1. *The British government and the Colonial Office.* Formal concern with problems of labor in the colonies began with the formation of a Colonial Office Labour Committee in 1930. It was during the tenure of Sidney Webb as Secretary of State for the Colonies that serious efforts were begun to lay the legal foundations for the development of trade unionism in the colonies. As a result of this initiative, Tanganyika and a number of British colonies adopted trade union ordinances in the early 1930s. The Colonial Development and Welfare Act passed in 1940, included, at the insistence of Labour Members of Parliament, a provision

requiring the adoption of legislation in the colony for the establishment of trade unions before financial assistance could be granted under the act. It was this provision that led to the adoption of Labour Ordinances in Nigeria, Kenya, and a number of other African colonies.[10]

2. *The administrative conferences of Labour Commissioners in East and Central Africa.* These conferences were initiated after World War II and served as an arena within which experiences could be exchanged between Labour Commissioners in the East African territories. As events took place within one territory and were reported to other Labour Commissioners, it became apparent that the others would have to begin to move to anticipate similar developments in their own territories. As a result of such meetings, workmen's compensation legislation was prepared in Tanganyika, for example, which was based on a Kenya ordinance but was influenced by recommendations from Nigeria and Northern Rhodesia.[11]

3. *Local developments.* Although the Tanganyika government or the Labour Department, or both, might provide impetus for administrative action, the greatest pressure for legislative action came as a result of local developments. Thus, legislation was passed in Tanganyika, restricting the right to strike in certain industries only after the strike of dockworkers in 1950. Similarly, new legislation was introduced affecting trade union amalgamations and industrial relations only after the general strike call of the Tanganyika Federation of Labour in 1956.

It was these three types of forces that led to the formulation of coherent and specific policies, embodied, as will be seen, in the form of several models of development. In some cases, these models actually were given legal form; for example, the original Trade Union Ordinance in 1932. In other cases, the models assumed the form of policies that the department sought to implement in order to control the development of trade unionism and industrial relations. The usual pattern throughout the colonies was to adhere as closely as possible to Colonial Office models in the early periods of transfer; to become more eclectic and selective at later periods; and, finally, as Africans began to participate actively in the social, economic, and political processes, carefully to select and emphasize specific models from the British reality.

In the particular case of Tanganyika, the initial introduction of a trade union ordinance constituted an almost literal accommodation to pressures and specific suggestions from the Colonial Office alone. The actual adoption of the new ordinance had no functional relevance in Tanganyika at the time because there were no organizations capable of being registered nor did there exist any urbanized proletariat that might take advantage of the legislation.

As labor problems began to develop after World War II, the Labour Department needed more clearly delineated policies with respect to trade unionism and industrial relations. The department's initial action when confronted by the development of an underground union of dockworkers in

35

Dar es Salaam in 1947 was to turn to an experienced British unionist. This was again, a response to external influences since, with the British Labour government in power, the exportation of trade unionists to serve as advisers was a common practice. The experience was apparently not a happy one and the Tanganyika government soon dropped the idea of having trade union officers and even, in most cases, those with trade union background within the department.

Increasing disillusionment within the colonial government with trade unionism in Tanganyika stemmed from the fact that the newly created Dockworkers Union was apparently not going to act in a "reasonable British" manner. There was the usual financial irregularity; the officers generally failed to understand the sanctity of written agreements; union funds were being dispersed for weird —at least to the British—purposes such as sacrifices of sheep and other magical practices; and the trade union officer was obviously unable fully to control the union. This was confirmed in the violent strike of 1950. Prompted by these events as well as by the probable criticism for its support of the unions to which the department was subjected both from the Tanganyika government[12] and from employers, the department formulated two clearcut models. One was concerned with the development of joint consultation as a substitute for collective bargaining; the other, formulated as a result of pressures by the Tanganyikans for unionism, called for the formation of localized, small scale, craft-based unions. A third model was also formulated as a model union constitution.

Supporting these models but coming later were several subsidiary models emphasizing nonpolitical aspects of unionism and the "right" way to approach industrial relations. These models were emphasized to varying degrees by the department. None of them, however, could encompass all of the aspects and problems of unionism, as it began to develop rapidly in Tanganyika.

MODELS

The Joint Consultation Model

Following its unhappy experiences with the Dockworkers Union, the department began in 1949 to examine new mechanisms through which the dissatisfaction of workers could be expressed to employers and which, at the same time, would give workers the basic organizational experience that would be necessary for the operation of trade unions at some time in the future. Reflection on recent experience called forth the following statement:

> It has become apparent that in the present early stages of the development of industrial relations in the Territory it is preferable to fix the remuneration and conditions of employment in industries by statutory authority rather than by any system of collective bargaining in which neither side of industry is as yet experienced; and to encourage employers to set up industrial councils whereat employees' grievances can be ventilated through their chosen representatives.

A Whitley Council was set up in the Department in June 1949, with the principal object of forming a model for other departments.[13]

This statement was only a harbinger of a more specific policy that took shape after the violent strike in February 1950 marking the demise of the Dockworkers Union.

> During the year steps have been taken to encourage individual employers to create machinery for the improving of "employer/worker" relations, particularly as regards matters affecting working conditions, and also to set up domestic or tribal councils to handle the many social problems which occur in the day-to-day life of their employees . . . a few of the larger employers of labour have accepted the advice offered, and have placed responsibility for the welfare of their employees in the hands of specially appointed compound managers or welfare officers.[14]

It was not until early in 1951 that government policy with respect to works councils was included in legislation. In a bill aimed at regulating wages and employment conditions, one purpose was to provide for the "encouragement and recognition of simple joint consultative machinery in the form of staff committees."[15] In its 1951 report, the department noted that workers were as yet unready for trade unionism.

> . . . the experience of the post-war years shows that the evolution of a responsible trade union movement must inevitably be a slow process and that the structure of industrial relations based on the principle of joint consultation will require to be built up in well defined stages. It is believed that in the existing circumstances a start can only be made at the lowest (e.g., workshop) level and it is here that the employer must provide opportunities for his employees to meet him or his representative to discuss matters of common interest.

The department spelled out the purpose of staff committees:

> a) giving the employees a wide interest and a greater responsibility for the conditions under which their duties are performed;
> b) providing a recognized and direct channel of communication between employees and employer on all matters affecting their joint or several interests; and
> c) promoting throughout the undertaking a spirit of co-operation in securing the efficiency of the undertaking and the contentment of the staff.

The department expressed the hope that joint consultative machinery would serve as a basis for later trade union development.

> It is thought possible that the existence of joint consultative machinery and the experience it will provide for Africans may assist in the development of a more mature attitude on their part

toward industrial negotiations. It is obvious that this or a similar educational process is necessary for the development of that type of African leadership which is an essential pre-requisite to the evolution of responsible trade unionism.[16]

It was not until 1953 that a full-fledged model of a works committee emerged. The statement of government policy in the report was almost identical to the language of the previous year, but pressure was brought to bear at least on government departments to organize staff committees. The pressure took the form of a circular letter from the Member for Social Services to all government departments employing industrial labor.[17] The letter pointed out that it was the aim of government to establish fair working conditions and maintain good relations between employers and employees. Much time of government officers, it was noted, was being devoted to the settlement of disputes between employers and employees which could be resolved by the parties themselves. This could be achieved by "starting at the lowest level by forming Works or Staff Committees in individual undertakings." The letter made clear "that Government and High Commission Departments are to be guided by this general policy . . ."

Accompanying the circular letter was a set of "Notes on Works Committees" which explained differences in nomenclature, the relevant legislation, and the formal functions of the committees. A suggested constitution was provided for representation of management and different segments of workers (including junior clerical staff, headmen, and laborers). The constitution also provided for regular meetings to be held with fixed agendas to be prepared in advance by prior submission of agenda items. It was forbidden to open new points for discussion unless there was agreement by both sides. A crude grievance machinery was included:

> When an individual employee desires to bring any question before the Committee, he or she should report to his or her departmental or sectional representative, who in the case of grievances, shall endeavor to reach settlement. Failing a settlement, the representative shall inform the employee's secretary. The latter shall endeavor to arrange a settlement. Failing a settlement the question shall come before the Works Committee.

The model constitution provided that "decisions shall be arrived at only by agreement between the two sides." No provision was made in case no agreement was reached.

The 1953 report completed the formulation of Labour Department policy, and there was little further development beyond the regular annual review of the progress made in establishing such committees within government units. In 1955, however, the year of the creation of TFL, the government sought to speed up the creation of joint consultative committees. Again, when the plantation

38

workers started to organize, the sisal employers began serious discussion of the establishment of joint consultative machinery.18

The most significant variation from the British original in the Labour Department's model of joint consultation is that consultation became a substitute for direct relationships in collective bargaining between unions and management. The model as developed by the department varied from British practice in two distinct ways. One, joint consultation in Tanganyika was seen as the stage preceding the creation of unions and therefore of collective bargaining. In Britain, in contrast, joint consultation began after unions were well established and collective relationships between unions and employers had been well institutionalized. Second, in Britain, because collective relationships were well established, joint consultation was organized from the top down so as not to upset existing arrangements and was regarded as auxiliary to bargaining rather than as a substitute. In Tanganyika, the department's model sought to organize joint consultative committees initially at the lowest levels.

These differences produced two consequences when joint consultation was transferred to Tanganyika. First, mechanisms resulted which were controlled essentially by the employers, since they were most aware of the operation of bureaucratic instrumentalities. Because the bulk of the African staff was unable to operate within a framework requiring agendas, the maintenance of minutes, or adherence to formalized rules, those parties with the necessary skills to operate a bureaucratic apparatus (in this case, the employers) had control. As will be shown in Appendix VII, Cases 9 and 10, the joint consultative committees therefore failed in their purpose, which was to handle lower level grievances. Second, as was only occasionally the case in Great Britain, joint consultation in Tanganyika became a main method by which the unions were excluded from the settlement of disputes by direct union-management relationships. Although employers did not seek to destroy the unions in a direct manner, they attempted continually and effectively to substitute joint consultation for collective bargaining.

The Structural Model

The disappointment with the Dockworkers Union led to the gradual formulation of a model of trade unionism that emphasized small scale organization in which Africans would be able to develop the skills necessary to the later formation of larger unions. In the preliminary stage, trade unions as such were to be discouraged, but experience with joint consultative machinery should be encouraged. Units should be organized and function at the shop or enterprise level. As unions began to develop they should be based on skill or occupation and should be organized locally rather than nationally. At a later stage, after these lower level bodies were firmly established, higher bodies would be developed.

Government considers it important that organizations should develop from craft or occupational union upwards, and that higher formations should rest upon these as the only stable foundations. Those wishing to form unions have been advised on these lines and the advice has generally been found acceptable.[19]

The Labour Department's model called for the formation of locally based craft unions organized on a small scale. It was opposed to the formation both of industrial unions, which would organize unskilled (and mainly illiterate and migratory workers), and of some central organization of the unions.

This structural model closely resembled the structure of unionism in its infancy in Great Britain and, in interviews with the writer, was frequently defended on that basis by officers of the Labour Department. Some of the deficiencies of trade unionism were attributed to too rapid development of the unions beyond the capacities of their leaders. This explained the leaders' irresponsibility in industrial relations and in financial arrangements. In Britain, unions had developed slowly over a long period and their members had had considerable time to gain experience. If the Tanganyikan unionists had only listened to the good advice of the Labour Department to go slow, it was argued, the unions would not be in such a mess.

The Model Constitution

Constitutions for unions that would satisfy basic concerns for internal democracy, internal administrative procedures, and financial regularity became essential once unions began to grow in size and significance. This was accomplished by the department in consultation with the TFL, primarily by the formulation in 1957 of a Model Constitution.[20] The constitution was fairly detailed and provided for annual conferences, elections of delegates and officers, secret ballots to be used on certain occasions, a structure of offices with fixed responsibilities, the organization of branches, the maintenance of financial records and the issuance of receipts, and the provision of financial reports.

The structure of offices and the responsibilities of each office were spelled out in considerable detail. Thus the general secretary was named the chief executive officer and official spokesman, and his duties in these capacities were defined. Similarly, financial procedures were quite fully specified. Less clearly developed in the model constitution were methods of democratic procedure. Such procedures as were delineated were aimed at establishing elementary organizational democracy in order to ensure some control by the members over the actions of the union and its officers. These ideas were also stressed by department officers who, in their contacts with trade unionists, emphasized the need for financial responsibility, the maintenance of democracy, and the holding of meetings to assess the opinion of the members.

Miscellaneous Models

The models of joint consultation, union structure, and the constitution were clearly defined in formal fashion—that is, in written reports—by the department. There were, however, a number of other models which were at most developed only vaguely in formal reports. They were largely formulated in the day-to-day interaction between the unionists and officers of the Labour Department, as the former sought advice on specific questions and as the latter sought to give trade unionism and industrial relations a "proper direction."[21] These models can be classified as being concerned with: one, separating unions from political activities; two, encouraging realism in the formulation of economic demands.

1. The nonpolitical character of unionism. Little reference to this characteristic can be found in formal reports of the department, the only exception being in 1953. "The importance at this early stage in the local development of trade unions of their devoting attention to the improvement of economic conditions of their members rather than the pursuit of political aims has also been emphasized..."[22] The implementation of this attitude took the form of innumerable informal exchanges between the unionists and officers of the department, in which the unionists were advised and warned about the consequences of political involvements. It is clear from interviews with the unionists as well as from an examination of the minutes of meetings of various union groups that the unionists feared the loss of union registration if they became politically involved. Thus when the anti-colonial Tanganyika African National Union (TANU) began to grow rapidly in 1954, and most unionists either joined it or sympathized with its purposes, there was hesitation to establish any organizational attachments to it. Indeed, it was with considerable trepidation that the unionists endorsed TANU's program calling for independence.

2. Realism in the Formulation of Economic Demands. Department officers soon discovered that union leaders formulated demands which, from the experience of unions in more developed areas, could only be considered as incredible.

> It is perhaps natural that there should be some evidence of discouragement on the part of members of trade unions if the formation of a union with which they are concerned has not resulted in the immediate alleviation or improvement of conditions of employment. This has sometimes been due to claims having been submitted which were clearly extravagant or unwarranted. Where, however, claims have been more realistic the employers concerned have generally been willing to consider them. An example of this is provided by the experience of the union of tailors who submitted

41

claims for increases in piece rates which in some cases amounted to as much as 200 percent over existing rates. When the employers ... offered to grant increases in piece rates amounting to fifty percent this offer was rejected.[23]

In most interviews conducted with labor officers by this writer, it was clear that they were continually advising the unionists to scale down their demands. Most union demands appeared to labor officers so unreasonable that they invited almost invariable rejection by employers. If union approaches to employers were to be successful, then economic demands had to be framed in some more realistic context.

Unspecified Aspects of Developmental Models

Although the Labour Department produced some fairly substantial and detailed models, many aspects of the operation of unions and of industrial relations practices could not be formulated in a transferable or consistent manner, but depended upon idiosyncratic experiences of individual labor officers. To a large extent, these unformulated aspects of trade unionism represent much of the normative processes found in any institution and are aspects that are known and understood by actors although never formally described. There were many reasons, of which the following are indicative, why some other aspects of union functioning were not embodied in models.

1. In formulating models, department officers concentrated on salient issues. Many problems that were incipient were unrecognized or regarded at first as insignificant. When they were later recognized, action was then taken to control the situation by formulating models. It was not until 1955, for example, that the department became aware of the fact that amalgamations were taking place among the unions, and that procedures controlling amalgamations became formulated.

2. Because department officers remained at a distance from the unions, they failed to understand some issues and did not fully appreciate the manner in which the unions were operating. Thus, for example, although secret ballots were required for strike votes, the conduct of many polls was far from satisfactory

3. The lack of experience of Labour Department personnel with industrial relations or unions meant that many officers had to depend on written literature or quick courses (taken usually when on leave in England) for their knowledge. During the entire period to be examined in detail (1947-1964), only three department officers had any direct experience with unions and industrial relations.[24] Thus officers could reproduce only the formal aspects of unionism in the models because they lacked knowledge about customary arrangements.

4. A good deal of transfer depended upon random factors such as the location of sympathetic or partially sympathetic labor officers, their willingness and ability to give out information, and the manner in which they treated

and dealt with African unionists. Even in the case of a labor officer who was sympathetic and able to pass along knowledge, there was always a substantial amount of movement from place to place of department officers so that there might be little continuity in the transfer of information.

Many aspects of trade unionism could not be transferred. It was not possible, for example, for the department to specify all aspects of relationships between officers of unions or the distribution of powers and responsibilities between the unions and TFL, the central trade union organization. Nor was it possible to explain many of the normative aspects of trade union officership—the need to work hard, the need for apprenticeship before people were elected to office, the dedication of officers that developed only after long apprenticeships. Similarly, although the model indicated the manner in which union policies were to be set, the actual mechanisms for making decisions could not be specified.

There were also other areas where models were not developed because of the policies of the department. Because the department sought to keep unions separated from the political movement, no attempt was made to formulate a model, based on British practice, of the relationship of the unions to a political party. The department simply stated that no relationship should exist. This meant in fact, that the Tanganyikans had to work out the relationship on their own. The department's ambivalence about international trade union assistance to the Tanganyikans precluded the formulation of a model dealing with the relations between the Tanganyikan unions and international trade union groups. In another area, its emphasis on joint consultation precluded the department from providing models for direct bargaining between the unions and management. Because of the department's commitment to joint consultation, serious dislocation was to take place almost continually in industrial relations, which might have been avoided if models based on experience had been provided.

The Labour Department did not serve as the sole source for models; existing institutions in Tanganyika also provided some models. In addition, union visitors from abroad made suggestions about improving union organization. When the Tanganyikan unionists traveled abroad, they also learned much about other forms of organization and frequently brought new models home with them.

CONCLUSION

With relatively inexperienced officers who manifested, on the whole, typical European attitudes toward Africans, the Labour Department was in the anomalous position of having to create the models and direct the development of organizations, which it could hardly have welcomed. It is a credit to the department's officers that they recognized the increased unrest of workers in Tanganyika and the corresponding need for institutional mechanisms to avoid situations involving riots and public disorders. This recognition led to the formulation of a model of joint consultation. The department was also concerned, however, with the maintenance of colonial government control, which led it to stress the organization of localized craft unions, once it became apparent that unions were inevitable. The department was prepared to reformulate its models as time and exigencies required. Each model, however, tended to emphasize the function of social control rather than the expression of dissatisfaction.

Because it was impossible for the department to specify all aspects of trade union development and of industrial relationships, the department had to concentrate upon limited and specific aspects, using the right to grant and to revoke registrations of unions as the primary means of obtaining compliance from the Africans. It was this power that made certain aspects of the model extremely visible to the Tanganyikans. On the other hand, since many aspects of unionism and industrial relations could not be reduced to models, vacuums existed which had to be filled by the Tanganyikans in the best way possible.

V Structural Changes in Tanganyika Unions

The Tanganyikan Labour Department's model of localized, craft-based unions without national organization to coordinate them was initially received intact, but was rapidly destroyed as the Tanganyikan unionists moved to create national industrial unions and a central federation of unions. This move began in the middle of 1955 and, by mid-1956, was well under way. Although the Tanganyikans also proposed a series of amalgamations in the years following 1956, only one was successful. A Tanganyikan model was, in effect, formulated that called for more broadly based unions. The original idea of creating a single union encompassing all workers was soon replaced by a more limited concept of a small number of unions, each with a substantial membership and financial base, and a central federation of labor. The structure of the unions that had emerged by the beginning of 1960 remained intact until January 1964 when drastic changes took place. By 1960 most unions were typical industrial unions. They recruited all workers, regardless of skills, working within broad industrial categories, such as plantation workers, railway workers, national government workers, or local government workers. There was also one general union, which included workers in road transport, light manufacturing, and construction, as well as two small craft unions. A central federation of labor was recognized as being preeminent by its affiliated unions which, however, remained autonomous.[1] This structure developed despite the pressures of the Tanganyikan government and contrary to the model formulated by the Labour Department.

THE TRADE UNIONISTS' MODEL

Unlike the officers of the Labour Department, the Tanganyikan trade unionists in the beginning constituted neither a coherent nor an organized group. Their lack of coherence was amplified by their relative inexperience in functioning in modern organizations as well as by their youth and comparatively low educational levels (see Chapter VII and Appendix III for data on the characteristics of the union leaders). Thus when unionism began to revive in 1954, the conscious planning of union structure through consideration of models was of little concern to the unionists. They were confronted with a situation in which, following the Labour Department's model, a number of small, localized craft organizations had proliferated throughout Tanganyika but were generally unable to establish relations with employers. The early preoccupation of the trade unionists was how to organize so as to make some impact upon employers. It was after the visit of Tom Mboya to Dar es Salaam in mid-1955 that the idea of amalgamation of the local craft unions and the formation of a centralized federation of labor crystallized. Despite the opposition of the Labour Department, the unionists actively organized on this basis. The officers elected by the founding conference of the Tanganyika Federation of Labour in 1955 were instructed to bring about the merger of the various localized crafts into national industrial unions.

It was only after the organization of the TFL and the creation of a number of national industrial unions that the future structure of the unions became a subject of discussion. The newly created industrial unions proved to have many weaknesses, and thus began to develop an interest in further amalgamations in order to create unions of a more general type. There was general dissatisfaction with the Labour Department because of its emphasis on a model based on British trade unionism. Speaking to the TFL Annual Conference in October 1956, General Secretary Rashidi Kawawa said: "The structure of our unions has followed that of the British despite the fact that conditions in the two countries were quite different. We copied the British because this was given to us by our masters."[2]

The two main issues concerning the trade unionists were: one, how should unions be developed—as industrial or general unions; and, two, what should be the relations between the TFL and its affiliated unions? To a considerable extent, the questions overlapped.

The main orientation of the unionists was that unions should be broadly based units that would be financially strong. This basic idea underlay Mboya's suggestions during his mid-1955 visit; it helped to produce the industrial union structures through a series of amalgamations in 1956. But many of these newly formed industrial unions continued to experience serious organizational weakness. Although most of the union leaders continued to subscribe to further amalgamations, the structure of the unions tended, after 1956, to become somewhat frozen. The question of further amalgamations was raised at the 1957 annual conference of TFL, and a vaguely worded resolution advised "all unions of the same nature to amalgamate and have one committee."[3] Since there was no specification as to which unions were to amalgamate, and some of the leaders were beginning to enjoy the positions of power as officers of their own unions, no further amalgamations were actually attempted.

46

The issue was revived in September 1958 after an upcountry tour by President Michael Kamaliza and General Secretary Rashidi Kawawa revealed a large number of moribund branches of unions. At a meeting of the Emergency Committee (the equivalent of an executive committee) of the TFL:

> The General Secretary reported on the weakness which had been found in unions upcountry. He pointed out that there are different unions of workers in the various towns but there are considerable relationships in the activities of these various unions. Because of the existence of so many unions, insufficient funds were available for union growth. The General Secretary therefore proposed that arrangements be made for amalgamation.

> After a long discussion a resolution was presented which proposed that "all unions which are alike and which are now functioning individually should amalgamate together to form strong unions."[4]

This resolution was adopted. Instead of leaving the situation vague, the emergency committee began a discussion of specific amalgamations and the following amalgamations were called for:

1. Transport and Allied Workers; Commercial and Industrial Workers; Building and Construction Workers; Tailors, Shoemakers and Garment Workers.

2. Railway African Union and the two dockworkers unions [the Tanga organization and the Dar es Salaam organization which included members in the southern ports of Tanganyika].

3. Government Workers Union and the Public Works Department Workers Union.

4. Remaining unions for which amalgamation is possible.

Each proposed amalgamation was voted upon individually and accepted by an overwhelming vote. The matter was then left to the General Secretary to implement.[5]

The proposed amalgamations, with one minor change,[6] constituted the model of trade union structure which the unionists saw as necessary in Tanganyika. The first two amalgamations would have produced general unions including within each of them all types of skilled and unskilled workers from a variety of heterogeneous industries. The significant element in the first amalgamation would be the lack of any dominant employer in these industries. The second proposed amalgamation would have brought together workers who were engaged in the transport of goods but, since there was no single employer for all dock and railway workers,[7] this amalgamation also would be described as general rather than industrial.

The third proposed amalgamation would have created a single organization of employees of central government. This would have been an industrial union since its base would have consisted of employees of a single employer. The remaining unions within TFL would have been mainly industrial in their structure.

As a model, this structure was far less clearly articulated than that of the Labour Department. Nor was the rationale underlying the model clear and explicit. The main impetus for this model appears to have been the crucial shortage of leadership upcountry. In each town, there were one or two people willing to take risks and make sacrifices to conduct the affairs of a union in the town. But, under the Labour Department system, the number of such people was inadequate for the number of branches in each town. The Dar es Salaam leadership recognized that amalgamation of the unions would permit the maintenance of unions in the smaller towns with reduced requirements for leadership personnel.

The model thus created by the unionists was based less on external models than on internal requirements. Yet the unions themselves were unable to implement their model's basic principle of continued amalgamation. It was not implemented, in fact, until the government action of 1964.

THE REALITIES OF STRUCTURAL EVOLUTION

In the early period of trade union revival, during 1952-54, the Labour Department was able to implement its model of union structure effectively. Beginning in 1955, however, pressures of changing political, economic, and social events overwhelmed the department, and a holding action was fought with little success.

The trade unionists followed a similar pattern of success and failure. At first without any serious consciousness of models, they were able to create a central trade union federation and industrial-based affiliates. As they became aware of problems of structure, the unionists were only partially successful in implementing the model they had developed.

A brief year-by-year account of union development shows the courses followed by the two groups.[8]

1952. The organizations emerging after the collapse of the Dockworkers Union adhered to the two criteria of the Labour Department's model:

1. The organizations were localized: Tabora, Kilimanjaro, Kigoma-Ujiji.

2. The organizations were craft-based: tailors, masons, clerks.

Organizations registered during this period did not take the name of "union" but were titled "associations." While no policy on this matter was revealed, there are indications that this followed internal policies of the Labour Department.

The African Commercial Employees Association was formed and sought registration. Indications are that the organization sought a national

48

jurisdiction, and registration was refused until its constitution was changed to limit its activities to Dar es Salaam. It was permitted to register in 1953.

1953. The situation existing in 1952 continued. Localized craft groups were registered as associations.

1954. A departure from the Labour Department model can be noted, in that one of the two organizations registered was a localized industrial organization, albeit formally functioning as a staff association rather than as a union. This was the African Staff Association of the Landing and Shipping Company of East Africa, Dar es Salaam.

1955. At the beginning of the year, there was a sharp increase in the number of unions registered. All of the organizations registered early in 1955 were localized craft organizations, but many used the name union instead of association.

Developments later in 1955, in effect, destroyed the Labour Department's model. The first of these developments was the organization of the central federation of labor, TFL, which was opposed by the Labour Department. In the opinion of the department, such an institution should have been the capstone of long range organization throughout Tanganyika. The department registered the TFL, but remained hostile to it. (See, for example, Chapter VI, p. 60, also note 9, p. 247.

The second blow to the department's model was the creation of national industrial unions. Three were organized and registered: the Local Government Workers, the Domestic and Hotel Workers, the Railway Workers. Although the members of these unions were actually concentrated in the capital, the unions claimed a national jurisdiction. In addition, as a result of the conference which founded TFL, measures were taken to combine the localized craft unions into a number of national industrial unions which were registered during 1956.

1956. Aspects of the department's model continued to be manifested in the registration of two localized craft groups—the Nzega Tailors Association and the Tanga Motor Drivers Union. The department used delaying tactics to discourage the amalgamations that were being effected under the TFL leadership. The registration by the department of two provincial-based unions reflected the department's attempt to yield a little to the pressure for broader based unions. Officers of the department recognized, however, that the pressure for the formation of national industrial unions was becoming intense and that complete refusal to register these unions would lead to serious conflict with the union leaders. Possibilities of influencing future developments would thereby be undermined. The registrations of national industrial unions for tailors and garment workers, for transport and allied workers, and for

49

commercial and industrial workers reflect the change. With reluctance, the department began to accept the idea of the demise of its own model.

1957. The department fought a rearguard action by attempting to prevent the organization of a national union for plantation workers. Two provincial plantation unions were accepted for registration for Tanga and Eastern Provinces. All three of the other unions registered during this year were national and industrial.

1958. Seven new unions were registered. Of these, four were national and industrial, one was provincial and industrial, and only two were craft organizations and, significantly, of rather skilled occupations (teachers and medical workers). The acceptance of registration of the Plantation Workers Union as a national organization marked the final collapse of the Labour Department's model. From this point on, the department aimed at controlling the structures of the unions by hindering proposed amalgamations of industrial unions into even broader based general unions.

The main tendencies in structural developments of the unions are shown in Table V.1 by the growth of the total number of unions in 1955 and 1956, the decline in the total number of unions in 1957, and the quadrupling of the average number of members per union. These figures reflect the mergers of the localized craft unions carried on by the TFL. Membership figures must be treated with considerable care since they are, at best, educated guesses by the Labour Department.

Post-1958 developments

Although there was general agreement on the principle of amalgamation at the November 1958 conference of TFL, it soon became evident that there were a number of problems involving actual implementation.[10] TFL General Secretary Kawawa indicated that some leaders were reluctant to accept amalgamation even though their members supported it.[11] Stated opposition to amalgamation seemed to stem from bitterness against other unions involved in the amalgamation or from fear that the leaders of the newly amalgamated unions would be unable to cope with running a larger organization. The rebuttal by the proponents of amalgamation was that some objections were really based on the fear of the loss of leadership posts through the amalgamation. In the vote that followed, three-quarters of the delegates supported the proposed amalgamations. In the following three months, despite many discussions, amalgamations were rejected by three of the unions.

The Medical Workers Union opposed amalgamation because, being a skilled group, its dissolution into an organization of government workers consisting almost entirely of unskilled and illiterate workers was unacceptable. This was a typical craft union argument. It is possible that the union leaders

50

Table V.1   African Trade Unions Registered in Tanganyika
1952–1962

| Year | Number of Unions by Size of Membership | | | | | | | Total Number of Unions | Total Estimated Membership* | Average Number of Members per Union** |
	Size Unknown	0-99	100-499	500-999	1000-2999	3000-4999	5000 or over			
1952		1	1					2	301	150
1953		4	1					5	687	147
1954	2	3	1					6	291+	48+
1955	2	9	7	1				19†	2,349+	124+
1956	1	11	5	2	5			24	12,912	538
1957		2	3	5	2		3	15	33,986	2,266
1958	1	3	3	4	2		5	18	44,600	2,478
1959		2	3	3	5		4	17	78,100	4,594
1960	1	2	1	4	3		5	16	91,770	5,736
1961	1	1	1		4		7	14	199,915	14,279
1962			1	1	2		8	12†	182,153	15,179
1963			1		4		7	12	147,177	12,265

* Membership estimates are provided by the Labour Department. Where a "+" is used this means that the department estimated the membership in excess of the figure provided.
** Averages are computed by dividing the total union membership by the number of unions.
† The Tanganyika Federation of Labour, registered as a union, is not included in this figure.
Source: Tanganyika, Annual Report of the Labour Department, 1952–1962.

did not want to lose their positions, but it is somewhat unlikely that this was the basis of rejection since the organization was small and unable to support any officer other than a secretary who was little more than a clerk. The union's main concern, therefore, appears to have been its desire to retain its craft identity.

The Building and Construction Workers Union was divided over the issue of amalgamation. The president opposed and the general secretary favored the move. When the new Transport and General Workers Union was formed, a number of branches of the Building Workers Union split off to join the amalgamated organization; others, particularly in Dar es Salaam and other large towns, remained with the original organization. The main argument against amalgamation was that it was being imposed from above without the consent of the members. In addition, there was resentment against the unions with which the building workers were supposed to amalgamate because of previous membership raids. The Building and Construction Workers Union was subsequently expelled from the TFL and continued its independent existence without the branches that had supported the amalgamation.

The Tailors, Shoemakers, and Garment Workers Union was a fragmentary organization with a scattering of members in several town. They were held together by locally based trade union entrepreneurs, but there was no coherent national organization. Refusal to amalgamate seemed to be based primarily on the fears of the entrepreneurs that they might lose their positions.

By mid-1959, the Transport and General Workers Union (TGWU) was formed through a merger of the Transport and Allied Workers Union and the Commercial and Industrial Workers Union, supplemented by several branches of the Building Workers and scattered members of the Tailors Union. Complications of TGWU's registration occupied its officers until early in 1960 when the new union was finally legally registered.

The proposed amalgamation of the two government workers unions took place, on paper, in mid-1959. The amalgamated union was not registered and could not function as a single body, however, because one of the units had not complied with the Trade Union Ordinance's requirements. In addition, a serious internal dispute wracked the Tanganyika African Government Workers Union. The merger of the unions was not actually achieved until mid-1960 when a European trade unionist, sent to Tanganyika to assist unions of government employees, became involved. The result of the merger was the Tanganyika Union of Public Employees.

The proposed merger of the dockworkers unions in Tanga and Dar es Salaam and the railway workers was favored by all parties concerned. Yet no merger took place and the amalgamation was never taken seriously by any of the unions involved. This presents a puzzling picture until the influences shaping the trade union movement are more closely examined, as is done below.

The unionists can hardly be said to have been successful in achieving all three specific amalgamations agreed upon by the TFL. In fact, the unionists found themselves only in a slightly better position than had the Labour Department in terms of the implementation of their own model. The reasons for this situation go to the heart of the problem of trade unionism in Tanganyika.

FORCES INFLUENCING THE EVOLUTION OF UNION STRUCTURE

Among the factors contributing to the formation of unions on a national basis were the availability of structural models other than that proposed by the Labour Department and the already existing national economic structures with which the unions had dealt. Contributing to the demise of the craft unions and the formation of industrial unions were the lack of skills in the African labor force and the corresponding lack of significant stratification. The initial movement toward amalgamation was partly inspired by the need for full-time union officials able to express the dissatisfaction of workers. Given the lack of sufficiently trained personnel, broader based unions, requiring a total of fewer officials, were more realistic than were the smaller, more numerous, organizations.

Once some of the financial problems were resolved, however, and union leaders began to appreciate their position both in terms of income and power, the trend toward amalgamation tended to stop. It is significant that of the two successful amalgamations, one (which created TGWU) consisted of unions that dealt with relatively small employers; the second was accomplished only because of the continuous efforts of an outside trade union adviser. An added deterrent to further amalgamation was the Labour Department's administrative interference to prevent mergers, which provided time for the institutionalization process to take place within the unions.

The Availability of Other Structural Models

Central government, a variety of other government organizations (High Commission agencies and local governments), large commercial firms, and the wage determining machinery of the sisal industry, all constituted models with which the trade unionists had contact as employees. Government—as an enterprise—served as a model for the trade union leaders, most of whom had worked in some government agency. (See Appendix III, Table AIII-16) The same is true of the sisal industry where wages and conditions were determined by a single agency, the Tanganyika Sisal Growers Association.[12] With approximately half of the labor force employed in highly centralized operations,[13] it would have been surprising if localized unions showed any degree of viability. Furthermore, much of the remainder of the labor force was employed by commercial and industrial concerns which were either national or East African in scope. Thus, employing organizations constituted a model for the burgeoning trade unions, emphasizing national control over localized units by the central headquarters.

What was, perhaps, the most visible structural model for the unionists was that of the mushrooming nationalist party, the Tanganyika African National Union (TANU).[14] These future leaders were cut off from their tribal background by their education, and rejected by the Europeans and Asians. TANU opened to them the exciting concept and hope of an African nation, which would be their own. The idea of nation stood out in sharp contrast to previous attachments to "home"—that is, the local community in which one was raised and where one's family still remained—and to tribe. Educated Africans, the trade union leaders among them, began to develop national consciousness and rejected anything that smacked of localism. TANU's appeal was as a national organization without differentiation according to occupation. But the Labour Department model's emphasis on local units was clearly antithetical to the new national consciousness. Parenthetically, the localized emphasis of the Labour Department was a reflection of broader colonial policy which, since 1947, had stressed the evolution of local government as a concrete embodiment of self-government. The reaction of the unionists against localized organization was as strong as TANU's opposition to emphasis on local government. The unionists, like TANU, wanted national organization since it was at this level that key decisions were made that determined local problems.

Structural Parallelism with Existing Economic Structures

Organizations that deal with one another on a competitive, as well as cooperative, basis sometimes duplicate the structure or activities of those organizations, a phenomenon that has been called "structural parallelism."[15] Unlike governments or businesses, the functional requirements of which are not primarily to deal with conflict, it is the fundamental responsibility of trade unions to represent the interests of workers vis-a-vis employers. If an employer commands a superior technology, the trade union will be at a disadvantage and will seek to deal with an employer by imitating his techniques as well as by developing new ones. If a union is successful in developing new techniques, an employer may in turn have to copy or innovate. A process of adaptation is continually taking place between organizations in conflict, as each seeks to maintain a position of advantage in relation to the other.

In Tanganyika, parallelism was manifested by a tendency to create organizations to deal realistically with power centers. If, for example, government servants in Mwanza wanted a wage increase, there was little point in going on strike in Mwanza because the decision on their case had to be made in Dar es Salaam, for the consequences of an increase would ramify throughout the country. Thus localized decisions were not possible and localized conflict was meaningless. The organization of government workers had to be national because no other form of organization would be effective. The same can be said of most other significant economic units.

The Labour Department did not consider the differences that existed between Britain and Tanganyika or that it was essential that unions reproduce the power structures of the units with which they were in conflict. In Britain, localized craft unions emerged in a period in which industry itself was localized and occupationally specialized. In Tanganyika, the structure of employment could only lead to a tendency to create national units with a broad occupational base and headquarters near the center of power of the industry. The need for this sort of national organization became apparent as soon as the localized organizations became active in 1955.

Homogeneity of the African Labor Force

On the basis of Britain's experience during its industrial revolution, the fundamental assumption of the Labour Department's model was that occupational differentiation was real and created differences in life styles. In a pioneering industrializing nation such as Britain had been, skills were developed

54

through a slow process of accretion of technological knowledge. Workers were proud of their skills: they dealt with craft-conscious employers who concentrated certain skills in limited forms of production.

By the time Tanganyika's unions emerged, a division of labor had been created by a relatively small number of skilled workers who, because of the lack of training facilities and educational institutions in the country, were largely recruited from Britain, India, and Italy. The unskilled character of the Tanganyika labor force and its consequent homogeneity are illustrated in Table II.4, page 20. A full two-thirds of the employed labor force was completely unskilled. And as was noted in the discussion of that table, the remaining one-third was composed largely of illiterate workers who, in other contexts would have been classified, at best, as semiskilled workers. Indeed, the only groups of workers with distinctly different life styles were clerks, medical workers, and school teachers; that is, Africans with higher levels of education and involved in the Western cultural system. Most artisans followed a style of life essentially the same as that of other African workers, even though they were more affluent. The orientation toward "one big union" stemmed from this lack of clear distinction between levels of skills or between occupations.

The educated Africans, however, were differentiated from the mass of the working population. They had better housing, accepted European standards, and sought the general values of Western culture. Yet, of this group which provided the leadership for the unions, only the teachers and medical workers created their own special unions. The more numerous clerks did not seek to differentiate themselves organizationally from the unskilled workers.

They did not seek their own craft unions because an African with skills, education, and a degree of westernization who sought to follow a European way of life was denigrated. Instead of being encouraged to escape his low status as an African, he was constantly told how badly educated, ill-equipped, incompetent, and inadequate he was. Thus, his identity with all other Africans was emphasized. In this respect, African experience in Tanganyika and in the British East and Central African regions was somewhat different from that of French-speaking Africa where many advantages existed for westernized Africans. Although Africans in the latter areas also experienced the colonial situation, mobility opportunities were greater (up to a point) and education could be translated into more significant material and social perquisites.

Educated Africans experienced considerable ambivalence about their situation. Although they regarded their more traditional countrymen as backward, the emphasis placed by the European-dominated social system on the racial identity of all Africans prevailed. Thus when a lengthy strike of railway workers took place in 1960, the educated clerks supported the unskilled workers—they were all African. In this way, racial factors in the colonial situation impeded the development of an internal stratification system among African workers in Tanganyika, so that unions based on occupational differences made little sense.

The Need for Full-time Personnel

Tanganyika is a large country whose urban population is concentrated in about twenty towns. Its plantation population is also widely dispersed. Too few leaders had to cover too much area. Aggravating this situation was the prevailing fear of victimization by employers shared by workers and leaders so that leadership of the unions became regarded as a full-time occupation. Yet, as long as unions were limited in size by occupational differentiation and locality, it was not possible financially to support full-time leadership. All of these factors produced a drive toward the creation of more broadly based structures to solve the leadership personnel problem.

There is a tendency, given the general political upheaval that was taking place and the reaction against British rule, to attribute the rejection of the department's model to sheer opposition to anything British. It is of course possible that there may have been some elements of this present. The overwhelming evidence is, however, that the trade unionists were subjected to forces which at that time they barely understood or appreciated.

Effects of Institutionalization and Administrative Interference

The Labour Department's delaying tactics involved the creation of an elaborate system of rules which made amalgamation administratively difficult. When the new Trade Union Ordinance was passed in 1956, amalgamation of unions was permitted as long as proper written notice was given to the Trade Union Registrar by the secretaries and six members of the amalgamating unions.[16] In new legislation passed in anticipation of the amalgamations, a secret ballot of the membership became obligatory, and all unions were required to complete and file a number of forms before a newly amalgamated union could be registered.[17]

The department was determined to implement this legislation vigorously. The unions that formed the new Transport and General Workers Union spent six months satisfying the department's requirements before the union was registered. During this period, relations with the employers were almost totally ignored. Similarly, the amalgamation of government workers unions was held up until one of the unions complied with requirements for a financial accounting. In both of these cases there was little doubt that the amalgamations would eventually be completed; the department was able only to delay its completion.

Meanwhile, the unions themselves were undergoing substantial change, as union leaders began to develop serious stakes in the maintenance of their organizations. The reaction to the proposed amalgamation of the railway workers union and the two dockworkers unions is an illustration.

The Tanga Dockworkers Union was directed by two strong leaders who, over a period of years, had worked out a modus vivendi between themselves. This union's relations with the Tanga port employers were quite stable, and the union had established a satisfactory system for handling grievances. The much larger Dar es Salaam union had been plagued by a long history of inadequate leadership and highly unstable relations with employers. Any merger of the two dockworkers unions might have imposed the unstable industrial relations of Dar es Salaam on the relatively happy circumstances of Tanga. The Tanga leaders felt therefore that amalgamation could only be achieved if the Dar es Salaam union became somewhat more stable.

A merger of the two dockworkers unions with the railway union raised additional questions because of the powerful leader who had emerged among the railway workers. Early in 1959, the Tanganyika Railway African Union (TRAU) had elected a new general secretary. Although young and inexperienced, C. S. K. Tumbo, hard-driving and a good organizer with a sense of the dramatic, soon made a serious impact not only on his own union but on the entire country. Tumbo took a heterogeneous collection of workers scattered over hundreds of miles of railway line and welded them into a powerful economic force. Through an 82-day strike which won substantial response from the workers, Tumbo developed a strong sense of union consciousness among his followers. Had amalgamation taken place, Tumbo would have had the best claim to a new union composed of dock and railway workers. Yet he was the newest of the leaders, and by far the most militant; the dockworkers feared that they might become subjects for mobilization on behalf of the railway workers rather than for their own purposes. In these circumstances, serious discussions concerning a merger between the three unions never materialized.

At the same time that the unions and their leaders were developing a stake in the maintenance of the status quo, the continued growth of the unions provided each with some kind of financial basis, albeit a perilous one. The major argument for continued amalgamation rested upon the need to support full-time personnel. Throughout 1959 and subsequently, the unions were continually building their memberships. Although financial problems and a shortage of experienced personnel remained crucial, the unions became able to maintain a full-time secretary at provincial centers, and some had one or more full-time people in each major town.

The sum of these developments was that the principle of amalgamation lost its viability after the amalgamations forming the Transport and General Workers and the Public Employees unions were finally registered in 1960.[18]

CONCLUSION

The form of any institutional structure can be expected to reflect both the functions of that institution and the social, cultural, economic, and political organization of the society within which it develops. No institution can be developed along preconceived lines without some adaptation taking place. The case of the structure of Tanganyika's unions is enlightening in terms of the model of analysis developed originally. Here was one situation in which a crucial group of agents of transfer—the officers of the Labour Department— sought to impose a structural model on an indigenous social group without heeding either the varying conditions under which the original trade union forms had evolved or the particular functions of the institution being transferred.

Although the Labour Department, in creating its trade union model, recognized the need of mechanisms to permit grievances to find overt expression, it sought a compromise solution in which organizations would be established but would not get out of hand. The intrinsic incompatibility of these goals precluded the success of the solution. In addition, because of colonial attitudes toward the Africans, the westernized elite, instead of forming an intervening layer, or middle class, provided the leadership for the burgeoning unions and the nationalist movement.

On their part, the unionists initially were not conscious of the problems of structure beyond an awareness of their immediate needs. Thus the early discussions tended toward "one big unionism." Neither this nor the subsequent proposals for amalgamation reflected ideological commitments: the Tanganyikan unionists were neither syndicalists nor ideological trade unionists. The overriding principle guiding their actions was eclectic and pragmatic. The failure of the Tanganyikan unionists to implement their model was only partially due to the hindrances thrown in the way by the Labour Department. These were manifold and annoying but not insuperable compared with the obduracy of the trade union leadership itself.

It was not until 1964 that structural changes occurred again and a "one big union" structure was created by the passage of legislation which made illegal the TFL and its constituent unions. In this case, the government itself was undertaking to revise the core functions of unions; the unions were converted from consumptionist to productionist activities.[19] The independent Tanganyika government thus carried on many of the former colonial government traditions of interference with the unions, but its power was considerably greater and it was able to impose structural changes that would have been inconceivable in the colonial period.

VI The TFL and Its Affiliates

Tom Mboya's original idea of a central federation of labor was immediately acceptable to the unionists, but he did not specify either any relationship between the central organization and the affiliated unions or the actual details of the TFL structure.[1] Because the Labour Department's model also failed to provide for a central trade union organization, the structure of the central federation and its relation to its affiliated organizations had to be worked out over a period of time by the Tanganyikan unionists themselves. Launching the central organization, the Tanganyikan Federation of Labour (TFL), in October 1955 was relatively easy, but difficulties soon developed in its relations with its affiliated unions. An unstable equilibrium was worked out in which the TFL emerged as the preeminent trade union body but the autonomy of affiliates remained relatively intact. Intervention by the central organization into internal affiliate affairs was tolerated only under limited and special circumstances.

TFL's strength with its affiliates stemmed from a variety of circumstances peculiar to the rapid growth of trade unionism in late-developing countries. Because it was the unions' representative in a series of important and influential relationships with external organizations (not including employers), the TFL acquired substantial powers in the distribution of support and assistance. The need to maintain order and effect coordinated action among affiliates that did not always get along together required organization at a higher level, such as the TFL, which could intervene at appropriate times. Finally, the TFL emerged as a significant body because of the relative expertise of its leadership.

The TFL position with respect to its affiliates gradually weakened as the affiliates developed greater skills in industrial relations and began, independently, to produce a series of small victories. Exacerbating the weakening process was TFL's chronic financial crisis. Although a dispenser of considerable patronage from a variety of external groups, TFL's financial organization and stability was, if anything, less reliable than that of its affiliates. After a period of considerable stability, the turnover of officers increased and TFL leadership was less able to influence the course of trade union events. In

1964 the TFL was replaced by a highly centralized structure, and stability, in effect, was imposed by the government.

THE FORMATION OF TFL AS A CENTRAL STRUCTURE

The British Trades Union Congress (TUC), which consists of a number of offices, an annual conference, a general council, and an emergency committee, served as a model for the relatively simple internal structure of the TFL.

The chief administrative officer of the TFL, like that of the TUC, was the general secretary. The president of the TFL was relatively less important than its general secretary. This was the form of TFL's internal organization from the beginning, and it underwent little change (aside from a brief experiment with an American structure in 1960-62, see page 74.

Far more complex was the relationship of the central trade union group with its affiliated organizations. A variety of possibilities existed, ranging from the weakly articulated relationship of the TUC to its affiliates, to the highly centralized organizations such as Norway's Landsorganisasjonen i Norge, or Austria's Oesterreichische Gewerkschaftsbewegung.[2] The objections to the TUC as a model for these relationships has been clearly stated: "British trade unionism has grown only through many years of hard labor. The unions are now very strong and do not depend upon the Trades Union Congress for assistance. This is quite different than in Tanganyika where the unions are weak and cannot be self-reliant without TFL assistance."[3]

Although it is likely that Labour Department officers assisted in the preparation of the first TFL constitution, the dapartment's only real concern was to be sure that the central trade union body did not emerge with too much power. The department clearly disapproved of the emergence of a central organization of labor at that time, before unionism had had a long period of development in the country.[4]

To the extent that there were any models for the relationship of the central organization to its affiliates, it was the Tanganyika African National Union that was most significant. But the idea of such a centralized, unified structure failed to be acceptable to the union leadership. Without a model, the relations between the TFL and its constituent organizations slowly emerged in response to various exigencies that came to the fore at different times.

The first limitations on the TFL were imposed by the Labour Department, which made clear that there was to be no strong central organization actively involved in industrial relations and other economic affairs. During the strike of December 1956, which developed as a result of a threatened general strike of domestic and hotel workers, the Labour Department intervened in a manner seen as favoring the employers. The TFL supported a number of sympathy strikes called by affiliated organizations, and threatened a national general strike in support of those striking workers who were discharged from their jobs. Meanwhile, in a number of unpleasant sessions held between TFL leaders and representatives of the Labour Department, the government stated that it considered TFL involvement in strike activities to be unconstitutional. Although the TFL officers stood by their general strike threat (ultimately withdrawn only after the arrival of two European trade unionists who helped effect a settlement), these early experiences weakened TFL's effectiveness in direct economic actions. The process of setting the limits of TFL action had begun.

THE EMERGENT REALITIES OF TFL-AFFILIATE RELATIONSHIPS

The early response of the unionists toward the TFL was one of dissatisfaction with the initial structure which they themselves had wrought. Although the formation of national industrial unions strengthened the movement enormously, the union leaders were unable to come to grips with employers. Frustrated by their continued lack of success, the unionists continually searched for stronger organizational forms, believing somewhat naively that the sheer fact of organizational structure would make employers give in to often incredible demands. (For discussions of union demands, see Chapter IV, pp. 41-42; Chapter VII, p. 90; Appendix VII, Cases 9, 10.)

The Single Union Idea[5]

The notion of a single union into which all existing organizations would merge was the product of a lengthy discussion[6] during the second conference of the TFL, in October 1956. The problems of the unions were probably exacerbated at that time by the ripening situation which was to culminate in the December strike. There was agreement among the delegates that the unions required strengthening: "Our objective in organizing the TFL is to have the strongest body of all. If there is any way in which the TFL can be given powers to assist the unions, let them be found. TFL is the father and the responsibility of fatherhood is to find food for the children."

Two basic strategies emerged. The first was a proposal to empower the TFL to work with affiliates, which was stated in a vaguely worded resolution that "TFL shall be responsible and shall help its unions in any matter at any time." The resolution was not sufficiently explicit about ways in which the TFL might provide assistance in union activities. The second strategy was evidenced in the suggestion of one delegate "that it is better if our unions follow the structure of the political parties, that is, have one trade union only catering for the entire country"; and in the substantial discussion, initial favorable response followed his remarks.

One of the few voices opposed to a single union warned that if the one union were banned, there would be no unions left in Tanganyika. The memory of the dockworkers' experiences must have been strong. The delegates referred the question of the single union to a special committee, and this effectively removed the proposal from further consideration. Although various unionists referred with some interest to the single union idea in interviews as late as 1959-60, the idea was never resuscitated in further discussions on structure.[7] The concern with strengthening the unions focused instead on the amalgamations, the results of which have already been discussed.

TFL and Amalgamations: A Case Study in Organizational Weakness

As has been indicated, the TFL was unable to be fully effective in carrying through the proposed amalgamations. An examination of a sequence of meetings illustrates the weakness of the TFL leadership.[8]

General Council, March 1956. There was general agreement on the value of amalgamation: "Unions which are alike should have similar names so that they can be combined more easily when they become stronger."

Annual Conference, October 1956. The discussion concentrated on the single union idea; there was little mention of amalgamation.

Annual Conference, November 1957. A resolution was adopted advising "all unions of the same nature to amalgamate and have one committee."

General Council, June 1958. The first agenda item dealt with amalgamation. The Council "agreed that TFL should continue advising all similar unions to amalgamate." A single union for all civil servants was urged. Further, amalgamation was seen as a solution to the "scramble among unions for membership."

Emergency Committee, September 30, 1958. As a result of the visit up-country by the TFL president and general secretary, amalgamation was once again raised as a solution to the problem of organizational weakness. The committee agreed on three specific amalgamations and one vaguely worded one.

Annual Conference, November 1958. A discussion of the emergency committee proposal and progress report led to agreement on the urgency of amalgamation. The affected unions were ordered to implement the resolution by January 1, 1959.

Emergency Committee, February 26, 1959. The general secretary reported progress on amalgamation, but that the Medical Workers and Building and Construction Workers had refused to amalgamate. Vague agreement was obtained to proceed with amalgamations of those agreeing and to "wait and see" the results.

General Council, April 1959, Following a discussion of the refusal of some unions to amalgamate, the council agreed that all unions that had been specified should amalgamate by June 1, 1959. The emergency committee was empowered to proceed after that date, with amalgamating unions that were willing to amalgamate. The newly amalgamated unions would have the right to include workers from the unions rejecting amalgamation—thereby permitting the raiding of membership.

Emergency Committee, July 22, 1959. Prior to this meeting, the Building and Construction Workers Union had been expelled from the TFL by General Secretary Kawawa. This meeting constituted an appeal against Kawawa's action. The appeal was referred to the annual conference.

Annual Conference, November 1959. After a three-and-a-half hour discussion, the expulsion of the Building and Construction Workers was sustained.

General Council, August 1960. There was discussion of the failure of amalgamation between the Railway Workers Union and the two dockworkers unions. Stating that votes favorable to amalgamation had been taken, the Railway Union and the Tanga Dockworkers Union insisted that the problem lay with the Dar es Salaam Dockworkers Union which had weak leadership. The executive (formerly emergency) committee was empowered to investigate and to call a unifying conference.

No additional documentation is available. Amalgamation became a dead issue as the focus shifted to other problems. In 1960, the vigorous opposition by a number of unions to a centralization proposal made by Michael Kamaliza, then general secretary of TFL, led to a serious split within the TFL that took the better part of a year to resolve. The Kamaliza move was primarily concerned with a proposal to centralize the financial organization of the unions and was seen by a number of unions as a threat to their autonomy. More importantly, they were concerned that the proposal might open them to control by the government and the nationalist political party, TANU. The solution to the dispute was to retain the basic structure of TFL intact.

If the central federation was unable effectively to amalgamate unions, it was because of the failure of the affiliated unions to allocate genuine power to the TFL. Had the representatives of the affiliated organizations attending TFL meetings carried back the policies agreed upon by the TFL, the central organization could have emerged with significant powers.

In addition to these deficiencies, the TFL was subject to conflicting demands. While demanding assistance and increased services, the affiliates complained about the number of full-time officers who had to be paid and in turn refused to pay affiliation fees. The TFL was seen as having external sources of support (see Chapter XI) and as needing support only on an ad hoc basis.

The Stabilization of TFL-Affiliate Relations

As the unionists obtained increased organizational knowledge, relations between the TFL and its affiliates became increasingly stable, and normative patterns began to emerge with increasing clarity. TFL intervention in the internal relations of affiliates became permissible under definite and limited circumstances.

When crises occurred within unions, it was recognized that TFL was best suited to intervene and try to bring about a peaceful solution. Thus, in 1959, when a conference of the Plantation Workers Union broke down, a TFL committee was formed to ensure that a reconvening of the conference would follow the union's rules. Similarly, when an internal fight broke out in the Domestic and Hotel Workers Union late in 1959, the annual conference of TFL established a committee to investigate.

The TFL also became the place where interaffiliate conflicts could be resolved. The unionists had learned at an early stage that they had considerable news potential and, all too frequently, when disagreements occurred, mud-slinging matches would occur in public and TFL committees would have to be created to try to restore harmony. In 1960, for example, serious disagreement developed over the future of the East Africa High Commission (see Chapter X, p. 126). The various unionists rapidly proceeded to the attack in the press, and the public display of disunity had to be resolved by the TFL. Indeed, much of the integrative activities, which became crucial after 1960 following the split in the unions, had to be accomplished within the framework of the TFL.

Intervention, to be legitimate, had to be specifically authorized by some TFL body. In cases where a specific committee was designated by the general council or the annual conference, rejection of that committee by TFL affiliates tended to be minimal. When, however, a TFL officer acted without specific authorization by one of these bodies, even though policy had previously been set, conflict was much more apt to occur. Thus, General Secretary Kawawa's own action to expel the Building and Construction Workers Union from the TFL was not only appealed but many union leaders felt that Kawawa had gone beyond his mandate, despite the indication by various TFL bodies that there would be punishment for those organizations not agreeing to amalgamation.

Except in cases where major splits developed internally and became public or appeared irreconcilable, TFL involvement in the internal affairs of the affiliates became minimal. The autonomy of affiliates was most significant in the case of industrial relations when, although TFL officers assisted the affiliates, the press of other activities precluded TFL's small staff from any serious involvement in the day-to-day business of grievance handling or disputes settlement.

The autonomy of the affiliates is illustrated by the innumerable meetings at which resolutions were passed, threats made, and cajolery used to find some method to induce affiliates to pay their fees to TFL. None were successful. Although the threat of nonrepresentation at TFL meetings had been made at almost every conference and meeting since the TFL was formed, it was not until the November 1959 annual conference that the threat was actually carried out.

Among the many resolutions passed by the 1959 annual conference, only one out of twenty-two prepared by the resolutions committee elicited discussion and opposition. This was a proposal to appoint TFL inspectors of accounts who would be empowered to inspect all books of all unions. The opponents argued that TFL's function was to advise and not to inspect. The resolution although adopted was never implemented.

Even after legislation was passed by the National Assembly in 1962 requiring all unions to be affiliated with the TFL (and, by implication, to pay their fees), TFL's financial crisis continued. The financial condition of the individual unions had improved as a result of the legalization of the checkoff, whereby the worker's dues could be withheld by the employer and forwarded directly to his union. Yet when the writer paid a return visit to Tanganyika in August 1963, all that appeared to have changed were the figures in the total debt owed to the TFL.

At the local level, the TFL played a slight role through the trades councils. Incorporating all branches of all unions in a particular locality, they were modeled after the British trades councils. They were proposed by the TFL initially in 1956 against the opposition of the Labour Department.[9] By mid-1960 there were twelve known councils centered in the largest towns in Tanganyika. The councils were not uniformly active, however, nor did they always work to resolve local conflicts between the unions. Indeed, national leadership of the affiliated unions became so dissatisfied with them that, at the 1960 general council meeting, it was suggested that the trades councils be replaced by four full-time TFL regional officers, a proposition originally made in 1958. By carrying on their work, the officers would gradually force the collapse of the trades councils. Although the trades councils never became important they helped to integrate local activities and created a forum within which the full-time leaders could exchange experiences and learn from one another.

Probably the most significant role that the TFL assumed was as spokesman in the foreign affairs of the unions. TFL's dealings with the government, TANU, and a large variety of trade union bodies outside Tanganyika gave the TFL considerable power in its relations with its affiliates.

The TFL emerged as the preeminent body in Tanganyikan unionism by 1958 and retained this position essentially until 1964, yet the affiliates retained substantial autonomy in most spheres. Compared with more established unions, the Tanganyikan reality came closer to the American system than to the British, but was far from the highly centralized pattern of the central labor organization in Austria or Norway. Both the forces contributing to

TFL's strength in its relations with its constituents and those forces contributing to its weakness are more closely examined below.

FORCES STRENGTHENING THE TFL

TFL and the External Relations of the Unions

Tanganyika's unions developed in a situation of world crisis and of extremely rapid social change. The gradual retreat of the colonial powers created a serious vacuum which a variety of external forces were eager to fill. Partly because of cold war conditions the unions could easily find the external support they needed and sought. Dealing with external agencies, however, required a relatively homogeneous point of view; this the TFL was able to present. When the British were still in control of Tanganyika, it was not possible for large numbers of external agencies to come into Tanganyika and manipulate indigenous splits to further their own points of view. Between 1955 and 1959, Western-oriented groups had an effective monopoly of contact with the unions. Although these often competed to influence the development of events, the East-West split had not yet caused the schisms that were to follow at a later stage. Thus, the unionists used the TFL to manage their external relations. This was illustrated in 1959 when the TFL confronted difficulties in raising its share of the costs to send a delegate to the conference of the International Confederation of Free Trade Unions. The Plantation Workers Union offered to let its delegate to an international conference of plantations unions represent the TFL, but the offer was turned down with considerable feeling by the annual conference, which felt that the TFL should be represented by its own officers.

In dealing with external groups the pace of events frequently required that decisions be made with dispatch. The presence, for example, of a roving mission from one of the international union groups presented many opportunities to pick up financial assistance if decisions could be made quickly. The TFL Emergency Committee was effective in this respect and, perhaps even more important, the TFL officers did not hesitate when necessary to make important decisions on their own.

Patronage

A large number of scholarships, opportunities to travel to Europe and elsewhere, the provision of cash for a variety of purposes, gifts of vehicles, subsidies to pay for the assistance of European advisers and to cover the salaries of Tanganyikan organizers, all had to be channeled by external groups into local sources known to be relatively reliable. It was possible, for example, for a Tanganyikan to return from travels with scholarships, tape recorders, and other emoluments which could be treated as personal equipment rather than as contributions to the unions. As the international trade union groups became experienced in providing assistance, they tended to channel aid through the central federations of labor—the TFL in the case of Tanganyika—and preferably through a few officers whose integrity was generally respected. In this regard, the TFL's first general secretary, Rashidi Kawawa, developed a reputation for dependability. But experience with TFL's first president, Arthur Ohanga, was less fortunate, because his questionable financial dealings soon meant that very few people trusted him. Several examples of TFL's handling of external assistance can be found in its experiences in strike situations.

Following the sympathy strikes in 1956, a number of strikers in the motor trade were discharged. The ultimate settlement returned to work those strikers with five years of service, but a substantial number who remained unemployed looked to the unions for the solution to their problem. Although the discharged workers were generally concentrated heavily in one or two unions, the financial assistance which was forthcoming through the American AFL-CIO was handled by a cash grant to the TFL rather than to the unions most seriously affected.

The 1960 strike of railway workers lasted a long time, and the union had no resources with which to assist the strikers. The financial assistance from international union sources was placed in a special account from which disbursements could be made only over the signatures of the general secretaries of both the railway union and the TFL. Thus the TFL had effective veto power over disbursements.

The TFL also exercised a different kind of veto power. In 1960, the Scandinavian construction unions made available a Swedish organizer to aid in the organization of building workers in Tanganyika. The expulsion of the Building and Construction Workers Union from the TFL precluded the workers belonging to this union from receiving this assistance. The organizer was invited to work with the "inheriting" union—the Transport and General Workers. Since the majority of the construction workers remained with the building union, this placed the organizer in a somewhat untenable position; it was resolved by his leaving Tanganyika to work elsewhere. TFL's veto powers resulting from the substantial volume of patronage gave the organization considerable strength in dealing with its affiliates.

The Integrative Activities of TFL

TFL's most significant strength developed out of the crucial need for integration of trade union activities in a period of extremely rapid growth. This growth, accompanied by a similar growth in the political movement, created enormous demands for educated manpower to staff the ranks of the administrative structures of these organizations. The demands were so great that it was necessary to employ as full-time unionists some persons who were almost illiterate, and many whose knowledge of English was negligible. The inexperience of these union officers and their tendency to undertake action on a personal basis without reference to union headquarters or proper committees made impossible meaningful communication by the unions. The TFL therefore tended to act as a center for communication particularly in crisis situations.

The TFL also acted as a force for integration in the real and threatened splits and conflicts within and between the affiliates. Initially there were jurisdictional disputes between the unions for marginal categories of workers. Later, after 1960, important policy differences separated the various affiliates. Because the union leaders had not yet developed sufficient organizational experience to make clear-cut decisions and stand by them[10] these conflicts placed the TFL in a central position in the early days, particularly during the tenure of Kawawa, whose skills as a mediator were irreplaceable after his departure. Indeed, after he left, the TFL became less effective in dealing with its affiliates.

The TFL integrative activities were continually put to a test as the unions sought to expand their memberships and move into new areas. TFL officers in 1956 effected the first amalgamations that produced the basic industrial union structure. Later, it was TFL that was primarily responsible for attempting further amalgamations. But more importantly it was through TFL that assistance was channeled to organize new sections of Tanganyika's labor force, particularly in the plantations and the mines. The organization of the Plantation Workers Union was fraught with considerable danger because the Labour Department was simultaneously encouraging the formation of provincial plantation unions, a move that fed the suspicions of early plantation unionists toward each other. It required considerable skill on the part of a central organization to bring the various quarreling leaders together long enough to launch Tanganyika's largest union. Similarly, as jurisdictional problems increased with the growth in size of the unions, they could only be resolved by a central body that demanded some degree of respect. When the African Commercial Employees Association, which had registered some early successes in organizing building workers, lost its jurisdiction over construction industries, the TFL played a central role in reconciling the damaged union.

At a later stage, when the unions were becoming stronger but were not yet sufficiently powerful to sustain many activities beyond basic internal communication, financial organization, and some industrial relations, demands increased for the expansion of peripheral services such as education, and propaganda. The existence of TFL as a central coordinating unit, particularly when combined with external assistance, made some such activities possible. For example, TFL obtained its first educational director in 1959, and a fragmentary educational program was organized for all the unions. In May 1959, after many years of discussion, a semimonthly newspaper *Kibarua* [Worker] was started and appeared sporadically until August 1960.

Finally, TFL gained some importance from the need to integrate union activities at the local level. Although the trades councils never became strong, they were a means by which unionists could be integrated in the same community. Because the trades councils were organized under the aegis of the TFL, community union leaders had an indirect connection with the central federation in addition to their contact with their own headquarters. The councils provided a center for discussion not only of local problems but also of the many inter-affiliate conflicts that raged in Dar es Salaam, and they tended to take positions in favor of unity and harmony when, frequently, conflict in Dar es Salaam had reached a breaking point.

TFL as a Source for Technical Expertise

The unionists were fortunate, at their founding conference, to elect as general secretary of TFL Rashidi Kawawa who became a most skillful trade unionist. Although he had had brief experience with unionism in the Tanganyika African Government Servants Association, Kawawa essentially learned his unionism on the job. He was, however, extremely knowledgeable and quick to learn. He also had unique personal skills such as his ability to mediate, to dissimulate skillfully when necessary, and to be extremely charming or tough as the occasion required. Most important, Kawawa and several of the other officers of TFL were quick to learn trade union tactics and strategy, to use the newspapers for effective publicity, and to manipulate what contacts existed locally or internationally to help the unions. Because TFL officers had more opportunities for gaining experience, the TFL soon became the most important source locally available to the unionists for technical expertise. The TFL was more efficiently operated than the others (although it too had serious problems of maintaining internal coherence) and its officers had some idea as to how reports had to be prepared, agendas constructed, financial accounts maintained, and files kept, as well as how to deal with the Labour Department and the Trade Union Registrar.

The TFL leadership was also more experienced and skilled than its affiliates in industrial relations activities, although this fact lost significance after the early days of unionism. Thus as crises developed, the TFL leaders were frequently drawn into negotiating sessions by leaders of the affiliated unions who felt some need for external support. TFL advice, on the basis of its expertise in dealing with international agencies, was also accepted after external assistance had been channeled to the affiliates.

FORCES WEAKENING THE TFL

Unquestionably the most significant factor isolating the central federation from the main stream of trade union activities was its exclusion from
direct involvement in industrial relations activities. Industrial relations activities became increasingly the bread-and-butter of the Tanganyikan unions as
they gained strength and began to register their first gains. The 1956 sympathy strike, the 1957 general strike threat, and the subsequent settlement
taught the unionists that a general attack upon the entire employer class
carried with it serious retribution and only small rewards. Thus the main economic action of the unions was defined within the jurisdiction of the affiliated organizations, and TFL's role became advisory or auxiliary. In addition,
the daily problems confronting the unions, such as the discharges, grievances
about pay, punishments, and discipline were beyond the capacity of the four-
man staff of the TFL. Gradually, as the union leaders increased their ability
to cope with these problems, the need for the expertise of the TFL declined.

Contributing to the TFL weakness was its chronic financial crisis.
Although patronage constituted an extremely important basis for TFL
strength, it was irregular and unpredictable. But the need for predictable
financial resources was as crucial to the TFL as it was to other organizations,
and TFL had to depend to a considerable degree upon its affiliates. The
affiliates, each with its own financial problems, found it all too easy to ignore
the perpetual financial crisis of the TFL. TFL officers were always available
for expert advice, and there was little incentive for the affiliates to change the
financial structure to give the central organization financial autonomy. Had
even some degree of independence been established initially, the TFL would
have emerged as an organization of great importance to Tanganyikan labor.

The dispensation of patronage was a somewhat mixed blessing because
at first TFL officers preempted a great deal of the early assistance; so it was
that most of the first scholarships went to TFL officers. While the position
of the TFL leadership made it inevitable that the large share of travel opportunities was used by TFL leaders rather than by affiliate leadership, this was
a source of strain which led to considerable criticism.

Other conflicts developed over the question of priorities in using occasional surplus funds; TFL officers were inclined to favor their use for central
purposes often contrary to the expectations of affiliates. After the sympathy
strikes of 1956, residual funds remained from the AFL-CIO grant after the
workers who had been fired had been resettled. A number of affiliates favored the distribution of the funds[3] among themselves, but the TFL leadership
proposed using the money to start a central newspaper.

Although the TFL constituted a source of expertise, this did not preclude considerable criticism of that expertise. The financial reports issued by
TFL officers caused much dissatisfaction, often with good reason. Experience

with Arthur Ohanga, the first TFL president, did not inspire confidence; discharged from his regular employment, much of his income came from the sale of a research booklet, *Expenditure and Consumption of African Labor in Dar es Salaam*, which he wrote for TFL publication, and from a lottery. His financial accounts of these affairs failed to satisfy the 1957 general council meeting and his suspension was supported by a substantial minority.

Delegates to TFL conferences or general council meetings generally indicated their dissatisfaction with the increasing number of full-time employees, but the small number of TFL leaders could not always fulfill demands for assistance. Despite their knowledge of TFL's lack of finances and staff, leaders of the affiliates were still dissatisfied when they could not obtain assistance at a crucial moment. Similarly, there were standing complaints that the TFL leaders ignored the upcountry unions and concentrated their energies in Dar es Salaam. These complaints were justified, even though the bulk of the work of the TFL was concentrated in the capital city.

It is obvious that there was always substantial dissatisfaction with the inadequacies of the TFL on the part of the affiliates. In sum, TFL relations with its affiliates were characterized by a desire for a strong TFL. But, although the TFL occupied a central position in Tanganyikan trade unionism, its initial strength was continually eroded as the main activities of trade unionism passed outside its sphere of involvement.

VII Organization Roles: Leaders and Members

Despite the formal definition of roles within the structure of trade unions, a great deal of flexibility exists for persons carrying on union activities. No matter how the rights and responsibilities of each office (as well as of membership) may be detailed in a constitution, participants, in fulfilling the requirements of office, may find it necessary to behave in ways not specified formally in that constitution.

The formal aspects of organizational roles delineated by the Labour Department's model constitution were adopted by the Tanganyikan unionists with few changes. The transfer of roles involved, however, somewhat different circumstances than the transfer of union structure. First, although the development of the overall structure of unions was crucial, it involved the Labour Department only in establishing long range policy and not in day-to-day activities of the unions. Second, the formal functions of any union office and criteria for membership could be specified by the department through the model constitution. The actual work, however, involved the Tanganyikan officers in minute-by-minute interaction when there were no specific guides available.

Thus the incumbents of the formal roles had to proceed beyond the formal definitions of their activities with behavior that would become normative over time.

Organizational roles can be divided into two basic categories: leaders and members. Leadership roles are superior and relatively active while membership roles tend to be passive. The distinction is important in Tanganyika because those in the roles of leaders were westernized and educated, and, therefore, there was less variation in transferring role models to this group than to the uneducated and tradition-bound members.

THE TRANSFER MODEL AND ITS RECEPTION

In the Labour Department's Model Constitution, the general secretary was designated the key officer of the organization—the same position he holds in Great Britain. The role of president, unlike that in American practice, was largely limited to that of presiding officer. Other typical British offices and their duties were copied by the Labour Department. A comparison of the duties of general secretaries in Great Britain and in the Model Constitution in Tanganyika makes clear the similarities. In Great Britain:

> As chief executive officer the general secretary is in charge of the union's administration, and all the work of the head office comes under his control . . . It will be the duty of the general secretary to see that the head office is properly staffed and equipped. Any purchase of property . . . will be negotiated by the general secretary . . . When officials are appointed . . . they will be responsible to the general secretary . . . The unions nearly always have some rule . . . that "the General Secretary shall obey the orders and be under the control of the Executive Committee," and they also prevent . . . their general secretaries from voting at executive council meetings . . . The general secretary is the chief spokesman for the union . . .[1]

In Tanganyika,

1. The General Secretary shall be the Chief Executive Officer of the Union and the official spokesman of the Union . . .

2. He shall be responsible for carrying into effect the declared policy of the Union, and shall conduct all the business and correspondence of the Union, and shall keep himself thoroughly acquainted with the affairs of the Union, and shall control the Head Office staff.

3. He shall be responsible for the keeping of the proper books and records of the Union, and shall supervise the duties of the General Treasurer in this connection . . .

4. He shall attend all meetings of the Executive Committee and Annual and Special Conferences . . . and shall have the right to speak on any matter . . . but not to vote.

Since the Model Constitution dealt with formal offices and duties, it was these rather than the less formal elements of organizational roles that served as models of transfer. Informal elements were emphasized, however, through personal contacts between the labor officers and the unionists. The idea of voluntary activity, for example, was stressed because of the weak financial condition of the unions. Also the British emphasized the importance of bureaucratic procedures in the operation of the unions. This was implemented by the legal requirement that the unions maintain financial records and make annual reports to the Trade Union Registrar. In response both to some careerists who assumed leadership roles and to the petty peculation that began to occur, labor officers stressed the idea of a moral commitment to trade unionism characterized by dedication, hard work, and honesty.

The socialist-egalitarian work ethic of British trade unionism was not, however, emphasized in Tanganyika. It was hardly to be expected that conservative-minded colonial civil servants would stress the socialist orientation of the British trade unionists. Nor did the few British trade unionists that came to the colonies carry over these ideas to any significant degree. The difference between their style of life and that of the Africans generally prohibited the development of the egalitarianism in interpersonal relations characteristic of Great Britain. Also the sense of dynamism, of social movement, failed to be transmitted to Tanganyika because labor officers deemphasized the idea of unions as key institutions of the working class.

Thus, only limited aspects of organizational roles could be developed as models for the Tanganyikan unionists and these were mainly the formal offices and duties. Other elements of British organizational roles were either unstressed or denigrated.

LEADERSHIP ROLES IN TANGANYIKA: THE REALITY

An overall examination of union leadership behavior throughout the world shows considerable homogeneity. The basic activities of unionists everywhere center upon communication, and the Tanganyikans were no exception. Much time and energy was spent in a great variety of meetings within the unions or between them and other organizations. Yet there were significant differences between unionists in Tanganyika and in Great Britain. Not only did social characteristics of union leaders differ but there were important variations in the ratio of leaders to union members, in the method of accession to office, in their work ethic, and in the creation of new roles concomitant with the cultural expectations of the Tanganyikans.

Formal Offices and Duties

From the success in effecting the transfer of formal organizational roles in Tanganyika, it can be generally concluded that formal offices and duties that can be specified in written form and legally enforced will transfer with little variation.

Only one significant variation in formal roles was attempted when the TFL experimented with an American type of structure for a two-year period. The change, which entailed slight rearrangements in personnel in various offices, was introduced after several unionists had visited the United States. A primary motive underlying the experiment was the limitation of the power of Michael Kamaliza who was, at the time, the TFL president. In changing to an American system of offices, the presidency went to Rashidi Kawawa, formerly general secretary, while Kamaliza became one of three vice-presidents. The British system was reinstated in March 1962, apparently because of the need to reduce the power of the presidency and to return to a system where the key administrative position was not so dominant; in this respect, the British system of offices was more useful than the American.

Social Characteristics of Leaders

British union leaders are, on the whole, representative of the union members.[2] The Tanganyikan full-time leaders, in contrast, reflect social origins distinctly different from the workers they represent. A measure of the difference between leaders and workers in Tanganyika is exemplified in a comparison of the skill distributions of the employed labor force with the occupational skills of the full-time leadership. Table II.4 shows that in 1958 only 5 percent of the male African labor force was employed in white collar occupations; 67 percent of employed males were unskilled. No satisfactory data are available on the characteristics of trade union leaders in Tanganyika, but a survey in 1960 showed that, of the full-time leaders interviewed, 83 percent had been white collar and clerical workers, 15 percent had been technicians (electricians or mechanics), and only 2 percent had been unskilled, manual workers (Table AIII-14).[3]

Unlike other developing countries, such as India, where union leaders often come from professional ranks and rarely have been employees,[4] the Tanganyikans were not outsiders. Almost all Tanganyikan leaders interviewed had been employed before becoming leaders, and over one-fourth stated that they had worked for ten or more years (Table AIII-19). Moreover, almost three-fourths of the respondents claimed work experience in the same industry represented (Table AIII-43) by their unions. This seemed particularly true of the Plantation Workers and the Railway African Union.

Tanganyika's full-time unionists are young, as might be expected in a union movement of short duration and rapid growth. Sixty-one percent of the leaders interviewed were under 30 years of age (Table AIII-1). Their educational background was mixed; 15 percent had less than eight years of education; 32 percent had ten or more years (Table AIII-2). Reflecting the wide diversity of tribes in Tanganyika, no single tribal group dominated the leadership, although the most populous tribes south of Lake Victoria were underrepresented and the tribes in the central sisal area around Tanga were overrepresented (Table AIII-5). Two-thirds of the union leadership was Christian, which was also a disproportionately high percentage. One-third of the respondents professed Islam, (Table AIII-11) but none adhered to traditional religions. The heavy concentration of Christians reflects the role of missionary education in producing westernized persons capable of being employed in the modern economy (Table AIII-3). Employment histories of the leaders show considerable mobility. Over two-thirds had worked for two or more employers (Table AIII-17) and a similar number had worked in two or more towns during their employment (Table AIII-18).

75

Although the leadership is undoubtedly provided by the westernized and educated elite, most of the leaders were the first generation to be westernized. Sixty percent had fathers who engaged in purely traditional pursuit, 22 percent of the respondents' fathers were educated and modernized (Table AIII-20). Other indications of traditional background are that only 56 perce knew the exact date of their birth (Table AIII-21) and 80 percent had been born in rural villages or hamlets (Table AIII-22). Wives of 63 percent of the respondents came, as tradition dictated, from their own tribe and an additional 13 percent of the respondents married women from geographically or culturally contiguous tribes (Table AIII-24). Of this latter group almost two-thirds had met their wives in the same village or area as their own (Table AIII-25). All had paid some form of *mahari* (bride wealth) at the time of their marriage but 44 percent claimed to have paid it without assistance from their fathers or other kin (Table AIII-27). Two-thirds of the respond ents envisioned a return to traditional pursuits, such as farming or fishing once they had retired from trade union activities (Table AIII-31).

Full-Time Leader-Member Ratios

In Britain, the ratio between full-time leaders and members has been estimated to be 1:3,700. In Tanganyika, by mid-1960, even small towns had at least one full-time official. On the basis of observations and examina tion of union records, this writer estimates that there was a minimum of 171 and a maximum of 448 full-time unionists in mid-1960.[5] Part of the difficulty in making such calculations is the lack of clear definition of the term "member." In 1961, TFL claimed membership among its affiliates of 43,460 members.[6] This total did not include those unions not affiliated with TFL, which would add several hundred more members. On the other hand, the Labour Department's *Annual Report* for 1960 listed total union membership as 91,770. Furthermore, considering the vague concept of membership, it could be argued that, by 1960, the membership of the unions included the total employed labor force. Such an unusual procedure provides a useful basis of comparison, since union leaders generally considered all employed persons as members of their unions. Using these three estimates and those of the numbers of full-time leaders, it is possible to construct a table (Table VII.1) summarizing the possible ratios.

If the maximum membership estimate is taken with the minimum estimate for the number of full-time leaders, the ratio (1:2,339) is still considerably higher than the ratio in Great Britain. This writer would estimate that a ratio of 1:400 (based on the membership estimate of 100,000 and on 250 full-time leaders) would be a fair representation of the ratio existing in 1960.

Table VII.1   Estimated Ratios of Full-time Union Leaders to Members—1960
(Number of Members to One Full-time Leader)

	Ratios to Full-time Leaders	
Membership Estimates	Minimum	Maximum
1961 TFL Estimate 43,460	254	97
1960 ARLD 91,770	537	205
1960 Employed Labor Force 400,000	2,339	893

The source of full-time leader estimates is given in Appendix V.

The Nonexistence of Voluntary Leadership

The difference between the ratios in Tanganyika and in Britain reflects
in part different notions of voluntarism. In contrast to Great Britain, Tanganyika
had an almost total lack of voluntary leaders, so that the work of the unions had
to be largely carried on by full-time employees of the organizations. This dearth
of volunteers was not simply the result of membership apathy, which is the normal state of affairs in Great Britain;[7] in Tanganyika, members, including the few
part-time volunteers, and leaders seemed to feel that leaders should carry on the
activities of the unions because they were employed and paid to do so. The lack
of voluntary involvement stemmed in part, also, from the relative inertness of
the rank and file membership, which was unable to read, write, or grasp the
fundamentals of modern voluntary associations. In sum, the paid employees
were responsible for the simple and routine activities, such as the collection
of dues, handling all grievances and disputes, as well as the more complex activities of determining policy, and maintaining communication.

Accession to Office

Accession to office in British trade unions, characteristic of associations
that are dependent on voluntary activities, normally comes only after a person
has proven himself by voluntary activity. Voluntary activity, in effect, constitutes an apprenticeship prior to full-time service. In Tanganyika, undertaking
full-time leadership meant engaging in the risk-taking that characterizes entrepreneurs, although in the case of the union leaders this represented an investment of time and energy rather than of capital. Essentially the prospect was
that the union leader would bring in enough dues and entrance fees to pay his
own salary.[8] At first, the union entrepreneurs themselves chose to assume that

77

role. Once the unions became more stable after 1958, new leaders were often appointed by incumbent officers, but still the entrepreneurship continued. The manner in which entrepreneurship operated can be seen in Cases 1 and 2 in Appendix VII. As unionism became widespread and additional entrepreneurs tried their hand at leadership, many were unsuccessful because they failed to understand the nature of the work and the need to invest energy. Others were successful and developed a constituency that provided rewards in the form of financial return or enhanced social status, or both.

Unlike practice in Great Britain and contrary to the provisions in most union constitutions, many union officers in Tanganyika were appointed and not elected. Of the full-time leaders questioned, 53 percent held their position by virtue of appointment and only 41 percent had been elected to office (Table AIII-34). The fact that so many officers were appointed did not mean that entrepreneurship was eliminated: individuals were appointed to posts if they were willing to undertake the risks involved. Salaries were not guaranteed and officers had to spend dues collected from workers to pay immediate bills and portions of their own salaries. This practice violated the formal procedures of most unions, which, combined with the administrative inefficiencies and weaknesses of most union officers, left them continually open to the possibility of legal prosecution for peculation. Indeed, the number of cases involving unionists in money shortages was considerable. Although understood to be a normal risk of full-time employment, the threat of prosecution undoubtedly discouraged continuous involvement with unions, particularly since regular salaries were not forthcoming and alternative employment opportunities existed.

Instability of Office Tenure

One index of the considerable turnover of full-time union leaders was obtained by examining the seven top offices of the TFL between 1955 and 1959.[9] In that period, there were three conferences following the founding conference at which TFL's first set of officers was elected. Since each of the seven top positions could have changed at each of the three conferences, a total of 21 changes was theoretically possible. In fact, 11 took place. Only two positions retained the same incumbents during this period—the general secretary and the assistant general secretary.

It might be argued that turnover reflected the desire by the unions to rotate the honorary offices of the TFL. An examination of the officers active in the unions in any capacity between 1955 and 1959 shows that this was not the case. Of the 16 people named, only five, or 31 percent, were still active in Tanganyika's unions in 1960. Ten of the others were not active in any way known to the writer and one was still active in the unions in Kenya. The data indicate a high rate of attrition.

Another indication of changing tenure is shown in the turnover rates of the two top offices in 13 unions between 1957 and 1960.[10] Of 25 officers in 1957, 15 were no longer active or involved in the unions in mid-1960. Only ten, or 40 percent, of those officers were still active. Since presidents of most organizations were not full-time, it might be useful to consider presidents and general secretaries separately. Of 13 presidents, seven were still active in 1960; of 13 general secretaries, only three remained active in the unions in 1960. The data indicate that the rate of attrition of officers in paid positions was considerably higher than of those in honorary positions. It might also be noted that, between February 1959 and August 1960, four general secretaries and the TFL Education and Publicity Secretary were dismissed from their posts with considerable publicity.

A still further indication of turnover is illustrated in the change in union officers between March and August 1960 in Korogwe, a small town in Tanga province. When the writer first visited Korogwe, there were nine full-time officers in the town and nearby areas; on the second visit, there were eight officers but, of these, only two were the same ones that had been in the town in March.

These data are supported by those obtained through the full-time leadership survey. Thus, 20 percent of the respondents questioned had held four or more positions in the union (Table AIII-38). Finally, interviews with 12 officers of the Plantation Workers Union were analyzed with regard to turnover in this union. The results are shown in Table VII.2. The average tenure in a position by the officers interviewed was just under 5.5 months. The consequences of such instability for branch activities, industrial relations, and dues collections can well be imagined.

The Work Ethic of Leaders

One difference in the character of leadership in Tanganyika compared with that in Britain is based on impressions and could not be empirically verified. There is an air of lassitude, of waiting or anticipation that characterized Tanganyikans in contrast to the sense of accomplishment or purpose that is present in Britain. This difference is reinforced by the differences noted between the Colonial Office in London and a government office in Dar es Salaam. In both places, the same files with the same identifying flags were circulated. In London, there was a sense of purpose and mission, a sense of empire (even if that empire had just about ended). In Tanganyika, the weary expression of messengers indicated that this was a routine to be suffered.

That there were Tanganyikan union leaders with a sense of dynamism, urgency, and businesslike activity is not denied. Some of the top-level leaders, the older risk-takers, the founders of many of the unions, worked strenuously at their jobs; for them, there were never enough hours in the day. Some, like

Table VII.2 Number and Length of Occupancy of Posts Held
by Twelve Plantation Workers Union Leaders

Officer	Total Time Employed by the Union (Months)	Number of Posts Occupied	Longest Period of Occupancy of One Union Post (Months)
1	30	6	12
2	19	5	9
3	30	5	7
4	25	5	12
5	22	2	21
6	10	2	9
7	32	7	10
8	9	2	7
9	7	2	6
10	13	3	7
11	15	1	15
12	15	2	9
Total	227	42	124
Average	19.9	3.5	10.3

Source: Author's survey

Martin (see Appendix VII, Case 1) kept books, typed correspondence, conducted meetings, made speeches, and operated the mimeograph machine when incompetent clerks smudged the ink badly. Yet such activity was infrequent. Dropping in on union offices around the country, one would often find a branch secretary simply sitting and waiting for members to come in.

Branch secretaries complained of the unwillingness of members to pay subscriptions. Yet there was ample evidence that workers would pay subscriptions and make fairly large contributions if sustained efforts were made to collect them. One branch of a union in Dar es Salaam was unable to support itself because members did not pay dues. When the branch secretary conducted a serious drive for one week in which he and other unionists went to places of work to meet workers, substantial sums were forthcoming. Similarly, around mid-1959, the TFL received a shipment of membership badges from the United States. A large quantity of these badges were "sold" to workers for a Shs. 5/- (70¢) contribution. Although the financial organization of this drive was chaotic, workers were willing to part with Shs. 5/- (a day's wages for an unskilled worker) to have a visible symbol of membership in the union. Yet many branch secretaries apparently could not be bothered to make sustained drives to collect funds. This is not to say that there did not exist massive difficulties in collecting funds. In the case of the plantation union, in particular, transportation facilities were extremely poor and there were great distances between estates. Even when officers visited estates, however, they rarely made dues collections.

This lassitude of officers, the feeble attempts to collect dues, the inactivity, represent a substantial difference from the behavior of trade union officials in Great Britain. Although many formal aspects of behavior (e.g., holding an office, attending meetings) were similar, there was a marked failure to adapt officership to the exigencies of Tanganyika's situation.[11]

New Kinds of Leaders

One puzzle in examining the types of leaders in Tanganyika was to account for those who were important in spite of having few skills or abilities relevant to their offices. When the selection process was examined, it became apparent that the criteria reflected indigenous cultural concerns. Some of these related to the ability to crystallize a consensus when crucial issues divided a body. Because consensus was highly valued by the Tanganyikans, to be able (1) to select the proper time to speak and (2) to verbalize a point of view that would be acceptable to the entire body were extremely important talents. In Tanganyikan unions, therefore, the consensus-molder emerged as a new role distinctly different from any role found in British unions. In the case of at least two union leaders encountered in Tanganyika, it was their ability to bring about consensus that accounted for their rapid rise to leadership. A member of a union's executive committee, described in Appendix VII, Case 3, sensed the trend in a discussion and brought it to a halt by proposing a resolution that embodied the consensus of the group. What was notable in the case of this consensus-molder was that he appeared able to form a consensus with some degree of regularity. A second example is that of an officer who had risen to national leadership in approximately one year. The talents of this leader, insofar as work was concerned, were questionable since his post required technical experience when it was patently obvious that he did not command the requisite skills. His accomplishments as a consensus-molder were solely responsible for his rise.

> The question of the continued existence of the High Commission became a burning issue in August 1960.[12] The conflict came to a head when several union leaders took conflicting public stands on the issue. A special meeting of the General Council of the TFL was called to reconcile the dispute. After over two hours of heated discussion, a resolution was introduced that ended the conflict for the moment. The resolution was the product of the intervention of one leader at the strategically correct moment. After hearing the discussion, he stood and talked about the real enemy of the trade unions—the newspapers and the employers who were trying to split the unions. Because of the "tricks" of these outsiders, the harmony of the unions was being destroyed.

This simple statement accomplished its purposes: it emphasized the need for internal harmony and directed attention to an external enemy. When the statement ended, spontaneous applause suddenly burst out—the first time that any statement was applauded in this meeting. The harmony of the meeting was thus reestablished and, though it took some time to work out the wording of the resolution, the group was reunited as a result of consensus-molding.

A consensus-molder—a role that reflected traditionalist orientations in the settlement of disputes—was rewarded with high positions. Leadership in a modern organization, however, requires other attributes, and the consensus-molder may find himself rising to posts where he is required to exercise administrative skills he does not command.

LEADERSHIP ROLES: SOURCES OF VARIATION

It is obvious that the differences between Tanganyikan and British leadership roles have their origin in differences in the social structures, cultural orientations, political, and legal-administrative systems of the two countries. What is less obvious is the manner in which these factors produced the specific changes that occurred. Before the manner of change can be considered however, it is necessary to indicate the special characteristics of Tanganyika's social system that are producing change.

Social Structural Factors

One important characteristic is that the population of Tanganyika was racially different from the political and economic rulers of the country and the employers. In addition, the history of European domination in all spheres of life had emphasized these differences and the ostensible social superiority of the foreign group. An educational system had also been introduced that had produced a number of marginal men—Africans who had been socialized along traditional lines but educated in mission and government schools along Western lines.

Cultural Factors

Almost all modern Africans have spent part of their formative years in a traditional society, which is reflected in much of their behavior. Socialization provides children with a set of answers to the dilemmas that human beings and societies confront, and Western education cannot be expected to submerge all facets and values of that traditionalism.

Political Factors

Tanganyika's unionism developed simultaneously with the nationalist political movement that split the country between its African inhabitants and the expatriates. Since the difference between the indigenous Africans and the foreigners was always visible, political and class awareness developed together; indeed, their separation was impossible. Yet class consciousness was different from that found in Britain since it was basically racial. It was the marginal, Western-educated Africans who developed and capitalized on this new awareness. Most Africans were unable to formulate their own feelings about the expatriates, in any kind of face-to-face situation, because patterns of subordination were deeply rooted in the colonial situation. That great dissatisfaction, however, did exist was evidenced by the incredible growth of the nationalist movement and its auxiliaries.

Legal-Administrative Factors

Combined with the other differences, the legal-administrative system helped to produce variations in the types of leaders: for example, the Trade Union Ordinance that made registration of unions compulsory and that gave the power of registration to the Labour Commissioner and also gave the Labour Department considerable authority over the unions. Similarly, the undeveloped state of the country and the lack of political-administrative experience of the indigenous population permitted the Labour Department to involve itself considerably in the operation of the unions.

Factors Contributing to Full-Time Leadership

Structural factors in Tanganyika limited the personnel upon whom union leadership might devolve, while the colonial situation prevented ordinary workers from expressing dissatisfaction. Unskilled workers were almost entirely illiterate and had neither experience nor ability to deal with the requirements of modern-day organization. Some manual workers were able to become voicers-of-discontent, but they were unable to give that dissatisfaction organizational expression. That they had done so in 1947 in the Dockworkers Union was only because of the sympathetic assistance of a tolerant government.

When government became unsympathetic and leadership personnel were needed to deal with the requirements of modern organization and to confront the coolness (if not hostility) of government officials, leadership roles fell to the clerks—the one group possessed of some of the technical skills required. For the Trade Union Ordinance required ". . . that no person shall hold the post of secretary or treasurer who in the opinion of the Registrar has not attained a standard of literacy sufficiently high as to enable him to perform his duties effectively."[13] The need to register, to keep books and records, conduct correspondence, and raise dues served as an imperative for the recruitment of westernized literates.

The emergence of leadership as an occupation took place because of the colonial context within which unionism was born in Tanganyika. The basis for leadership roles lay in the emergence of a distinctly new role, that of a

83

voicer-of-discontent. The process of institutionalization of these leadership roles depended upon the existence of social groups that would provide support —that is, a modern working class.

As Africans increasingly became committed workers, the old system of social cohesion lost its relevance. Tribal attachments did not die out, but they were relevant only for particular and limited relations between Africans.[14] In their interaction with employers, a new consciousness emerged of Africans vis-à-vis Europeans. A revolution of expectations came as Africans saw the possibility of obtaining a higher standard of living. They were not surprised, originally, that such things as autos were beyond their ability to command. The broadening experience of World War II, however, made them question why they could not have such things also. As this kind of question began to be asked by a very few Africans, and to have meaning to others, the role of voicer-of-discontent began to find social support.[15]

The voicers-of-discontent in the early days of British trade unionism came from among the manual workers and received education and support from the intellectuals and social reformers of their day. In Tanganyika the working class was divided between a westernized group of clerks and the vast bulk of unskilled, illiterate workers with no organizational skills. There was no intellectual group in Tanganyika, other than a handful of expatriates. Furthermore, the period of the revolution of expectations was too short to permit the lengthy process by which British voluntary union leadership had emerged.

The period following the catastrophic dock strike of 1950 was relatively quiet. The clerks, however, more than any other category of Africans in the labor force, were dissatisfied and began to speak against real and fancied injustices. Some of those that complained found themselves referred to a labor officer. The labor officers normally explained that the employee had to settle his problem for himself; the department could not intervene unless some law had been violated. But some officers broached the idea of a trade union as a means of solving grievances. In this manner a few clerks began to organize. Their first activities were to approach an employer with petitions to correct injustices, but few employers looked with friendly eyes on the development of a group that might threaten their authority. The constant underlying factor of race made it even more difficult for the African to confront the European in a face-to-face situation which was intolerable to Europeans. To voice dissatisfaction was therefore a hazardous and a full-time job, for which compensation was necessary, rather than a voluntary activity carried on after working hours.

Because workers were unwilling or unable to carry on union activities on a voluntary basis, the entire responsibility for the operation of the union rested on the shoulders of the full-time officers, which accounts for the relatively high ratio of officers to members. There were no shop leaders, such as stewards, to handle low-level shop problems or sustain the union's internal life. These circumstances account for the full-time as well as the entrepreneurial nature of the role of union leaders. When risk-taking proved successful, additional entrepreneurs tried it and, in this manner, the role became institutionalized.

The Subsistence Work Ethic

The lassitude of many of Tanganyika's union leaders is strikingly similar to the subsistence orientation found in many traditional societies. This orientation is not peculiar to Africa; indeed, Weber found this traditionalism prevalent among European workers in the early stages of capitalist development.

> One of the technical means which the modern employer uses in order to secure the greatest possible amount of work from his men is the device of piece-rates . . . The attempt has again and again been made, by increasing the piece-rates of the workmen, thereby giving them an opportunity to earn what is for them a very high wage, to interest them in increasing their own efficiency. But a peculiar difficulty has been met with surprising frequency: raising the piece-rates has often had the result that not more but less has been accomplished in the same time, because the workers reacted to the increase not by increasing but by decreasing the amount of his own work . . . This is an example of what is meant here by traditionalism. A man does not "by nature" wish to earn more and more money, but simply to live as he is accustomed to live and to earn as much as is necessary for that purpose.[16]

Traditionalism, which refers to the "psychic attitude-set for the habitual workaday and to the belief in the everyday routine as an inviolable norm of conduct,"[17] was regarded by Weber as a major impediment to capitalist accumulation. This traditionalism will be identified as a subsistence orientation because, in many traditional societies, there is acceptance of an economic organization that permits only minimal satisfaction in terms of food, clothing, and shelter.

Traditionalist orientations in Africans are, of course, modified by education, but there is no reason to assume that in a single generation they can be supplanted by a work ethic in keeping with the Protestant ethic, especially since so few British civil servants embodied this model. In fact, aspects of the subsistence orientation continued to manifest themselves when African trade union leaders were left to their own devices to support themselves and their national organizations.[18]

The subsistence orientation of many union leaders is evident in their failure to collect dues, to wait in offices, to be relatively quiescent in many activities. All too often national headquarters received a monthly accounting without funds since the small amounts that were collected were consumed locally for part of the wages of the local secretary and some minor office expenses.

Nor did the situation change to any extent after the checkoff was legalized in 1962. Unions had to obtain authorization of workers to have employers check off their dues and forward them directly to union headquarters. Interviews in 1963 indicated that only a relatively small percentage of workers had actually signed the authorization forms. A major reason for the small percentage appeared to be that a systematic drive to reach all the workers had not yet been conducted; now that most unions had a relatively satisfactory volume of income, no new efforts were made to increase the number paying dues.

The similarities and differences in the character of union leadership in Britain and Tanganyika and the sources of the differences are summarized in Chart VII.1.

ORGANIZATIONAL ROLES: MEMBERS

Although associations cannot operate without members, the role of the members in the continuous operation of the organization is less significant than that of the leaders. Yet trade unions are membership organizations and being a member implies a certain pattern of behavior.

Because the labor officers had continual contact with the union leaders, models of leader roles were more clearly delineated than those of members. Models of members' roles were formulated only to the extent that organizational dilemmas became manifest. Thus when members failed to pay dues, union leaders were urged to establish procedures to collect funds. This, in effect, provided the basis for a model of membership, but the model was not as clear as in the case of leadership roles. The role of the member was further attenuated by the difficulty, owing to their lack of westernization, that members had in grasping the essence of their position.

A Model of the Member Role

Membership in organizations such as trade unions is made up of three elements: (1) the voluntary nature of being a member; (2) certain duties and obligations; (3) certain rights and privileges.

1. *Membership as voluntary.* An individual voluntarily associates himself with a trade union organization and can sever this relationship when he wishes.[19] Economic necessity requires that men work; the type of work in which they engage, their social associations both at work and outside it, are achieved within certain limiting social frameworks. Membership in a trade union or a club is therefore not an ascribed status but one that is obtained through deliberate action of the person himself.[20]

2. *Duties of membership.* The requirements for joining an organization and continuing in membership are generally minimal. In most cases, membership

Chart VII.1 Comparison of Tanganyikan Leadership Roles to Other Models

Element under Analysis	British Pattern	Labour Department Model	Tanganyika Reality	Source of change
Formal offices and duties	President, general secretary; duties constitutionally delimited	Same as British	Same as British	None
Occupational experience of leaders and members	Similar to each other's	No relevant models	Dissimilar white collar leaders and unskilled workers, but from the same industries	Characteristics of social structure: racial differences of population and political rulers and employers; social superiority of expatriates; colonialism; marginal Africans produced by educational system; bulk of the labor force unskilled and illiterate.
Full-time officer-member ratio	Low	Low	High	
Voluntarism	High	High	Low	
Accession to office	Apprenticeship; election, appointment, examination	Election	Entrepreneurship	
Stability of office	High	No relevant models	Low	
Work ethic	Socialist-Protestant	Morality	Subsistence orientation	Traditionalism
New roles	—	—	Consensus-molders	Traditional orientation toward consensus

requires formally and legally only: (a) the voluntary act of association and (b) payment of certain fees at certain times, which are constitutionally specified. There are frequently other duties for membership that are not basic and usually not required, but they are stressed normatively to some degree. These are: (c) participation in meetings of the organization and (d) occasional voluntary activity on behalf of the organization.

3. *Rights of membership.* Members have the right to participate in the making of decisions of their organization at some level. It does not matter that these rights may be denied in practice in some unions; the basic right of the membership role is to be consulted on the determination of certain policies. This is accomplished by periodic meetings, at which the members vote on issues and by elections of candidates for offices and of delegates to attend the union's conferences. Another right of membership is to share in the benefits obtained by the organization. This might consist of a wage increase or burial benefits.

Membership in Tanganyika

When the role of the member was examined in the Tanganyikan situation, it became clear that the reality diverged from the model.

1. *The character of membership.* If membership is seen as an achieved status in most Western trade unions, the situation was far less clear in Tanganyika. The ability of union leaders to command a following and their inability to collect dues from "members" creates an inconsistency in the reality of "membership." A Provincial Commissioner in Tanganyika reported that "The hold of the unions on labour is out of all proportion to the number of *genuine and contributing members . . .*"21

Great confusion exists over the concept of membership. To Africans, membership in traditional society is an ascribed characteristic; tribal Africans do not voluntarily associate themselves with clans, tribes, and age grades. When the traditional African goes to work for wages, he continues to view membership in most associations as ascribed and not achieved. This is indicated, for example, in a paper prepared by a westernized African trained in the social sciences. The writer was discussing whether or not benefits won by an African trade union should apply only to the members of the organization. "Quite recently, five boys were issued with heavy overcoats to protect themselves against cold at night . . . Overcoats were issued to nonmembers as well as members. Indeed, it is part of the Union's policy that *members outside the organization* should also benefit from its work."22 Ascribed membership may not make sense legally and constitutionally, but if Africans operate on the basis of this belief, as W.I. Thomas noted, "it is true in its consequences." Thus when the general secretary of one union was in conflict with the employers because he was unable to prove, by Western standards, that at least one-third of the employees belonged to the union, he said: "You will know how many members we have in five days' time when we strike."

Although no systematic examination was made of attitudes of workers toward membership, the evidence indicates that Africans assumed membership to be an ascribed status obtained by virtue of employment. When a worker went to work in a particular firm, he apparently believed that he automatically became a member of the union that organized for that firm.

Leaders, of course, had a stake in maximizing the number of their members, and there are indications that leaders tended to think of their constituency as all workers employed within the jurisdiction of their union. Yet leaders also had a stake in maximizing the payment of dues by members. The ambiguity in membership status was reflected, therefore, in the speeches of upper level leaders who urged members to pay their dues, but who refused to exclude from union meetings and the decision-making process those who had not paid their dues.

Three types of members could be found in Tanganyika:

a. *Constitutional members.* This refers to the concept of membership in voluntary associations held in modern societies. A person becomes a member of an organization by paying certain specified fees, adhering to certain rules of the organization.

b. *Occasional members.* This describes the situation where a person may pay an initial fee to join the organization, and possibly one month's dues. Or he may make a contribution to one of the ubiquitous special drives of the organization. Such people consider themselves as members and are considered to be members by the leaders of the organization. Many Africans in Tanganyika, for example, purchased the TFL badges and considered themselves members of the TFL.

c. *Ascribed members.* These are workers who consider themselves to be, and are considered by most leaders to be, members because their employment is within the jurisdiction of the union.

The vagueness of membership concepts led Labour Department officers to attempt to deal with the social realities by formulating a concept of adherents —those workers who followed the lead of the union officers but who were not constitutional members.[23]

2. *Duties of Membership* The idea that union membership entailed a conscious act of voluntary association appeared to be barely understood by workers and leaders because they viewed membership largely as ascribed. Nor was the obligation of regular payment of dues clearly understood. Workers paid occasional sums to the union, but they did not appreciate the need for regular payment of dues to retain union membership. The idea that a regular payment once a month provided returns in the form of benefits which the union won (the so-called "slot machine" theory of trade unionism) was also not clear. If one did not pay dues (taxes) to the government, one went to jail.

But this was not true of the unions. Accordingly, members paid dues only when they were dunned by their officers.

Similarly, attendance at meetings was seen only as a vague obligation. Participation was not significant and workers were only barely aware of the operating procedures. Thus, ignorance of modern organizations limited the ability of workers to exercise their duties of membership.

Finally, the idea that a worker should voluntarily engage in activities on behalf of his organization hardly existed and, indeed, the worker hardly knew how to go about doing voluntary work. Thus the bulk of the membership of the unions was inert.

3. *Rights of Membership.* The right to make decisions was only vaguely understood by workers. Decision making was substantially different from that in British unions and consisted of informal ratification processes. Since the machinery used to ascertain membership sentiments was crude, it was not clear how workers could go about rejecting a decision made by their leaders.

Expectations of the benefits of trade unionism were high. In fact, members' expectations were frequently raised to levels beyond the realm of economic reality. This can be seen in the demand for a minimum daily wage of Shs. 7/75 ($1.08) when the monthly wage on the railways was under $12.00 a month. Trade union leaders generally found that workers followed the union leaders' call when demands were very high. As a consequence demands were frequently made that had little relationship to reality.

The retention, intact, of many of the formal aspects of organizational roles supports the proposition that formal aspects of roles can be transferred with relatively little variation, especially if coercive powers and administrative structures exist to enforce transfer. However, the above examination of organizational roles also reveals the extent of variation from these formal roles as the model was received in Tanganyika.

VIII Organizational Processes in Transfer: Decision Making

The primary concern of most studies of decision making is the way in which different strata in organizations assemble information, make assessments, and reach decisions on organizational problems.[1] To a considerable degree, it has been the form rather than the substance of decision making that has preoccupied most scholars. The present chapter, although following along these lines, focuses primarily on the variations produced in decision making by differences in cultural expectations. The study of decision making in Tanganyikan unions is limited to formal contexts, not because it was only in formal ways that decisions were made, but because it was in formal contexts that the process was clearest and the accumulation of data most feasible.

Membership organizations, in contrast to business organizations, claim to involve their members in the process of decision making by the creation of ostensibly representative bodies which have regularly scheduled meetings. Practically speaking, decisions are made at two levels: by leaders or officers and by members. The daily work of the organization is carried on by a relatively small number of leaders who deal with organizational problems in very specific and immediate terms.

Surprisingly, the models for the decision-making processes in Tanganyikan unions generally were not derived from Britain's trade unions via the Labour Department, but from the parliamentary procedures followed in Tanganyika's Legislative Council and in the other formal organizations to which Tanganyikans had been exposed. These relatively clear models of decision making did not come from any specific and direct source which exercised any degree of administrative control over the unions. Acceptance of the general parliamentary model by the trade unionists can therefore be called voluntary.

The present chapter examines decision making in Tanganyikan unions at both the leadership and the membership levels, which permits consideration of the influence of such factors as Western education. Thus it can be anticipated that the leaders' activities reflected British experience more accurately than did those of the members.

91

AN IDEAL-TYPICAL MODEL OF BRITISH DECISION MAKING

The British parliamentary system of decision making has served as a model for formal organizations as well as for British unions. Parliamentary decision making is based on long-standing traditions that have become embodied in highly formalized procedures. In trade unions and most modern membership organizations, the decision-making process is specified in writing in the constitution or a set of rules. Frequently there are, in addition, the standing orders (by-laws) and a systematic guide for the conduct of formal meetings.[2]

These various written instruments[3] follow British parliamentary practice but in a variety of substantially simplified forms. Control begins with the specifications of an agenda and carries on to definitions of who can participate and the various roles of participants.

There are four distinct aspects of the formal process of decision making that have developed in British experience and that are followed in most public and private Anglo-Saxon parliamentary institutions, including trade unions.

1. *The presentation of the motion.* A motion, normally a resolution,[4] outlines a course of action or orientation to a problem which is believed to express the correct decision of the body. Typically it is submitted before discussion in writing or, when given verbally, is entered into the records.

2. *Procedures to change the sense of the motion.* Strictly controlled opportunities are provided to make amendments to the motion. They are normally submitted in writing or are committed to writing as they are proposed.

3. *Debate of the motion.* Discussion is limited to the motion or amendment, and can take place only after the motion has been introduced.

4. *The vote on the motion or amendment.* Majorities normally rule unless provision is made for some different proportion.

Underlying this process are a number of distinct assumptions.

1. Universalistic rules exist that are applicable to all decision-making situations.

2. Corporate decision-making groups are expected to have within them divergent points of view which should be permitted expression.

3. The corporate decision-making group consists of a majority and at least one or more minorities. The process is oriented toward the determination of the will of the majority. It is pluralistic: any social unit is composed of non-homogeneous groups that will compete with one another for power and authority.

This ideal-typical model is not followed consistently at all times. The reality adheres most closely to the model in large scale bodies. Thus parliaments follow the model more closely than do executive committees of trade unions. As groups become smaller and more homogeneous, the model becomes less relevant. Indeed, in many small scale organizations, this model of decision making is replaced by an informal search for consensus.[5] Nevertheless, even in such situations, where intense conflict breaks out, there is recourse to the formal system.

DECISION MAKING IN EXECUTIVE UNION BODIES IN TANGANYIKA

The most striking fact to an observer of Tanganyikan unions at the time this study was being conducted was the extent to which Western forms of parliamentarism were reproduced intact. There were also, however, variations. For example, while the chairman presided, he was normally accorded more respect and deference than is found in British unions.[6]

At annual conferences the agendas of the more experienced organizations were fairly well organized. Less experienced groups, however, might use several agendas simultaneously. Most agendas consisted, as they do in British unions, of a long series of items, many of them duplicates of others, submitted by the union's branches. Unlike British agendas the Tanganyikan agenda items were not well-developed resolutions or statements of policy, but were attenuated and generalized views of problems. A typical agenda consisted of a large number of items such as the following (printed verbatim):

> Responsibilities—African workers be granted more responsibilities in their posts.
> Employment—
>   a. Women should not be employed by the union.
>   b. A leader expelled from another union should not be offered a job in our union.
> Indians—Membership of Indians in the union.[7]

The usual practice in British unions of controlling and ordering the resolutions submitted by the branches through the standing orders committee[8] was not found; indeed, no Tanganyikan union had a standing orders committee. The usual practice was for the conference to proceed with the agenda for several days until it was realized that the agenda would not be completed in time and then an ad hoc resolutions committee would be appointed to combine, order, and rewrite resolutions. Even this latter practice had not yet developed in some of the less experienced unions.

As each agenda item was reached, the chairman read off the subject to be considered, and discussion was opened. No motion was put nor was a resolution introduced. Discussion continued for a period, after which motions began to be proposed. If delegates felt that discussion had been inadequate, they refused to consider resolutions and the debate continued. After a time, when someone felt that he understood the sense of the discussion, another resolution might be proposed. If the resolution embodied the sentiments of the delegates, the chairman would accept it formally and again read it or have it read.

93

Once a motion or resolution was accepted by the chair, discussion came to an end. Following this, a vote might or might not be taken. In most cases the chairman scanned the delegates to determine whether or not the resolution was acceptable. If he saw no visible objection, the motion was entered in the minutes as having been adopted. In some cases a vote was taken by a show of hands.

This procedure inverted the normal procedure used in most Western unions where the motion initiates rather than closes the debate. The inversion of the procedure was usually explained on the basis of the organizational inexperience of the Tanganyikans. All leaders agreed that the introduction of the motion did in fact signify the close of the debate.[9]

The position of the motion as the closer of debate meant that the Tanganyikan unionists had a different conception of its purpose, with the motion being viewed as an embodiment of the consensus of the meeting rather than as the sentiment of the majority. The process is exemplified in Appendix VII, Case 3. It is always possible that the inversion of the motion to close rather than initiate debate was a random change or was due to organizational inexperience.

It is more likely that the inversion represents a reflection of the consensus orientation of most small scale, homogeneous, unstratified societies. When the motion closes debate, it must represent the consensus of the group achieved through discussion. When a motion initiates debate, policy is being formulated through the division of participants into those favoring and those opposing the policy. The position of the motion thus reflects either monist or pluralist views of society.

TRADITIONAL DECISION MAKING: AN AFRICAN IDEAL-TYPICAL MODEL

If traditional decision making is to be analyzed as a general phenomenon, a model that extracts the basic elements of the process is necessary. Because of the paucity of relevant materials dealing with Tanganyikan tribes, examination was concentrated on literature dealing with Bantu tribes of East, Central, and Southern Africa. During this search it became apparent that similarities existed in most societies despite differences in social structures. Although some tribes had complex structures and others had attenuated political systems,[10] common characteristics appeared in court proceedings, arbitrations, discussions, and disputes.

1. Discussion was open and not usually limited to the immediate parties involved. Most frequently, all available adult males participated in the decision-making process. Even where there were headmen, decision making was an open process in which all could participate. Although in some cases the actual judgment was rendered by headmen, open discussion normally occurred in which all males participated.[11]

2. Discussion was lengthy and exhaustive. The function of extended discussion was to permit all feelings to be expressed so that an eventual consensus could be achieved. Thus most court procedures, trials, and arbitration of disputes took a considerable amount of time. It was difficult to find cases in the literature where participants experienced pressure to speed up decision making. It was rare, also, that a vote was taken for or against a proposal.

3. Decisions had to reflect public opinion. The length of discussion permitted public opinion to coalesce and form a guide for judges or arbitrators. Even in highly centralized political systems, such as the Zulu, in which the position of the chief is exalted, the chief must rule according to advice.[12]

The traditional process of decision making reflects the relatively undifferentiated social structures and the homogeneity of the value system. It also shows the concern for the maintenance of consensus, which is characteristic of decision making in most small scale traditional African societies where social relations are intense.[13] The maintenance of consensus when conflict occurs helps to prevent schisms within the tribe.[14]

Typically in traditional societies there are no differentiated or specialized roles for the settlement of conflicts. Among the Soga, for example, Fallers notes the lack of specialization and shows that there was an expectation that everyone would know customary law.[15] The participation of large numbers of people in the settlement of disputes not only helps to crystallize public opinion, but provides an enforcement mechanism for the decision eventually reached.

The search for consensus is also found among the Mashona.[16] Disputes are settled by elaborate trial procedures in which most people participate, taking the role of plaintiff or defendant, arguing the case for one side or the other. The purpose of this role-taking is to search for the facts involved in the conflict. Underlying this method is an assumption that if the truth is known there can be only one decision that the group can render. This is clear in the case of the Bantu Kavirondo. "The old men then listen to the case as presented by the two disputants and any witness. The decision could be announced by any elder present as, with the facts ascertained, there was only one possible judgment, which was the common knowledge to all,"[17] The overwhelming evidence is that the use of voting is insignificant.[18]

For most traditional African societies, then, conflicting interests do not exist, particularly those based on economic distinctions. There are of course a number of relatively complex societies that do have conflicting interest groups. Among such societies as the Ndebele, Swazi, Lozi, and Ganda in Eastern and Southern Africa as well as among the kingdoms of the Sudanic belt and several other societies of West Africa, stratification exists in various forms, and conceptions of interests have been developed in varying degrees. In much of sub-Saharan Africa, however, economic organization was and continues to be simple and the concomitant social patterns are largely unstratified. In such societies, the search for truth can be based on the assumption that a single answer is valid for all parties concerned. Similarly, the idea of majorities and minorities is not developed. The majority consists of the entire social group; a minority, by definition, consists of a deviant individual or group that threatens the existence of the larger social unit.

CONSENSUS IN TANGANYIKAN TRADE UNIONS

Residual value orientations of African union leaders have meant that consensus rather than majority decision was sought in the solution of problems. As experience is gained and as leaders come into contact with the techniques used by other trade unions abroad, it is likely that the decision-making process will evolve and possibly will eventually resemble more closely that found in Western organizations. An imperative for evolution along these lines is the pressure of time experienced in modern society. Consensus can be afforded only when time is not valuable. One characteristic of preindustrial societies is the relative insignificance of time as calculated in industrial societies.[19] Time is of considerable importance, however, to conflict groups. Trade unions invariably face deadlines in the form of expiration of collective agreements, so that indefinite discussion of problems cannot be tolerated. Hence there will be pressures on trade unionists to achieve decisions before consensus has been reached.

Working against such evolution of the decision-making process are the values of a cultural system geared to the idea of the homogeneity of the corporate group. This idea, while not simply traditional, reflects the lack of stratification and social homogeneity characteristic of many traditional African groups. The basic egalitarian outlook, which argues that African society is not stratified,[20] can be partly regarded as the rationalization of an African elite to justify its maintenance of political power. Yet there is evidence that many Africans in the modern period retain a unitary view of society. This view underlies much of the behavior of the Tanganyikan trade unionists.

The belief that, from a given set of facts only a single conclusion can be drawn makes it impossible for traditional African societies to recognize that there could be conflicts of interest.[21] In modern form, Tanganyikan trade unionists are extremely reluctant to admit the existence of any disagreements not only among themselves but also between themselves and employers. Invariably, conflict is explained as "misunderstanding." The word "disagreement" is an extremely strong term, and one which, in traditional society, is to be avoided, unless there is a serious breakdown in social relations.

The extent to which this term is avoided is illustrated by the minutes of a meeting of the TFL Emergency Committee at the time of a strike and riot at the Mjesani plantation in 1958.

> On Tuesday, the manager of the estate wanted to disperse the strikers who had gathered at the football field, but was unable to do this. He then called the police, who came immediately. One had a pistol, nine had guns, and the others had shields. The police began their aggression by shooting at our brothers who ran away, and many were hurt. Some women dropped their children, and this caused further deaths. The results of such *misunderstandings* was due to the fact that the employers do not respect the union at all.[22]

One frustrating experience of Europeans engaged in industrial relations was that trade unionists continually repeated the same arguments. Many European managers complained during interviews that negotiations were fruitless. African unionists came in with problems, stated their case, and awaited an answer. The Europeans would rebut the unionists' contentions after which Africans would repeat their previous argument. The rebuttal would again be repeated, to be followed again by the same initial argument. The African unionists, when their argument was rejected, concluded that they had not *really* communicated to the employer and must therefore restate the case. Once the problem was *really* communicated, there could be only one decision—that which the union leader favored.

Consensus in decision making, however, was not the only way in which decisions were made: votes were taken, and majorities and minorities existed. The problem remains to explain the circumstances under which each system was used. A hypothesis can be formulated which will require further testing: *The more an issue appears to affect the viability of the organization, the stronger will be the effort to solve the problem by consensus.*

There was a plethora of simple organizational problems having little relevance for organizational viability that could be settled by simple votes. The size of appointed committees was frequently in question. The matter was usually put to a vote, and the issue was quickly passed over. When, however, a major conflict developed within the unions in 1960 over the continued existence of the East Africa High Commission, the issue was debated until consensus was achieved. The delegates did not seek a vote on the issue.

The search for consensus has been seen as a value orientation in relatively homogeneous, unstratified, traditional societies. As African societies modernize, they exhibit modern patterns of social stratification. Indeed, one of the major problems of modern African societies is the massive gap between the educated elite and the rest of the society. Yet an ideological characteristic of the modern African political elite has been the attempt to argue away the existence of such stratification. In practice this viewpoint is used to justify the maintenance in the society of a single source of political, social, and economic power and to legitimatize the undermining of competing or independent sources of power. Most of the political elite in Africa are intolerant of political minorities and autonomous centers of power, and seek continually to bring them under control. Thus the carryover of traditional orientations toward social homogeneity and consensus are given the modern-day garb of "democratic centralism."[23]

DECISION MAKING BY THE UNION MEMBERSHIP

When the process of decision making at lower levels of the unions was examined, variation from Western models became considerable[24] because the process had been extensively adapted to fit the cultural experience of union members. By lower levels is meant the branch or estate that equates, in the United States, with the local union or shop meeting. The participants were the leaders and the rank and file members or adherents of the union. Formal roles involved in decision making were somewhat meaningless to the members. To most workers, the majority of whom were illiterate and without experience in modern organizations, the differentiation of the office of chairman from that of secretary was unclear.[25] In many cases, the branch secretary acted as the de facto chairman, even though invariably there was a chairman who nominally presided. Beyond this, little transfer of institutional forms had taken place and extensive adaptation had occurred. Because of their inability to grasp the nature of modern bureaucratic organization, members experienced difficulty in grasping the idea that there were limits to action by virtue of the existence of constitutions or other written instruments.

Two important variations from Western procedures were found in decision making by the rank and file:

1. *Failure to delineate a decision-making constituency.* One major difference between the unions of Tanganyika and those of Great Britain was that the concept of the branch meeting did not yet exist. Instead, mass meetings were held.[26] Thus when problems had to be taken to the rank and file, leaders experienced difficulty in delineating the decision-making group; the problems were in fact not brought to the branch but rather to "the members." Since membership was so loosely defined, union meetings were effectively open to all.

The failure to delineate the decision-making group did not lessen the pressure felt by union leaders to have their actions ratified by the members. Mass meetings were held with considerable frequency at which leaders reported to the members, and sought approval for their actions. The ratification procedures commonly used to achieve decisions, however, varied greatly from Western models.

2. *Differences in ratification procedures.* Decisions were not made by the presentation of formal instruments (motions) but through verbal

explanations by leaders of past or projected courses of action for which ratification from the assembled mass was being sought. Ratification was not achieved by means of a vote of any kind—by show of hands or voice or ballot —but rather through a dialogue between the leader and the followers. The leader explained some event, his own course of action, or what he proposed to do in the future. At various points while delivering his address, the leader asked of the audience: "Mmesikia?" ("Have you [plural] heard?") The audience, as a group or discrete individuals or subgroups within it, answered: "Tumesikia." ("We have heard.") This procedure, typically used at mass meetings of the unions, served as the main instrument by which the leaders obtained authorization for action from their followers.

This type of decision making can be highly inaccurate since a leader will consider his actions authorized if he receives responses from even a small segment of the audience. Underlying the assumption of acceptance is the idea that if any person in the audience responds, he is speaking for the whole. That this form of decision making can lead to organizational difficulties soon becomes obvious.[27]

A major cause for many internal conflicts between African union leaders can be traced to the continued dependence upon this unsatisfactory method for the ratification of decisions. Since the decision-making group was rarely accurately delineated, anyone could simply walk in and participate in the decision-making process.

In addition, a course of action could be accepted by a minority "having heard." Thus several leaders could propose contradictory courses of action and all could be ratified. This led to the feeling among leaders that the members were fickle, which was not altogether unjustified.[28] It is possible that, given the lack of organizational skills and failure to understand the complexity of proposals, members did not understand the subtleties of the differences between their leaders, and therefore, authorized conflicting courses of action. It is also likely, however, that authorization came from different elements of the same constituency, or indeed, from differing constituencies.

The particular form of vocal ratification represents a major variation from the model of Western decision making. It reflects traditionalism but is also partially a function of the organizational inexperience of union members.[29] This process becomes increasingly inadequate as agreements with employers become more complex, because the uncertainties involved in this type of decision making are intolerable to leaders seeking some degree of stabilization in their membership and their courses of action. Thus the type of decision making encountered during the period of field research can be anticipated to change, as there are increased pressures for more reliable ways of making decisions. When more Tanganyikans are educated, complex documents such as wage agreements can be circulated in writing and the members will be better able to understand them.

IX Industrial Relations: Core Functions in Transfer

Trade unions are institutions primarily concerned with the regulation of employment relations. Unions came into existence as workers sought means of controlling these relations which had hitherto been regulated either by government or employers, or some combination thereof.[1]

Since the time when unions first developed in Britain, the methods of collective bargaining have proliferated and become more complex. In the early stages of trade union development in any country, unions are primarily concerned with the formulation, presentation, and legitimization of worker protest. When unionism was transferred to Tanganyika, the British, concerned with developing controllable mechanisms for the expression of dissatisfaction, established a model of joint consultation rather than of collective bargaining, thus precluding direct employee-employer relationships. But to the Tanganyikans the structures the British created were inadequate to deal with the grievances as they came more and more to the surface.

On their part, the Tanganyikans were primarily concerned with attempting to bring employers into direct relationships with the unions and did not wish to use intermediary units such as joint consultative committees. Anxious to find the most effective means of expressing the grievances of workers, the unionists were strongly oriented toward dramatic mechanisms that emphasized the power of the workers. The strike was therefore their most popular weapon regardless of the other available instrumentalities through which they might communicate indirectly with employers. Thus, the Labour Department, by committing itself to joint consultation rather than to collective bargaining helped to increase conflict and left gaps in a model of industrial relations which the unionists had to fill for themselves.

Industrial relations systems are extremely intricate mechanisms which, even in the most advanced societies, frequently come close to breaking down. In Tanganyika, the strain placed on the system was greater than normal. The usual difficulties of employers, in adjusting to the fact that workers were suddenly making demands through their union leaders, were exacerbated in the colonial environment by the expatriate employers' view of Africans as being "just out of the trees."[2] The inexperience of the unionists increased the tension because it accounted both for their emphasis on the strike threat, the strike, and the boycott to express conflict and for their inability to distinguish between crucial problems—perhaps involving a great many workers and substantial victories—and insignificant matters which might pertain to only a small number and produce at best paper victories. Nor were the unionists able thoroughly to prepare cases in advance with evidence and orderly documentation. In addition, in direct relationship with employers, the unionists were unable to understand the roles of employers, which led to excessive concentration and repetition of a single argument even after employers had produced reasonable responses.[3]

Finally, the Labour Department manifested inexperience in industrial relations by its failure to take seriously many of the disputes which might have ended sooner had there been more appropriate intervention. By ignoring the changing political and social situation, the department contributed to the increased hostility of the unions.

EMPLOYMENT RELATIONS: THE BACKGROUND TO INDUSTRIAL RELATIONS

Except for the limited trade carried on by some groups in the Arab network, in 1888 the indigenous population of Tanganyika depended largely on subsistence agriculture and pastoral activities. When the Germans introduced a number of enterprises requiring labor such as plantations and railways, initially there were few incentives for Africans to enter into paid employment. Because of the resulting manpower shortage the Germans and later the British employed such strategies as forced labor (especially in the early days) and taxation to obtain the labor they needed. Taxation stimulated the movement of Africans from subsistence pursuits into employment and gave rise to substantial population movements throughout Tanganyika. No reliable data are available on migratory labor; an index of its magnitude and significance, however, can be obtained from a comparison of the number of Africans accommodated in government transit centers with employment figures, (shown in Table IX.1). Although indicative of the importance of migratory labor, the data must be interpreted with care since it appears, for example, that between 1951 and 1956 half of the labor force was migratory but, in fact, most workers would have used several transit centers.

As long as the bulk of the labor force was migratory, the employers largely controlled employment relationships although there was some government regulation in the form of weak inspection systems and specification of minimum conditions of employment, such as housing and a food ration. African employees could resort to four unreliable methods of protest.

Table IX.1
Migratory Labor in Tanganyika

Year	Number of Africans Employed	Number of Africans Accommodated in Government Transit Centers	Number of Africans Recruited Through Recruitment Organizations
1951	455,398	225,949	38,300
1952	443,597	282,878	34,393
1953	448,271	269,241	32,388
1954	439,094	243,975	30,610
1955	413,100	224,240	27,777
1956	424,209	265,950	26,472
1957	430,470	199,106	23,930
1958	430,547	173,601	32,840
1959	428,268	177,795	22,740
1960	387,475	135,288	11,614
1961	442,092	76,771	3,967
1962	398,816	45,328	5,693

Source: ARLD, 1951–1962.

1. *Personal addresses and petitions.* Except in the large and highly organized industries and plantations where direct access to employers was essentially impossible, employees had occasional opportunities to approach employers with personal grievances and petitions. Many employers did, in fact, seek to keep channels of personal appeal open. Although it was a legitimate means for the presentation of grievances, petitioning had to be approached carefully, usually humbly with a variety of forms of deferential address to the *bwana mkubwa* [big boss].

2. *Councils of elders.* On some plantations the employer formed a council by appointing from among the various tribes present "elders" who might or might not have legitimate authority over their fellow tribesmen on the estates. The employers frequently organized such councils to facilitate communication with their employees, but the councils could also operate to express dissatisfaction of workers to employers.

3. *Desertion and evasion of contract; boycotts.* If conditions became unbearable, the common, albeit illegal, method of escape by African employees was desertion. Word about conditions would be passed informally by migrating workers with the result that "A concern with a bad reputation is speedily boycotted, and it is remarkable for how long a period a bad reputation will cling."[4] Conversely, where employers were reputed to be good, the word would also be spread. Certain tribes came to favor certain estates, and workers from these tribes always sought work at the favored estates.

4. *Strikes, riots, and disturbances.* If a number of workers shared a common grievance, a more organized form of action was possible, and strikes occasionally took place when employees spontaneously[5] struck. The

pre-union strikes inevitably became riots since no mechanisms existed for the orderly presentation of collective grievances. Because there was no leadership, workers sought out their employers en masse—a frightening experience that resulted in calls to the police for protection.

These four methods of protest were adequate as long as most workers worked for wages for limited periods, but as workers became employed for longer periods, other means of settling disputes became necessary. Following World War II, attempts to organize workers began, and changes in the handling of disputes were inevitable.

The 1947 strike of Dar es Salaam dockworkers prompted the Labour Department to organize a union, but, on the basis of the violence of the 1950 strike, this experience was considered premature and the department consciously formulated a model of industrial relations based on joint consultation (as discussed in Chapter IV).

Table IX.2 shows the growth in the number of joint consultation units and the increase in the number of workers covered by such arrangements. The first substantial increase in 1958 resulted from the creation of joint consultative arrangements in the sisal industry following an investigation for the employers by C. W. Guillebaud, a British industrial relations specialist, who advised the development of a complex system consisting of four levels of consultation (see Appendix VII, Case 9). Ninety-eight units were added to the total number of committees listed by the Labour Department. In 1959 the increase from 87 to 142 estate-level committees in the sisal industry and 19 new committees set up in the tea industry, following an agreement between the plantation union and the tea growers, accounted for the spurt. The increase in 1960 was the result mainly of ten new consultative units for local government structures.

The existence of a number of informal consultative organs, the so-called "councils of elders," was noted by the department first in 1952; and they continued to be counted through 1957 after which the department made no mention of them. Their minor role and lack of significance is discussed in Appendix VI.

It would appear from the number of committees that both joint consultation and the transfer of the model of industrial relations had been successful. The figures, however, fail to reflect the fact that during the entire period in which nominal success was being noted by the Labour Department in its *Annual Report,* the joint consultation system was in fact responsible for increasing industrial hostility, making industrial relations in Tanganyika a daily battleground, failing to resolve the acute pressures at the workshop level, and finally abetting a series of crucial strikes.

Table IX.2
Joint Staff Committees and Workers Covered by Joint Consultative
Arrangements in Tanganyika, 1952-1962

Year	Total Number of Committees	Number of Committees Organized in Government and High Commission Agencies	Estimated Number of Workers Covered
1952	8 (?)	?	?
1953	44	28	20,000
1954	53	37	23,000
1955	64	45	25,000
1956	80	59	35,000
1957	87	55	38,000
1958	188	64	114,000
1959	248	55	220,000
1960	271	52	260,000
1961	286	60	270,000
1962	No information given	--	---

Source: ARLD, 1952-1962.

THE STRUGGLE FOR DIRECT RELATIONSHIPS

Joint consultation came to be regarded as a mechanism both to under-
mine the development of direct relationships and to avoid direct confrontation
between employers and employees for purposes of collective negotiations. At
first, employers saw the staff committees—the concrete embodiment of the
joint consultative machinery—as legitimate organs for dealing with their employees and as a substitute for trade unions. The unionists followed the advice
of the Labour Department but became increasingly disenchanted with consultation because it did not permit them to negotiate directly with employers at
all levels. The gradual rejection of the model took a variety of forms at different stages and in different industries, but there were three general areas of
dissatisfaction.

1. *Union recognition.* Although the growth of unionism in Tanganyika
stimulated employers to form joint consultative structures, employers hoped
that if the unions could be kept out until the mechanisms were established,
there would be no need for unions as such. The unions, on the contrary, were
concerned with obtaining formal recognition from the employers in the form
of an agreement that the employer would deal with the union when it presented demands and employee grievances.

The handling of union recognition varied considerably from industry
to industry. On the whole, the larger employers, including those in the sisal
industry, posts and telecommunications, and railways, sought to evade direct
confrontation with the unions. Many small employers, particularly Asians,
were willing to deal with the unions directly. Because some of the trade

union leaders were entrepreneurs, many employers wanted proof of their leadership and the loyalty of their constituency before the employers would deal with them. The unionists saw this reaction by employers as evasion and they countered by trying to obtain formal recognition of the unions from the employers.[6] The traditional means of proving union control over the labor force has been strike action. Thus, in the sisal industry of Tanganyika, the Plantation Workers Union struck to prove that the union rather than the worker delegates to the Central Joint Council represented the sisal workers.

It became increasingly clear to most employers that the unions were able to bring workers out on strike, and direct recognition was accorded to most unions by 1958. In the sisal industry, however, the price of recognition was that the unions accept the system of joint consultation that had already been organized.

2. *Mechanisms for consultation rather than negotiation.* Consultative procedures have always strictly limited what can be discussed. In Tanganyika, consultation frequently did not permit discussion of the important area of wage structures. Management in the major consultative organizations of the sisal and railway industries refused to permit discussion of problems at the national level unresolved at lower levels, which meant that grievances could not be discussed at the level where the union leadership had direct access to employer representatives.

3. *Direct relationships.* As the unionists gained experience, they began to demand direct relationships with employers at all levels, and the problem became a major source of conflict in industrial relations. For example, the Tanganyikan Railway African Union (TRAU) realized that it had little control over the Local Department Committees (LDC) which were unable to resolve the grievances that were being channeled to them. Since union leaders were excluded from participation in the LDCs, the committees were composed largely of illiterate and organizationally inexperienced workmen who were unable to deal effectively with the European management representatives. Grievances unresolved in the LDCs were channeled to the union's branches where they accumulated over a period of time. Four full-time district secretaries appointed in 1960 by TRAU General Secretary Tumbo to process grievances were refused recognition by railway management on the grounds that they had been appointed and not elected. The management, however, did recognize Tumbo, who had been elected, so that even the most trivial grievances, were channeled to him in Dar es Salaam. A major concern of the union was therefore to obtain recognition of its full-time district officials so that grievances could be handled directly at the local level.

The same problems on the sisal plantations were exacerbated by the refusal by estate owners and managers to permit union officials to enter the estates, which were private property. Owners and managers were prepared to recognize estate committees, but the exclusion of union leaders from the estates meant that the employers controlled the grievance machinery. The clerks represented on the estate committees were unwilling or unable to risk contradicting the expatriate employers. Grievances were channeled away from this controlled mechanism of joint consultation, directly to the full-time union secretaries who were, however, not considered legitimate.

Among government employees, similar problems existed. The formation of joint staff committees was strongly encouraged by government in its various agencies. However, the union's branch officers might be voluntary officials from a different government unit or full-time officers not employed by the government, which in either case meant that they would be excluded from most joint staff committees. The result was that persons with grievances appealed not to their representative on the joint staff council (who was not, most often, a union officer) but to the secretary of the union who was excluded from meetings of the joint staff committee.

Despite the fact that the policy of joint consultation was supported by the government, a considerable number of employers turned to direct negotiations with the unions. In some cases such as the tea growing industry, these direct relations were encompassed within the joint consultative structures. The Tea Growers Association signed an agreement with the Plantation Workers Union in 1959 which recognized the union and provided for its direct participation in a three-level negotiations machinery. At the lowest, estate level, employee representatives were elected by the employees, but "there shall be one member who shall be an estate employee nominated by the Union." At the district and national levels, the union was directly represented and designated its own representatives. The Labour Department summarized the differences succinctly:

> The view taken by the Tea Industry is entirely opposed to the attitude of the Sisal Industry. The former favours the complete recognition of the Union and direct negotiation with that union while the latter accords very limited recognition which has in the short time the machinery has been established led to considerable trouble. It remains to be seen which is the better course.[7]

Relations between the tea growers and the Plantation Workers Union were relatively harmonious in contrast with relations in the sisal industry which continued to be stormy throughout the entire existence of the Plantation Workers Union. Much of the conflict in the sisal industry indicated in Table IX.3 concerned, first, recognition and, later, inability to negotiate directly at all levels between the union and employers. In 1961, for example, the Labour Department's *Annual Report* noted deadlocks between the Plantation Workers Union and the sisal and tea plantation employers over wages; the 1962 *Annual Report* stated that joint consultation mechanisms were not

Table IX.3
Industrial Disputes in Tanganyika's Sisal Industry, 1956-1962

Year	Number of Disputes	Number of Workers Involved	Number of Man-Days Lost
1956	22	3,596	9,101
1957	48	29,470	125,459
1958	76	51,314	228,908
1959	88	56,082	258,279
1960	82	59,970	552,863
1961	25	9,955	45,646
1962	59	27,486	186,975

Source: ARLD, 1956-1962.

operating because the union refused to recognize the system. The employers and the union "were unable to agree . . . on the establishment of suitable alternative negotiating machinery for the industry."[8] Where unions were able to obtain direct recognition as among tea growers, sugar plantations, and many small manufacturing concerns organized by the Transport and General Workers Union, difficulties were still experienced, but they were not aggravated by the system.

Joint consultation, in which the Local Government Workers Union usually had some form of representation, was most successful in local governments. Beginning in 1957, the number of councils increased rapidly and by 1960 thirteen townships and native authorities were covered. Appendix VII, Case 12, describes joint consultation in local government and also illustrates how more experienced and modernized personnel were better able to manipulate the consultative machinery than were the ordinary workers and, in the case cited, the union representative. On the whole, however, the model of joint consultation proved to be a failure and eventually had to be scrapped.

That the Labour Department held longer to its joint consultative model than to its structural model may have been due, at least in part, to the retention of joint consultation by the Tanganyika Sisal Growers Association, the largest group of private employers in the country. The fact that the executive director of the association was a former Labour Commissioner may also have played some role in encouraging the department to keep the model for so long.

Nevertheless, the continual conflict, as unions sought to obtain direct representation with the employers, led to a gradual evolution of policy, albeit unacknowledged by the department. *Annual Reports* until 1957 continually noted the successful growth of consultative committees, and it was not until 1958 that the beginning of a shift was noted.

> With the rapid growth of the trade union movement . . . trade unions play an ever increasing part in the determination of conditions . . . by direct negotiation and collective bargaining

with employers. Labour/management relations nevertheless continue to be based mainly on the relationship and degree of cooperation and consultation which existed in individual undertakings or establishments.

The *Annual Report* then stated that direct negotiation more nearly approached the realization of government policy

that the conclusion of freely negotiated collective agreements would be possible between organizations of workers and employers which provide for terms and conditions of employment which are acceptable to the majority of workers in a craft or industry and are also economically practicable from the point of view of their employers.[9]

By 1959 the Plantation Workers Union had developed direct negotiating machinery with the tea growers and the major sugar plantations, and the *Annual Report* noted "the notable increase in such direct negotiations," and again stated that this constituted progress toward realization of government policy.[10] The *Annual Report* in 1960 noted the success both of joint consultation, which "has continued to be a major responsibility of the Labour Division," and of direct negotiations, since 56 percent of the working population was now covered by collective agreements between unions and employers.[11]

The joint consultative model sustained a major blow in 1960 when a commission of inquiry, established in the wake of the major strike of railway workers early in the year, called in its report for the establishment of direct negotiating relationships between the railway management and the unions.[12] The 1961 *Annual Report* commented that "it is regrettable that no direct negotiating machinery has yet been set up in the East African Railways Administration and the East African Posts and Telecommunications Administration for the purpose of considering conditions of service . . . as recommended by the Report made by Mr. H. Whitson . . . "[13] Finally in 1962, the *Annual Report* was able to report that negotiating machinery had been set up in both administrations and "appears to be working satisfactorily."[14]

Until 1962, the department had noted annually the increase in the number of joint staff committees, the number of workers covered, and the list of joint staff committees. Significantly, the 1962 *Annual Report* omits this information, and joint consultation, which had previously been a separate section of the *Annual Report*, was now incorporated into a single section titled "Joint Consultation and Negotiating Machinery."

Thus by 1962, joint consultation ceased to be significant in the determination of relations between employers and employees. The struggle for direct representation and negotiation had been won by the unions, and the nature of industrial relations problems changed. In the remaining years of autonomous trade unionism, conflict developed over the operations of the negotiating machinery and, in particular, over the increased need for third party involvement in the settlement of disputes which could not be resolved through normal bargaining procedures.

CORE FUNCTIONS AND MECHANISMS

For the unionists, the Labour Department's policy encouraging joint consultation as opposed to direct negotiation constituted an attempt to remove from the unions their core function. Our earlier discussion (in Chapter I) defined core functions as relative to the viewpoint of specific social groups. In the case of Tanganyika, the activities that the union leadership considered most meaningful required direct involvement in the presentation of demands and the processing of day-to-day grievances. The model of joint consultation, however, excluded the unions from both activities and became a focus of hostility as unionists moved toward direct confrontation.

Unions as Demanding Organizations

That unions existed to make demands on employers was a revolutionary concept in Tanganyika when Mboya presented it on his visit there. Previously, the idea that unions should make demands on employers was nonexistent. When, for example, the memorandum that the African Commercial Employees Association forwarded to the Dar es Salaam Chamber of Commerce and the Indian Merchants' Chamber in 1953, raised questions about "salaries, provident fund, cost of living . . . discriminatory treatment of African employees . . . " it consisted of information about the conditions of African employees, but it made no demands. Typical for that time, this early memorandum to employers was a petition requesting redress of grievances, and there was no threat of strike action even after "acknowledgment of the memo was received from the Dar es Salaam Chamber of Commerce, but there seems to be no action taken by them."[15] Similarly, in the same year, the association processed a grievance to one of the oil companies when an employee was discharged while in the hospital. Instead of threats or hostile language, four representatives of the association called on the employer to inform him of this situation.

In August 1955, Mboya made clear to the Tanganyika unionists that unions had the right and responsibility to approach employers not simply as petitioners but as legitimate spokesmen of the demands that the workers wished to make of the employers. This new approach was perhaps best exemplified in the personal experience of Rashidi Kawawa, then president of the Tanganyika African Government Servants Association (TAGSA). Kawawa stated[16] that, although he had been encouraged by the Labour Department to register TAGSA as a trade union, he had refused to do so because

109

department officers had not been able to explain to him what advantage there would be in a registered union. Kawawa's explanation for their behavior was that the labor officers were forbidden to make clear that unions existed to make demands on behalf of the workers. This concept became clear for Kawawa and the other unionists in the classes held by Mboya. From then on, instead of listening with respect to the advice of the labor officers, the unionists became more independent and, according to the Labour Department, increasingly irresponsible; in fact, the leaders began to formulate demands for substantial wage increases.

Employers everywhere have rarely taken kindly to the sharing of authority over their employees with external organizations such as unions, and Tanganyikan employers were no exception. The colonial situation helped neither employers nor the British government officials to adapt to the changes. A small segment of the African population in Tanganyika was just beginning to challenge colonial rule, and the reaction to this early nationalism by many expatriates was to attempt to hold the line against concessions to Africans. The reactions of employers to the demands of what they considered to be self-proclaimed labor leaders, were also negative with regard to recognition of unions and to dealing with the full-time union leadership.

This in turn produced strong reaction in the new and still inexperienced labor leadership, many of whom had misinterpreted Mboya's concept of the right to make demands to mean that employers had to agree to those demands. As hostility and opposition were encountered, the unionists turned increasingly to the strike threat and the strike as major weapons. The action of the Local Government Workers Union against the Dar es Salaam Municipal Council in mid-1956 demonstrated publicly the shift in attitude of the unionists. After several months of fruitless discussion on a wage claim, the municipal employees issued a strike notice which became effective on the day that Princess Margaret was to begin an official visit to Tanganyika. The unions were obviously no longer petitioning organizations but had already developed an acute sense of strike tactics.

The strike by the Local Government Workers Union was averted at the last minute but it increased the hostility between the unions on the one hand and government and employers on the other. In Dar es Salaam, the Domestic and Hotel Workers Union had been presenting demands to the hotel keepers, and a small incident during the royal visit triggered a threat of a general strike, but the Labour Department intervened in what was considered an unwarranted manner by the TFL. A two-day sympathy strike by many TFL affiliates intended to support the Domestic Workers Union led to wholesale discharges and, two months later, to a threat of a national general strike, which was subsequently averted.

During 1957 and 1958, as the pace of union organization accelerated and Africans drew courage from the growth of the nationalist movement, militant action was used by most unionists, sometimes effectively but many times inappropriately. By 1959 and 1960, the strike threat had become an almost daily occurrence in the local press. The unions were determined to make demands of the employers and, all too frequently, these were put in offensive form. However, the continued exclusion of the unions from direct participation in joint consultation did little to resolve disputes and appeared to the unionists as means of employer evasion.

Day-to-Day Expressions of Discontent

The resolution of grievances by personal petition to employers, in which the petitioner consciously demeaned himself, became increasingly unsatisfactory to ordinary workers as the political revolution began to deepen in Tanganyika and workers' expectations began to rise. Such petitions all too frequently were rejected and now, in addition, the African workers were being told by the political and trade union leaders that certain things belonged to them *by right*. Not only were they being exploited by the colonialists and the employers, but they should and could live better, send their children to school, have better housing and food, and be able to purchase such things as bicycles.

The problem in industrial relations was that the full-time trade union leaders, who were best able to transmit those issues that were meaningful to workers, were excluded from the joint consultative machinery, particularly at the lower levels. Thus, small grievances either became lost in the mazes of procedural detail or accumulated and caused festering dissatisfaction which the full-time union leaders could manipulate to mobilize the workers.

An example of this situation was the chronic grievance over upgrading in the railway workshops in Dar es Salaam. The Local Department Committee, a joint consultative organization, was unable to solve this problem satisfactorily and it was referred to the union. Correspondence then flew back and forth between Nairobi and Dar es Salaam between the railway administration and the union. Eventually, the workers took action on their own and the union was officially brought in to return the workers to work. Following the strike, the administration, in line with its policy of recognizing only elected officers, continued to refuse to deal with district and regional officials assigned by the union to handle the dispute; thus the day-to-day issues continued to fester with no effective mechanism to solve them.

Joint consultation in this typical example increased hostility and daily tensions by preventing the resolution of small scale grievances. Controlled effectively by the expatriate employers because of the exclusion of full-time unionists, the mechanism stimulated the desire by workers to ease their

111

grievances but it inadvertently worked to channel them for resolution, not through the official structure, but directly to the unions. As the unionists gained experience and began to understand the consequences of being bound to a system of joint consultation, there was increasing conflict and a series of major strikes after 1960. Thus the joint consultative model failed because it could not handle the core functions of trade unions as seen by the unionists—that is, the presentation of demands and the settling of day-to-day grievances.

PROBLEMS OF INEXPERIENCE

The establishment of a modern system of industrial relations implies changes in past relationships between the main parties concerned. In particular, the shift in attitudes and behavior from the colonial situation to one in which the indigenous population stands on the brink of political power is a significant one. With the rapidity of change it is not surprising that all parties to industrial relations suffered from lack of experience in their new relationships. The lag between attitudes and behavior on the one hand and the rapidly changing political situation on the other was responsible for many of the problems of inexperience in Tanganyika.

The Employers

The main adjustment facing the employers was to the fact that they could no longer act unilaterally and with impunity in their own establishments. During the colonial period, while there were legislative limitations on employers these were not onerous nor was their enforcement rigorous. The impunity with which employers could act was reinforced by the behavior of African workers, which constantly emphasized the superior status of the expatriate employers.

Until the elections of 1958, which established TANU as the sole party with a mass base, few expatriates took the African political movement seriously. Indeed, even after this time, except for leading elements in the civil service, most Europeans and Asians remained oblivious to the significant changes taking place. Both the letters of the African unionists and the meetings demanded by them were therefore largely ignored or treated with disdain, and it was this treatment that goaded the unionists into the wholesale issuance of strike threats. Even when the employers began to meet with the union leaders, their approach frequently retained the old colonial attitudes; for example, they expected the customary signs of deference from the African unionists. On their part, the union leaders often overacted their new roles, becoming abusive and unreasonably demanding.

The employers lacked some of the simplest ideas of the conduct of industrial relationships. Thus the consultant to the sisal growers,

112

C. W. Guillebaud, had to advise them not only on the formation of their consultative apparatus, but also, in the simplest terms, on how to deal with unions. In a memorandum prepared for the employers for the first meeting of the Central Joint Council, the consultant explained that the employees would probably ask for a substantial increase in wages, and employers must be prepared to make some wage adjustments if they wished the consultative mechanism to work. Guillebaud advised, however, that the employers' offer be lower than that which the employers were actually prepared to give in order to provide bargaining leeway. A further indication of the employers' lack of experience was their carelessness in leaving copies of the memorandum where the unionists could pick them up after the meeting had adjourned. Some employers were so inexperienced in industrial relations that they simply panicked and sent for the nearest Labour Department Officer when approached by a union leader for even the simplest kind of grievance settlement.

In a number of relatively modern firms, management took the view that unions were probably there to stay, and either imported or trained local personnel in industrial relations to handle grievances and to deal with the unionists on a continuing basis—which method could lead to the establishment of relatively harmonious relations. In some of the large government organizations, however, there already existed a personnel section with expatriate welfare officers who created a lag in the development of new relationships because it was difficult for them to remove themselves from the colonial social situation.

It was within those organizations where troubles existed that the main tone of industrial relations was set. Thus, even though the unions had relatively peaceful relations with such employers as the tea growers and the local tobacco and flour companies, the prevailing tone of industrial relations was set in the railways, the sisal plantations, and the Dar es Salaam docks where continuous hostilities occurred.

The Union Leaders

Many of the difficulties arising from the inexperience of the full-time unionists have already been indicated: the problem of the maintenance of a coherent internal administration, the uselessness of their files and records, and the enormous turnover of leadership. In addition, the significant factor compounding the difficulties of the full-time leaders in dealing with employers was their simplistic approach to grievance handling. The unionists could not formulate a battery of arguments; in most negotiations witnessed by the writer, they had either a simple single argument or several arguments compounded. Appendix VII, Cases 11 and 12, indicates some of the difficulties of the unionists.

113

The union leaders experienced an almost total inability to occupy the role of the employer imaginatively and to envision beforehand the response to their own arguments. In those negotiation sessions observed, no unionist ever made the approach to an employer that "this is to your advantage." The inability of African union leaders to grasp the position of the employer and deal with him on his own terms was only one index of their difficulty in assuming new roles. The complexities of driving an automobile, becoming a possessor of a bank account, or being a trade union leader, all presented problems of learning. In dealing with employers, the union leader was unable to vary the hostile style of approach even when, no matter how justified the hostility, the situation indicated the efficacy of nonhostility.

The Labor Officers and the Labour Department

In a situation in which employers and unionists were largely inexperienced, the labor officers constituted the main body of experience, such as it was, in industrial relations. The Labour Department, however, also suffered from its colonial past and the inability of its officers, as late as 1960, one year before independence, to adapt to changed circumstances.

The spirit with which most officers approached industrial relations was exemplified by the Labour Commissioner during the 1960 railway strike when, instead of pressing both sides to reach a settlement, he allowed conciliation proceedings to continue inconclusively. Even when pressure for settlement was reinforced by the arrival of two unionists representing international trade union bodies, the Labour Commissioner did nothing to conciliate the dispute. In permitting the situation to persist without resolution, the commissioner was, in effect, contributing to a weakening of the union since it had few financial resources with which to sustain the strikers.

The changing political complex had little meaning for most labor officers; the syndrome of the club remained intact, and the personal relationships developed between the European labor officers and European employers tended to sustain the traditional colonial attitude toward the African unionists.

Although the labor officers were in a position to contribute to the evolution of the system of industrial relations, most did not know how to assist and few actually did contribute. This situation, added to the department's rigid adherence to the joint consultation mechanism, accounts for the substantial hostility between the African unionists and most of the labor officers.

CONCLUSION

The attempt to transfer joint consultation as the key mechanism of industrial relations proved to be unsuccessful for the Tanganyikans because they viewed the core functions of trade unionism differently than did the government and the employers. The union leaders' belief that unions were a means of expressing dissatisfaction of the workers was reinforced by the changing political situation which emphasized the legitimacy of their goals and therefore provided social support for their activities. The Labour Department, on the other hand, conceived of consultation essentially as an instrument of control to be achieved by the exclusion of the full-time unionists from at least the lower levels of the joint consultative apparatus.

The failure of the Labour Department demonstrates the consequences of the effort to obtain institutional transfer without sufficient attention to either the circumstances of transfer or the institutional forms being transferred. The transfer model of the Labour Department proved to be meaningless to the Tanganyikan unionists and, indeed, was actually dysfunctional since it excluded the unionists from involvement with the constituency to which they were addressing themselves and which, increasingly, constituted their social base. Unions that cannot express discontent become meaningless, and the Tanganyikan unionists could not permit such a situation to occur.

X The Unions and Politics

"Seek ye first the political kingdom and all things will be added unto it."
Kwame Nkrumah

The thesis of this chapter is that the Tanganyikan unions did not in fact engage in political unionism or, indeed, in politics at all to any significant degree, but that even when the political arena—Nkrumah's "kingdom"—was eschewed, political consequences could not be avoided. The Tanganyikan unions were economic in their approach and in the success of their appeal, yet there existed a close symbiotic relationship between them and the political movement. As the union leadership struggled to develop a constituency and build the organizations, every economic action had political significance, if only by virtue of the interpretations given to it by the expatriate employers and the colonial government. This does not mean that the unionists were unaware of the political implications of their economic actions; but, as the model of union-party relationships that had been formulated by the Labour Department emphasized the need for separation, the unionists were apprehensive about moving in political directions. Accordingly, they deemphasized the political content of their economic activities, often taking a public stand to make clear that a specific economic action was purely economic. Indeed, in the early days of unionism, although almost all of the unionists were TANU members and supporters, relatively few played prominent roles in the political movement.

As Tanganyika moved closer to independence, the relative uninvolvement of the unions in political questions began to change so that the unions became increasingly embroiled in political issues. The issue of the continued existence of the East Africa High Commission, a central political issue, began to trouble the unions. Out of a purely economic problem—the lengthy and difficult postal and railway strikes—came a political issue in which the unions soon found themselves embroiled. Other economic issues pitted the unions directly against the first TANU government which took power in September

116

1960. In addition, a number of leading unionists began to play prominent roles in government; some of them left their union posts when they became members of parliament; others did not. At the same time, the unions recognized the grave dangers in embarking on a political course, so that trends toward the formation of an anti-TANU labor party were invariably rejected by the union leadership. To enter directly into the political arena was recognized by the unions as an opening for TANU to enter the union area in response,[1] and, therefore, the union leadership explicitly denied political orientations.

The original Labour Department model of autonomous and politically independent unions was accepted with an ill will by the Tanganyikans; it was enforced largely by the threat of suppression of the unions. Once the unions proved successful, however, the unionists strove to adhere to the model and preserve the autonomy of the unions. As independence drew closer, and union activity was interpreted politically as anti-TANU, the TANU government sought to establish control over the unions in varying degrees. When most strategies failed, a direct takeover was effected in January and February 1964, following the mutiny of the Tanganyikan army.

POLITICAL UNIONISM: MODELS AND REALITIES

The Labour Department emphasized at an early stage that the unions should follow a separate development from that of the political party. Although a few early TANU activists made forays into the organizing process of unions, they were effectively discouraged. For example, consultation by some workers with Oscar Kambona, later organizing secretary of TANU, was followed by a subsequent visit to him by the police,[2] which action conveyed the idea that political persons were not expected to meddle in union matters. By the same token, from the beginning of trade union development in 1952, the Labour Department made it clear that direct political involvement by unionists was unacceptable. The fact that the founders of the TFL concerned themselves entirely with internal structural questions argues persuasively that the message emanating from the Labour Department had been received.

Even if weak on the reasons why such separation should take place, union officers down to the local level were able, in interview after interview, both to explain the separation and to provide operational definitions for the difference between their own sphere of competence and that of the party. As was explained in one interview, if a worker came to the union to complain of having been beaten by his employer, this was considered within the jurisdiction of the union; if he had been beaten by the police, he was referred to TANU.

To a large extent, therefore, the modus operandi of the unions was nonpolitical and autonomous with respect to TANU, yet the unions like those in most developing nations were continually accused of being involved in politics by representatives of the colonial government, by employers, and, indeed, in a subsequent period, by academic analysts. In order to assess the amount of political unionism in Tanganyika objectively, it is proposed to use an ideal-typical model of political unionism against which to test the empirical realities of Tanganyikan unionism.

An Ideal-Typical Model of Political Unionism

A substantial literature has developed in recent years on the subject of political unionism in developing societies.[3] The concept of political unionism itself evolved out of European experience based on fundamental Marxist notions of the development of the working class movement in which unions were seen as a mobilizing device auxiliary to the political movement.[4] Political and economic unions became clearly differentiated when the working class movement developed in the United States, in large part independent of political concerns; the greatest successes of the movement in the United States were marked by concentration on narrow economic issues. It would be a mistake to characterize the American unions as apolitical, yet integration with political organizations was negligible, and is today, and concern for the achievement of political goals was small. Although there was considerable variation in the extent of political unionism in Europe, there was widespread acceptance of the idea that it was essential for unions to engage in political activities. The basic model of political unionism in the European context rests on three criteria: (1) political unions are formally affiliated with a political party or adhere to its points of view on a broad spectrum of subjects; (2) overlapping leadership is found between the unions and political parties; and (3) political unions engage in political action either by pursuing economic goals for political purposes or by using economic actions for political goals.

Students of labor in developing countries, using this kind of model, have demonstrated that unions in those countries have become political, by contending that, since unions developed in a colonial situation, they grew as auxiliaries to the anticolonial political movements. These views have been supported in the African countries by political leaders who have metaphorically described unions as branches of a tree in which the party constitutes the roots and trunk.[5] This has also appeared typically in Tanganyika. One scholar has noted, for example, that:

> The party gave financial aid to assist the setting up of the union centre, and the first president of TFL was a prominent party member. The two organizations shared the same office facilities, arranged joint action on issues of common concern, and conducted joint recruiting campaigns.[6]

Julius Nyerere, leader of TANU, referred to the unions and the party as "legs" of the same nationalist movement.[7] Yet the following examination of these and other contentions leads one to doubt their validity.

The model of political unionism embodies the experience of a variety of countries, but there is some doubt that it can be applied to many African situations. In a recent study of African unionism, Berg and Butler concluded that African unions have not been political and that, in fact, although unions were continually described as political by friendly nationalists and hostile employers, the success of unionism was contingent largely on the degree to which concentration was focused on economic goals. Berg and Butler also were led to believe that the unions, to the extent that they became political prior to independence, were usually unsuccessful; and that in the postindependence period, any tendency of the unions to engage in political action was rapidly constrained by the new governments, so that the political role of the unions has in fact been negligible.[8]

The Tanganyikan case supports the thesis of Berg and Butler, in that the success of the unions was based on their relatively narrow focus on economic goals, but this emphasis overlooks the fact that economic action has political consequences. In Tanganyika, this writer contends, the unions were successful in developing a significant base among employed workers because they eschewed political unionism, but many, if not most, of the purely economic actions took on political coloration albeit inadvertently. In this sense, the contentions of Millen and other students of unions in developing countries have validity, but their emphasis is wrong. Further conceptual clarity is required to differentiate the type of political unionism characteristic of Europe from that of Africa, and especially Tanganyika in which the unions' struggle for economic goals had political consequences.

POLITICAL UNIONISM AND THE TANGANYIKAN EXPERIENCE: THE THREE CRITERIA

Party Affiliation and Support of Party Policies by the Unions

Historical consideration of union-TANU relations illustrates that while the TFL endorsed TANU's goal of independence at an early stage, its commitment to TANU organizationally was extremely hesitant.

The earliest recorded discussion of TFL-TANU relations occurred at the first annual conference of TFL held in Dar es Salaam in October 1956. Resolutions were adopted attacking the colonial government for its lack of consideration and protection of workers, but TFL-TANU relations occupied only a small part of the discussion. General Secretary Rashidi Kawawa formulated what was to be TFL's basic position for the next few years: although union members were also members of TANU, the two organizations were separate and distinct. Most delegates felt that the unions should avoid politics, but there was a strong feeling that the unions should be directly represented within the Tanganyika Legislative Council. Some of the representatives recognized the potential for conflict with TANU if the unions were directly represented in the same body in which TANU was demanding representation. Unable to find a satisfactory formula for the union's representation in the Legislative Council but anxious to avoid potential conflicts with TANU, the conference adopted a resolution which provided that "no Trade Union which is affiliated with the TFL should affiliate itself with TANU at the moment." Another resolution stated that, at the moment, trade union leaders should not accept positions of leadership in political organizations, and the trade union movement should be represented in the Legislative Council. The TFL Emergency Committee was directed to study the means of implementing this idea.[9]

By the time of the TFL General Council meeting in July 1957 the political tempo of the country had quickened. TANU's rapid growth had led to the formation early in 1956 of a political countermovement, the United Tanganyika Party (UTP), sponsored by the government but dominated by expatriate settlers, particularly the larger sisal plantation owners. To express its support of TANU and opposition to UTP, the TFL General Council adopted a resolution which endorsed TANU's main feature, a call for independence, without actually supporting TANU:

> Africans must be left free to govern themselves . . . To be ruled is absolutely unjustifiable today. A date for independence of Tanganyika must be fixed without delay . . .

> We want all citizens of this country to be given the right to vote so that there can be government by the majority . . .

> Workers and unions cannot keep away from government affairs because we are citizens like other people. Our unions are not political but we must be given the opportunity to express our views and be heard on all issues concerning our lives and the progress of the country. Our unions must have representatives in the legislature of the country to speak on our behalf and defend the rights of workers.[10]

While unionists supported TANU's program, they feared government suppression and therefore did not suggest closer organizational alignment. As it was, this resolution enraged the government and the settlers because of its endorsement of TANU's program. A spokesman for the government's public relations department warned that "it was not in the best interests of the Trades Union movement . . . for the TFL to become involved in politics or to attempt to take over the mantle of any particular party." The unions were similarly criticized by the *Tanganyika Standard.*[11] Kawawa repudiated any orientation of the TFL toward party politics, stating that the TFL "policy is to see that the trade union movement is entirely independent and that is also the policy of the ICFTU [International Confederation of Free Trade Unions] to which it is affiliated."[12]

There can be no doubt that the unionists were constantly aware of political activities and the work of TANU; but the work of the 1956 TFL Annual Conference and the 1957 TFL General Council meeting cannot be said to have been especially concerned with political matters. For the 1956 annual conference, four of 29 pages of minutes were devoted to political matters; the remaining pages were concerned with trade union questions which, although attacking government or calling on it for action, represent traditional union demands for minimum wages, provision of security, control of child labor, and other benefits. For the general council meeting of 1957, only three of 53 pages of minutes were devoted to political questions.

During 1958, the unions moved closer to TANU, for the TFL agreed to support financially a proposed TANU college, and Kawawa became a TANU candidate for the legislative council. As the election approached, the TFL urged workers to register as voters. By the end of the year, TFL had established its first organizational tie with TANU through its formal representation on TANU bodies although the character of this link is vague.[13]

That the sympathies of the unionists obviously lay with TANU was made clear during many 1959-1960 interviews but, though a number of TFL leaders were members of leading TANU bodies, it was not until February 1961 that TFL obtained formal representation on TANU's National Executive Committee. This formal representation, however, did not result from the closeness of the organizations but from the divisions between the unions, TANU, and the government. In spite of this new tie the unions still were not formally affiliated with TANU and, although provision for such affiliation existed, no unions ever formally became part of TANU.[14]

The "Kanyama affair" illustrates that although the unions hesitated to become affiliated directly with TANU, they would not countenance union officials who appeared to support political opposition to TANU. E.N.N. Kanyama was the general secretary of the Tanganyika Railway African Union (TRAU) and by 1958 had achieved prominence as a union leader and as an active participant in TFL affairs. His problems with the development of an important opposition group centered in the Dar es Salaam branch of his union were amplified by his endorsement of an Asian candidate, Dr. Daya, for the legislative council elections slated for February 1959. Subsequently TANU endorsed another candidate, and Kanyama's action was repudiated by the TFL and the TRAU Annual Conference. Despite public apologies and appeals, Kanyama was first refused recognition by the TFL and then expelled from TRAU. Nyerere refused Kanyama's appeal to intervene on the grounds that the unions had to be independent.[15]

The attack upon Kanyama was probably based only in part on his political act, for he was a relatively conservative unionist who had incurred strong opposition from his own union and from TFL circles. The violence of the attack, however, was probably based largely on his political behavior. The TFL was unquestionably sensitive to any actions that might be interpreted as hostile to TANU since, by 1959, it was commonly accepted that TFL would support TANU's program until the attainment of independence.

Overlap Between Political and Union Roles

To determine the amount of overlap between political and union roles necessitates consideration of both the extent of the involvement of the TANU leadership in the formation of the unions and the degree to which union leaders played prominent roles in the political movement. Let us consider, first, the question of the involvement of TANU in the formation of TFL in 1955 and then turn to the question of overlap in roles.

If TANU played any role in the formation of the early unions or TFL, the labor officers involved in the development of unionism in Tanganyika were unconscious of it, though they were sensitive to any political activities of the unions. Neither notations by Labour Department officers, interviews with leading unionists, nor persual of TFL files indicate any TANU involvement. It is conceivable that TANU may have provided some financial assistance to TFL but it was either insignificant or carefully hidden. In fact, TANU, which in 1955 was experiencing considerable growth and substantial internal problems, probably could not have mobilized significant financial resources on behalf of the unions.

Whether Tom Mboya met with TANU personnel during his historic trip to Tanganyika is unknown, but political considerations played no part in his discussions with the unionists or in his public meeting. Of the early TANU leaders, only one, Bhoke Munanka, later discouraged from organizing unions by a local labor officer, was involved in the formation of unions, and then it was in a number of small craft unions in the Mwanza area before 1955. A few union leaders came to the unions from TANU; none played a significant role in the TFL or in the important unions.[16] In sum, the degree to which TANU played a part in the formation and organizing of the TFL or of any unions was minimal.

The prevailing evidence is that after the unions began to grow there was some overlap between union and party roles, but this overlap has been exaggerated. Scott's suggestion, for example, that the first president of TFL was a prominent party member is erroneous. The first president of TFL was Arthur Ohanga, a Kenyan originally employed by the railway administration in Tanganyika. If Ohanga was a TANU member, it did not appear in the press at the time so that it is unlikely that he was a prominent party member. Were he a member, the local press, inordinately sensitive to the rising nationalist movement, would surely have noted the fact.

The reference may be, actually, to Rashidi Kawawa, the first TFL general secretary who played an important role in TANU and became a member of the TANU Central Committee in 1957, but his rapid rise within TANU was probably owing to his prominence as a union leader as well as to his undoubted personal abilities. Kawawa, indeed, did not become a member of TANU until early in 1956 when he assumed the TFL leadership on a full-time basis. Before that time, because of his employment by the government, he could not belong to TANU although he certainly sympathized with the party. There are some indications that Kawawa may have been active in the TANU Youth League at an early stage, but this was hardly an important or long term activity.[17] It is possible, of course, that Kawawa was nominated to the legislative council at the suggestion of TANU[18] but it is equally likely that the governor appointed him either because it seemed desirable to give burgeoning unions representation or because it was hoped that this would lead to tensions between TANU and the unions.

Other unionists were active in TANU affairs during the early days of growth. Maynard Mpangala, one of the first full-time unionists and general secretary of the African Commercial Employees Association (ACEA) worked on TANU recruiting drives during his free time and was reported to be a member of the first TANU Central Committee. TANU also provided ACEA with office space for a period of time. Patrick Mandawa, another TFL activist, was discharged from his employment with the railways for organizing for TANU and TRAU.

When unionists such as Kawawa and Michael Kamaliza, at the time general secretary of the Commercial and Industrial Workers Union, were engaged simultaneously in political activities and union affairs, some doubts were raised in the minds of union leaders as to the appropriateness of their actions. In 1958, for example, after returning from an upcountry organizing tour, Kawawa and Kamaliza were questioned about their participation in a TANU meeting in Mwanza. Both responded that they had spoken as individuals and not in their capacities as union officials.[20]

One way of determining the degree of overlap in party and union roles is to examine employment histories, political affiliations, and involvement of unionists in party activities. Data bearing on this subject were collected in the leadership survey conducted in the field. While all of the 64 full-time union leaders interviewed stated they were TANU members, only five had previously been employed as full-time TANU officials.[21] Of the 64 respondents, only nine at the time interviewed held offices in TANU, and the total having held offices previously was eight. Table X.1 summarizes the data.

Table X.1

TANU Involvement by Full-time Union Officers, 1960*

Level of Office	Formerly Held Office	Holding Office at Time of Interview	Total
National	2	1	3
Provincial, District, or Branch	6	8	14
Total	8	9	17

*The table shows the highest office occupied. It includes only those respondents with formal offices in TANU, which does not preclude the possibility of other respondents being very active.

Source: Author's survey.

The Character of Union Action

Another criterion for political unionism is contained in the answer to the question: do unions engage in economic actions for political or for economic goals? It is contended here that none of the major union actions between 1956 and 1960 had either specific or general political purposes.[22] TANU played a role in some disputes, but the unions set the goals and were, in most cases, responsible for their implementation. That the economic actions of the unions had political implications is accurate and central to the thesis being developed here, but the mobilization of workers for economic goals should not be confused with the political implications of that mobilization. For example, the Plantation Workers Union may have been stimulated to engage in strike actions because many of the employers were supporters of the United Tanganyika Party. To mobilize the workers, however, the union leaders did not use political symbols or political goals because the unionists had learned that economic goals had the desired effect, and therefore adhered to them. At the same time, the leaders specifically rejected the implications of political goals made by the settlers, the government, and the *Tanganyika Standard*.

Demonstration of the economic character of some of the important conflicts in which the unions engaged between 1956 and 1960 involves consideration of the nature of the issues, the parties to the conflict, the overt goals being sought, the degree of success, and, in the political realm, the involvement of TANU and the political implications of economic actions.[23] Other illustrations concern cases already dealt with at length, such as the railway strike, the sisal workers' strikes, and others.

1. *The Local Government Workers dispute, (September and October 195* This dispute with the Dar es Salaam Municipal Council concerned wage increase and a cost-of-living allowance. It involved no political demands. The strike deadline of the union expired, however, on the day that Princess Margaret

was scheduled to begin a formal visit to Tanganyika, and the strike thus took on political import. The many attacks on the union criticizing its timing did not interpret the strike politically or as a manifestation of the nationalist movement; the criticisms were largely for bad manners and "not being cricket."

2. *The DMT strike (March-April 1957).* This strike, following on the heels of the 1956 general strike, indicates that workers felt sufficiently encouraged to respond to the call of the Transport and Allied Workers Union for a strike against the Dar es Salaam Municipal Transport Company (DMT). This strike was economic: demands were made for simple (if large) wage increases. It was effective in that African workers heeded the call of the union; the ability of the management to use European and Asian employees to maintain the operation of services led the unions to call for a boycott of the busses. In this, TANU played a significant role, organizing the communications network calling on Africans to support the boycott. Because of the success of the boycott, the strike ended after 24 days in a victory for the union.

3. *The brewery strike (April-May 1958).* This strike, which involved the entire African staff of 270 workers of the East African Breweries, took place after the Commercial and Industrial Workers Union rejected an offer of a wage increase following a long wage dispute. The brewery responded to the strike by organizing the European and Asian staff to continue production, at which point the union called for a public boycott of European beer. TANU became involved when it published a leaflet written by Nyerere in which he supported the boycott and the strike. Thus, a minor industrial dispute over wages became inflated to a full scale political issue, during which the original economic issues became somewhat submerged. The potential harvest for TANU of increased mass support to be reaped from its association with the boycott became explicit at the trial of Kawawa, who was charged with intimidating two strikebreakers. Nyerere's presence at the trial attracted public attention and, following Kawawa's conviction in which he was fined Shs. 101/- ($14.14), a mob of an estimated 600 to 800 persons demonstrated their support of the whole affair in which TANU was involved.

4. *The postal strike (December 1959-February 1960).* Although this strike developed political implications almost immediately, the issues that brought out 1250 workers were strictly economic. The political implications of the strike centered on its economic failure, for the postal administration maintained basic services throughout the strike despite the fact that over 90 percent of the African employees heeded the strike call. This phenomenon pointed up the fact that, because the postal service was part of the East Africa High Commission, the commission was politically inaccessible at the time, and the leadership of the union therefore became hostile to the High Commission and demanded its dissolution.

These cases illustrate that the political movement was involved in various ways in union affairs, but it was economic considerations that largely motivated strike activity and the support of the workers. TANU was clearly cognizant of the value of union activity to help mobilize the African population against the colonial government and the expatriate employers. The boycotts called by the unions, for example, provided TANU with an opportunity to support the unions and unite broad segments of the population on issues seen as involving the "foreign exploiters," and yet avoid a direct challenge to the government.

The Conflict Between TANU and the Unions[24]

During the preindependence period, although some economic actions had political implications, the unionists tended to move very carefully whenever political questions arose. As Tanganyika moved toward independence, the relations between the unions and the political movement began to change drastically, for new political responsibilities undertaken by TANU created a strain between it and the unions.

The TFL-TANU conflict began as a result of the major, economically unsuccessful strikes by postal and railway workers in 1960. The unionists were enraged that, on the eve of TANU's accession to power, the management of the High Commission services remained politically inaccessible, which led to the demand for the end of the High Commission and the assignment of responsibilities for the services to ministers in the Tanganyikan government. A shift in TANU's position on the commission after June 1960 was indicated by Nyerere's public support of the formation of an East African Federation, and it became clear shortly afterward in speeches by Nyerere and Oscar Kambona that the High Commission was to be retained to form the skeletal structure for the future federation.

TANU's stance vis-à-vis the High Commission precipitated a split within the TFL. On the one side was the group of unions organizing government workers, including the postal and railway workers—a group that was opposed to the High Commission and therefore increasingly anti-TANU. On the other side, the pro-TANU wing was made up primarily of transport and domestic workers and was formed largely in opposition to the anti-TANU group. There was also a center group consisting of plantation workers, dockworkers, and mineworkers which, on various issues, swung from one side to the other.

The split became public in August 1960 when Michael Kamaliza gave qualified support to the retention of the High Commission. Temporarily patched up at an emergency meeting of the TFL General Council in August 1960, the split was soon reopened by the Mwadui strike of the African Mine Workers Union. The union and the management had signed a fifteen-month agreement in April 1960, and the union proposed, in effect, to violate the

126

agreement by calling a strike to demand increased wages and improved working conditions. The unionists fully expected the new TANU government to support their side in this first major industrial dispute since TANU had come to power, but they were disappointed when the Minister for Commerce and Industry took a public stand against them. This led to bitter attacks by the union leadership on the minister, and others in TANU; feelings became so strained that a committee of three government ministers and five trade unionists was formed in January 1961 to resolve the issues. As a result of this, in February, TFL was allocated two seats in the TANU National Executive Committee and thus obtained its first formal representation in TANU at the top level.

The conflict over Africanization was less dramatic but more significant than the Mwadui dispute. The position of Nyerere and the Minister for Health and Labour favoring "localization" rather than "Africanization" was unacceptable to either the unionists or, indeed, to many TANU backbenchers in the National Assembly. The issue began to develop as the first TANU government was constituted in September 1960 and continued through a series of crises, in which the unions implicitly threatened an ultimate seizure of the railways and the sisal plantations, until the army mutiny occurred in which one of the demands was the Africanization of the officer group.

A third issue that divided the unions was the attempt by Michael Kamaliza, who succeeded to the presidency of TFL in October 1960 after Kawawa took a ministerial post in the first Nyerere government, to centralize the unions by giving TFL substantial financial control over the affiliated unions. The government workers unions vigorously opposed the Kamaliza proposals for they realized that they would lose substantial autonomy to the TFL. Not only was Kamaliza believed to be TANU's main supporter within TFL but his stand supporting the High Commission and his conspicuous silence during the Mwadui strike had been considered a betrayal. Kamaliza's approach to centralization violated TFL procedures and this, added to Kamaliza's pro-TANU history, led the anti-TANU group to view his efforts as the start of a TANU takeover of the unions. This dispute could not be resolved internally and eventually necessitated an outside mediator.

Later, in 1963, after he became Minister for Labour, Kamaliza proposed, in private discussions with the unionists, that the TFL and the unions be incorporated into his ministry. The unionists, recognizing that this would constitute a takeover by government, rejected the proposal by an overwhelming vote. Other incidents contributing to union-TANU or union-government hostilities were a dispute between the TANU-led Dar es Salaam Municipal Council and the Local Government Workers Union in October 1961, and the dissatisfaction of the unions with government actions concerning the establishment of a minimum wage.

127

In June 1962 the National Assembly passed three bills, one of which, by naming the TFL a designated federation, effectively gave the government control over TFL because it could be "undesignated" in the future. A second bill severely limited the right to strike; the third made civil servants earning annually over £702 ($1965) ineligible for union membership, thus effectively removing many important leaders of the government workers union.

Nor did the adoption of legislation in November 1962, intended to help plantation workers, improve union-government relations because the legislation was interpreted as in fact detrimental. A series of wildcat strikes, possibly organized covertly by the union's leadership, began in late December 1962, as a result of which two prominent Plantation Workers Union leaders, including TFL president Victor Mkello, were rusticated by President Nyerere. The rustication, which lasted approximately two months, created a permanent insurmountable barrier between the unions and the government. The deterioration of relations between the unions and the TANU government prompted the government to take advantage of the January 1964 army mutiny to detain approximately 200 trade unionists.

The next month, while most of the union leaders were still detained, the government introduced legislation that ended autonomous trade unionism and created a new union, the National Union of Tanganyika Workers (NUTA). There were no affiliates of NUTA; instead it comprised industrial sections. The general secretary and the assistant general secretary were to be appointed by the President of the Republic to serve five year terms "at his pleasure." The general secretary in turn appointed all subordinate officials, subject to some controls, except delegates to the annual conference. The annual conference was to review policy rather than, as it had in the past, determine it. The government, by this legislation, finally brought under control the obdurate trade unionists who, having developed an autonomous economic base, between 1960 and 1964, had become an increasingly recalcitrant opposition.

In sum, throughout the period between 1960 and January 1964 the various disputes between TANU and the unions and between the factions within the unions were based almost entirely on economic considerations, although their form increasingly became political. The reactions to the High Commission originated in the failure of the unions to obtain economic access to the employers. The Mwadui strike involved issues of wages and working conditions, and the Africanization disputes concerned advancement of Africans into higher level occupations occupied by expatriates. The hostile reaction of the unions to the legislation of June 1962 was to protect both their right to strike and their autonomy. The plantation strikes of December 1962 began when workers felt that their economic situation was threatened by the legislation adopted in November. Finally, the unionists wished to protect their own organizations from being taken over. Throughout this period, while the dispute raged publicly and privately, the unions rarely proposed a political course for themselves. Indeed, this was specifically rejected on a number of occasions by the TFL and other union officials.

POLITICAL IMPLICATIONS OF ECONOMIC ACTIONS

There are four major reasons why economic action by the unions inevitably had political consequences. First, the government itself was a major employer; second, it set the standards for wages and salaries in the private sector. Third, the government's new responsibilities for capital accumulation led it to try to control the efforts of the unions to increase the propensities of their members to consume. And, finally, the government had to ensure the stability of the administrative structures.

Government as a Major Employer

As Table II.3 shows, the Tanganyikan government employed almost one-fifth of the labor force and was therefore an organization against which unions could be expected to direct hostilities. But any time that a government workers union sought the traditional economic demands of unions, political implications existed.

In the preindependence period, the unionists could direct their energies against government units with the encouragement of TANU. It would have been difficult and embarrassing for the British Colonial government, as the administering authority of a United Nations trust territory, to suppress the unions for pressing for economic goals. After independence, the government workers unions wished to see some of the benefits of independence directed to their members. In its capacities as both major employer and government, the TANU government had to resist the pressures of the unions and, ultimately, to control them.

Government as an Industrial Pace-Setter

Whenever government raised wages and salaries, employers in the private sector generally followed suit. This meant that unions had to confront government not simply as an employer but as a source of improved benefits for organized workers as a whole. Thus, most unions gave support to the demands of government workers unions against the government because they recognized that increases for the government workers would be translated into increases for their own constituents.

Furthermore, the unions continually pressed the government to establish minimum wages, wage councils to regulate wage minima in certain industries, and other benefits because the unions themselves had such difficulty in dealing with employers. Government was thus not only sustaining pressure from the unions as an employer but also as their source of protective legislation.

The Problem of Capital Accumulation

After independence, capital accumulation becomes a critical problem for any government that must both improve a relatively undeveloped economy and distribute economic resources as equitably as possible. Organized workers, because of their strategic location in the urban centers and in the modern economy, are able to exert greater influence on government to obtain larger percentages of national income than are other pressure groups in society.

Since the colonial government knew that its tenure was limited, the rapid expansion of the economy was not the burning issue for it that it was for the African nationalists. The colonial government could therefore afford to make some concessions to the organized workers. Once independence was achieved, the TANU government had to confront its former partners in the unions from the other side of the bargaining table as both major employer and, in the interests of accelerated economic development, chief barrier to union demands. The government argued that, inasmuch as employed African workers constituted only five percent of the total population, they would become—if they were to take the bulk of any increase in national income—a privileged class within Tanganyika.

> Tanganyika, today, is a poor country. The standard of living of the masses of our people is shamefully low. But if every man and woman takes up the challenge . . . Tanganyika will prosper; and that prosperity will be shared by all her people.

> But it must be shared . . . if members of any group within our society are going to argue that, because they happen to be contributing more to the national income than some other groups, they must therefore take for themselves a greater share of the profits of their own industry than they actually need; and if they insist on this in spite of the fact that it would mean reducing their group's contribution to the general income and thus slowing down the rate at which the entire community can benefit, then that group is exploiting (or trying to exploit) its fellow human beings. It is displaying a capitalist attitude of mind.[25]

It was believed that wage increases, if not regulated, would be expended on improvements in living standards. But in order to achieve the necessary capital accumulation for economic growth, the government had to ensure that workers saved whether they wanted to or not. This can be effected partially through forced or other forms of savings or through taxation by which the increased productivity is not passed on to the workers.

The Administrative Responsibilities of Government

In a colonial society, the native political party in opposition need not concern itself with the maintenance of order nor with the consequences of its demands. Once in power, the party has the responsibility as the director of the government to maintain order and to deal with the consequences of demands made upon the government.

For example, in the preindependence period, TANU favored Africanization, if only implicitly, by pointing out that the best jobs were occupied by expatriates. As the political changeover took place, the unionists and many TANU leaders believed that not only should the decision-makers at the very top be African but Africans should be employed at all administrative levels of government and, indeed, of private employment. A rapid changeover of personnel, however, could lead to a total collapse of the administrative and economic structure of a country, as the experience of the Congo had shown. Thus one responsibility of a new government is to ensure that the switch of personnel occurs so that administrative efficiency is maintained, and remaining expatriate personnel will stay on for a time.

The demands of unionists for Africanization in Tanganyika constituted a potential threat to the security of the state and to the economy. Since the TANU government now directly controlled the rate at which Africanization occurred in government service and influenced considerably the rate of change in private employment, the question of Africanization became a burning political issue.

CONCLUSION

Although few unionists understood the reasons for the separation of unions from political activities which the Labour Department had insisted upon, the significance of the separation was understood and used by the union leadership. The unions developed as autonomous units and, by limiting action to the economic sphere, mobilized workers in a highly successful manner. When TANU took over the reins of government, however, the political implications of economic activity assumed more significance. The insistence by the unions for their share of independence placed them increasingly at loggerheads with their former political allies while, at the same time, they rejected the efforts of the government to control their activities. Thus the unionists found themselves seeking to adhere, with some support from external union groups, to an outmoded British model of organizational autonomy so that they might maintain their source of power in society. But the continuing pressure from the unions constituted too serious a threat to the political movement. The presence of British troops to end the army mutiny of January 1964 was used to suppress autonomous trade unionism by the African government, which thereby effected the final demise of the models of British trade unionism.

XI   The International Base of Tanganyikan Unionism

Tanganyika's unions, because of weaknesses in internal resources, administration, leadership and economic power, were able to continue their industrial relations activities only by substantial dependence on external resources. In the previous chapter, the external contributions from the political movement were examined; here we turn to a different form of external support, that of the international trade union movement. The circumstances leading to international concern with the development of Tanganyikan unionism, and the forms that concern took, as well as the internal conditions that led the unionists to seek external involvement, must be examined.

CIRCUMSTANCES OF INTERNATIONAL TRADE UNION INVOLVEMENT

Prior to World War II, the interest of international trade union organizations in the underdeveloped areas was negligible. A few countries such as India had begun serious trade union growth but most of the underdeveloped areas had not yet developed a working class base upon which modern unionism could be built. The development of a committed proletariat in Africa following the war provided the base for trade unionism, and country after country witnessed the foundation of unions of African workers.[1] The political split between East and West was paralleled in international trade unionism by a split in the World Federation of Trade Unions (WFTU). Created in 1945, WFTU included unions from most of the allied countries, but the marriage was uneasy because some of the most anticommunist organizations, such as the American Federation of Labor, committed to the idea that unions must be independent of governments, were convinced that their Russian counterparts were not genuine trade unions. When the WFTU split, the Western unions accompanied by most organizations from underdeveloped areas, created the International Confederation of Free Trade Unions (ICFTU). The WFTU continued to exist and encompassed the unions of the Soviet bloc and the important national union centers[2] in Italy and France.

The natural interest that trade unions elsewhere would have in the new African unions was accelerated by the cold war, as both WFTU and ICFTU sought to establish connections with the nascent unions and to exercise some degree of influence over them.[3] WFTU was largely unsuccessful and eventually abandoned direct activities in Africa to support the All-African Trade Union Federation, a continentally limited trade union organization.

With the exception of a few French areas, WFTU had limited influence in Africa during the time that Tanganyika's unions began to develop, but the presence of WFTU provided a constant goad to the ICFTU to expand its contacts. In 1953, ICFTU opened an office in Accra, on the Gold Coast, with a full-time European field representative; another representative was sent to Nairobi to encourage the development of the Kenya unions. Active concern with Tanganyikan unionism did not begin until February 1957 when Albert Hammerton, ICFTU representative in West Africa, and Walter Hood of the British Trades Union Congress Colonial Department went to Tanganyika at the request of the TFL to help resolve the threatened general strike. From that time, ICFTU maintained a close and continuing interest in Tanganyika.

The international organizations did not constitute a single monolith which maintained clear-cut and well-defined policies in Africa. The Western-oriented international trade union organizations were composed of a variety of often dissonant forces. In addition to the ICFTU itself there were the international trade secretariats (ITS)—international organizations of unions engaged in the same trades (e.g., International Metal Workers Federation, International Transport Workers Federation)—which, although affiliates of ICFTU, retained their autonomy and were frequently concerned with problems other than those of interest to the ICFTU. Also involved were national trade union centers such as the British Trades Union Congress (TUC) which had become interested in colonial labor problems and had formed a committee to deal with the subject as early as 1937. By 1950, TUC activities in the colonies were so advanced that colonial labor problems became a formal administrative responsibility.[4] Other national centers became involved somewhat later, but the multiplicity of contacts developed by the national centers, each concerned with its own problems and interests, did not lend itself to an orderly situation. ICFTU sought to bring the competition under control, but this was hardly possible when the only agreement among the many competing elements was that WFTU should be prevented from gaining a foothold on the continent. For example, ICFTU, convinced that one of the best ways to aid the growth of African unionism was by education, created the African Labour College at Kampala, Uganda, in 1958, but the ITS believed that union organization could be facilitated by placing experienced non-African unionists with their affiliates in the African countries. The TUC was interested in training small numbers of unionists in Britain and arranged scholarships for Africans and, on behalf of the colonial unions, also did a great deal of "fire fighting" at the Colonial Office, which pressure was passed on to the colonial governments. The United States organizations generally provided financial subsidies to pay off debts or purchase equipment such as automobiles, mimeograph machines, and film projectors. This variety of activity from a multiplicity of agencies made it possible and productive for the African unions to play different groups against each oth

TANGANYIKAN REQUIREMENTS FOR AN INTERNATIONAL BASE

Three general considerations encouraged the Tanganyikan unionists to look to the international trade union movement for support. First, there was both the lack of coherent internal organization and the continual financial crisis. Second, the unions were confronted from time to time with serious crises in industrial relations for which their slender internal resources were inadequate. They turned in those cases sometimes to their cohorts in the nationalist political party for assistance but at other times to extremely powerful non-Tanganyikan forces which the nature of the particular crisis seemed to require. Finally, because of the inadequacy of the models available to them, the unionists felt the need to obtain more detailed models from more experienced sources. Thus the external union groups served at times as agents of transfer.

Because the union leadership looked to a wider world of international trade unionism for assistance, the base of many unions, particularly in the financial area, became established externally. The TFL, for example, by receiving external assistance, provided an excuse to its affiliates not to pay their affiliation fees, which, in turn, reinforced TFL dependence upon external resources.

Financial Crisis

Until 1960, dues collections in Tanganyikan unions were conducted largely by branch secretaries frequently assisted by "union agents" who received a percentage of the money collected. From the funds collected, branch secretaries usually deducted their own salaries, salaries of other union employees, and office expenses. The residue then sent to the national office was usually very small. For example, of the annual income of a provincial unit of an important union, 50 percent was spent by the regional office for salaries and other local expenses, 42 percent was expended by branches within the region, and only 8 percent was remitted to national headquarters. This union's national office was deep in debt at the time, with over $4000 owed for printing bills alone. In such circumstances, national offices of unions commonly used credit facilities for all possible expenditures except salaries. Asian merchants were prepared to extend liberal credit, and most unions normally functioned, therefore, while owing massive debts.

The shortage of cash meant that most national unions could not afford the "luxury" of giving cash to TFL to pay affiliation fees. The TFL, therefore, which also had to pay salaries, maintain an office, purchase stationery, and publish a newspaper, was in a perpetual state of financial crisis. Nor did the introduction of the checkoff in 1962 resolve the financial problems. Some national unions became relatively affluent, but their tendency was more to expand their field staffs than to pay their affiliation fees to TFL. Creditors would sometimes create crises by threatening the unions with court action if payment was not forthcoming. Unions would hastily appeal to other unions, the TFL, or, if circumstances were propitious, to an ITS or other external agency; sometimes an international trade union visitor or delegation might be persuaded to assist in the payment of debts.

Industrial Relations Crises

One example may illustrate the importance and variety of external assistance to the conduct of industrial relations activities by the Tanganyikan unions. In December 1956 when a number of unions called a strike of their members in protest against Labour Department involvement in the strike of domestic and hotel workers, a large number of the sympathy strikers were discharged. The union leaders did not know how to extricate themselves from this situation and so decided that external help was imperative. An ad hoc collection of money enabled Rashidi Kawawa to go to Europe to seek assistance from the ICFTU. When the issue remained unresolved, Kawawa successfully sought additional assistance while attending the first regional conference of the African Regional Organization of ICFTU in Accra in January 1957. Later, a cash contribution from the AFL-CIO permitted TFL to send back to their homes those strikers who were not rehired as a result of the settlement.

External Organizations as a Source of Detailed Models

The need for external sources of detailed models was less vital for the Tanganyikans than were the other external needs discussed above. Nevertheless, the lack of detail in the models available locally led the Tanganyikans to use European and American experience in the organization and maintenance of Tanganyikan unions and in the search for new ways to resolve their problems.

The analysis of transfer in these cases is extremely difficult because models were rarely presented in the form of policies, as they were by the Labour Department. In some cases, the presence of a foreign visitor might stimulate a discussion of a local problem and the visitor might respond with suggestions as to how such problems had been resolved in his own union. In other cases, Tanganyikans traveling abroad would absorb ideas which they would bring back and attempt to implement. Not all of these suggestions were viable and there naturally were no records kept of innovations originating from external sources. In one

135

documented instance, successful transfer occurred as a result of the attendance of a Tanganyikan at the school sponsored by ICFTU in Brussels. Another Tanganyikan leader who had visited the United States was less fortunate in his attempt to install an American type of multilevel grievance machinery based on written grievances. Although the proposal was ludicrous both because of the lack of literate personnel and the small size of the organization, management took fright and successfully discouraged the union and its leader. Other highly detailed models of administrative procedures were transferred when, for example, a representative of an ITS spent over a year in Tanganyika working with government workers' unions primarily to organize coherent financial records and to create respectable bookkeeping systems.

TYPES OF INTERNATIONAL ASSISTANCE

Financial Assistance

Some financial assistance was given in direct lump-sum unrestricted contributions, the distribution of which was left to the discretion of the Tanganyikans. One example of this was the contribution of the AFL-CIO to the TFL to help disperse discharged strikers in 1957. A variation on this form of assistance was the American shipment of thousands of TFL badges which were sold to workers for a contribution of Shs. 5/- (70¢), the money to be put into a "Solidarity Fund" maintained by TFL for serious emergencies. Many union organizations—ICFTU and the ITS for example—felt that this kind of assistance was very dangerous and irresponsible, for experience had shown that most lump-sum contributions were badly handled.

Second, and more often, financial assistance would be provided for specific purposes. An occasional visitor to Tanganyika might have discretionary funds with which he was permitted by his organization to pay a collection of back debts. Funds were also occasionally available to purchase automobiles, mimeograph machines, or other equipment, legal title to which might remain with the international body. Sometimes funds were available for the maintenance and operation of equipment. In these ways, the external groups sought to provide the Tanganyikans with much-needed equipment but to keep some external control over its use. Sometimes, funds were allocated to a project, such as paying the salary of an organizer whom the Tanganyikans would designate. External support was made available in this way by international groups to pay for a plantations organizer and a mines organizer; similarly, AFL-CIO paid the salary of the TFL education director for a period.

Special blocked bank accounts, dispersal of funds at fixed intervals, and similar devices were frequently utilized in an attempt to control the use of funds for only those purposes intended by the external source. Some unions were more reliable than others, but the perpetual financial crisis of all tempted the unions to use funds for regular operating expenses. Thus the funds from TFL badges, intended to build up the Solidarity Fund, were largely consumed for normal operations.

Technical Assistance

Far more significant and costly than direct financial assistance were the various programs undertaken to upgrade the technical-administrative skills of the Tanganyikan unionists. These programs were directed, almost entirely, toward raising the quality of the leadership and therefore concentrated almost exclusively on the full-time officials upon whom the unions were wholly dependent. Technical assistance came in a variety of forms which can be identified as follows.

1. *External specialists in crisis situations.* Specialists provided to help in various crises could take advantage of these situations to educate the Tanganyikans somewhat in the operation of their unions and the working out of industrial relations. In 1957, for example, the foreign visitors involved in the settlement of the general strike organized classes for the unionists.

2. *Technical experts for long range programs.* The use for educational purposes of specialists in crisis situations was limited because, once the crisis was resolved, the external unionists left the scene. At a fairly early stage, some international organizations set up long range programs of technical assistance in which experienced European unionists spent extended periods in the country. Thus one expatriate assisted for several months in plantations organization and negotiations; another was sent by the ITS of public service workers to assist the government workers unions in their unification efforts and to help them straighten out financial procedures and controls.

3. *Programs of external training.* Opportunities for study abroad were available to the Tanganyikans from the time the TFL was formed. Shortly after Rashidi Kawawa became general secretary of TFL, he was sent to England to attend a study conference and a short course on unionism organized by the TUC. Through contacts made on this visit, Tanganyikans were invited to attend courses sponsored by the World Assembly of Youth in Japan and Ceylon. This was only the beginning of an influx of invitations to study abroad.

One of the most important of the external training programs was that of the ICFTU African Labour College which opened in Uganda in 1958. Thirty-three Tanganyikans had attended the eight three-to-four month courses held at this facility through 1963.[5] Some Tanganyikans were invited to study in the United States. ICFTU also sponsored study programs in Brussels. After the Israelis opened the Afro-Asian Institute, a number of Tanganyikans were invited to attend study courses. Other Western countries provided scholarships and travel assistance. After Tanganyika became independent, the unions opened relations with counterpart organizations in Soviet-bloc countries, and Tanganyikans have had the opportunity of studying in Eastern countries as well.

137

4. *Programs of internal training.* There have been fewer internal than external programs supported by external resources. Classes were held for full-time leaders, for example, by the staff of the Kampala Labour College in 1959. In 1960, again through the Kampala College, a program directed toward reaching rank and file leadership was initiated.

5. *Globe-trotting.* The cold war created a situation in which there was a continuous demand for the presence of representatives from unions in under-developed countries at conferences and meetings. In addition, the desire of various countries to win friends led to the extension of numerous offers to unionists to travel abroad. The international trade union bodies required an African representative at their congresses; in the national unions, no annual conference of the British TUC, the German DGB, or the AFL-CIO was considered complete without its complement of representation from trade union groups from exotic places. Invariably, invitations to the TFL were accompanied by a return-trip ticket and all expenses paid. After 1961, the return-trip tickets began frequently to appear from communist unions as well. Nontrade union organizations: governments, private nontrade union groups, and others from many countries sought at various times to win friends abroad by inviting Africans to come to their countries for study tours.

Although Tanganyika's unions were hardly parochial, travel abroad provided new perspectives and suggestions for changes to the inexperienced leaders. Such trips, however, continually removed the leading unionists from their jobs for extended periods of time, and all too frequently general secretaries or other officers might be absent at crucial times in a union's negotiations. Provision was usually made to have the absent official's position taken by another unionist, but the lower ranking replacements rarely had the experience and knowledge of the peripatetic leaders.

CONCLUSION

The external involvements of the Tanganyikan unions illustrate the dependence of new organizations on sympathetic outsiders to provide financial and technical contributions. Colonial unions, unlike British unions in their infancy, had relatively little support from humane liberals;[6] and the number of labor officers who were genuinely sympathetic to the development of unionism in Tanganyika was small and could contribute little.[7] In this respect, the British colonial territories differed considerably from the French territories in which French communists and socialists substantially helped the developing labor organizations.[8] In addition, if Tanganyikan unions were to confront the powerfully organized, centrally controlled employers, they had to create strong organizations rapidly, which, acting independently, with limited resources was almost impossible. The Tanganyikan unionists soon learned to use with sophistication the available external resources

The attainment of Tanganyikan independence and the developing conflict with TANU increased the dependence of the Tanganyikan unions on external sources of support. Some of the financial problems lessened, to be sure, after the introduction of the checkoff, but the continual drain on the leadership of the unions, as substantial numbers left for important positions in the government, weakened the unions because the vacancies increasingly were filled by inexperienced and unsophisticated Tanganyikans. As the conflict with TANU developed, the anti-TANU unions recognized that an important source of support for their own autonomy vis-à-vis the government could be developed through the strong commitment of the Western-oriented international union groups to the freedom of unions from government domination. The anti-TANU unions generally worked, therefore, to retain their ties with ICFTU. When TFL was abolished and NUTA created in its place, the Western-oriented union groups protested as strongly as they could, but NUTA soon affiliated itself with the All-African Trade Union Federation.

Although dependence decreased as the Tanganyikan unions developed, they were never free from their need for external sources of support, a fact which they recognized. Nevertheless, they resented the limitations on assistance, the careful mechanisms established to control the dispersal of funds, and the lack of trust by the external groups such as ICFTU.

XII Organizational Change in Institutional Transfer

The present study has undertaken an analysis of a situation in which institutions, developed over a long period of time in one sociocultural context, have been transferred to another society previously devoid of such institutions. Indeed, the receiving culture had few of the social prerequisites of modern institutions at the time of transfer since it was only in the post-World War II period that the social, economic, and political structures of Tanganyika began to modernize. Colonialism initiated a process of social change which undermined traditional institutions, created the basis for a new nation and society, and ultimately gave rise to various forms of protest that required institutionalization. The study has shown how different models for channeling the protests of labor were formulated, received, and subsequently altered by Tanganyikans. In this chapter, the character of change is summarized and the sources of change examined.

CHANGES IN TANGANYIKAN UNIONISM

Structural Changes

During the period of rapid development between 1957 and 1960, the structure of Tanganyikan unions differed both from the model conceived by the Labour Department and from the structure desired by the unionists. Unions were neither locally based nor were they, structurally, craft unions as desired by the department, nor did general unions, the primary aim of the unionists, emerge. National industrial unions were formed in Tanganyika despite considerable effort by the Labour Department to implement their own proposed structures. Lack of acceptance of the Labour Department's model was owing both to its inappropriateness to Tanganyika's economic and social structure, and to the significant political changes that were taking place in Tanganyika.

Although Tanganyika's economy was underdeveloped, it did not consist of small scale enterprises relatively independent of one another. In proposing a model of trade unionism based on the craft unions of the early industrial revolution in Britain, the Labour Department ignored the concentration of economic power in the hands of a small number of employers in Tanganyika and the significance of government as an employer. The department's model was based on the concept of a society that was occupationally heterogeneous. Tanganyika's workers, on the other hand, were almost uniformly unskilled except for a small number of westernized and educated Africans. The racial differences between employers and workers made for additional and unique considerations. The department's model, directed toward administrative control of the evolution of trade unions, failed to take cognizance of the political maelstrom into which the country was hurled in 1954. Once the political revolution began, the unionists could only reject a structure that undermined their organizations' integrity by placing them under the guidance of the department.

The variations that ensued reflected more clearly than had the department's model the structure of economy and society and the changing character of political life in Tanganyika. The unionists themselves attempted to formulate vague structural models of general unions but found them difficult to implement, as leaders developed a stake in the maintenance of existing organizations. By preventing amalgamations, the Labour Department had encouraged the institutionalization of existing organizations. As a result, after one successful and one partially successful merger in 1959, there were no more efforts to create a few large general unions.

The relationships between the national center (the TFL) and its affiliated unions evolved to a large extent in the absence of a coherent model formulated by the Labour Department which opposed the formation of a national center. To the extent that any model existed, it consisted of a fragmentary set of ideas developed during Mboya's brief visit to Tanganyika supplemented by the example of the Tanganyikan African National Union.

TFL emerged as a prominent but weak central union organization with little actual authority over its affiliates. It was unable, for example, to obtain compliance either on the question of amalgamation or on financial commitments from its affiliates. Such strength as it had, derived from its contact with the international trade union world, the patronage it could dispense, its coordination of union activities, and its expertise. As experience developed among the leaders of the affiliates, the exclusion of TFL from industrial relations weakened the organization vis-à-vis its affiliates.

Organizational Roles and Decision Making

Clear-cut models were formulated only for formal offices and duties, and these were reproduced in Tanganyika with no significant changes. Other aspects of organizational roles were vague or unspecified and many differences were found when comparing Tanganyikan unions with Britain's. Most striking in Tanganyika was the high ratio of full-time union leaders to members and the difference in the social characteristics and the occupational background between the leaders and the members. Most Tanganyikan union officials were white-collar clerks who achieved their office through entrepreneurial self-selection and their tenure was generally unpredictable. Both the subsistence orientation and the new leadership role of consensus-molder reflected the traditional society of Tanganyika.

Membership roles also differed from those found in Britain. The traditionalism of the uneducated members in Tanganyika made concepts of voluntary association difficult to grasp. As they had been socialized in societies where membership is an ascribed characteristic, members and leaders experienced difficulty in adjusting to achievement orientations.

Variation from modern models of decision making was noted at all union levels, most notably in the carryover from traditional society of the emphasis on consensus. The desire for consensus is characteristic of small scale, highly integrated tribal societies. The difficulties of decision making at lower levels stemmed from inexperience with both modern organizational techniques and, more important, with the concept of membership as ascribed. The importation of traditional concepts of social cohesion into the modern organization also created problems.

Industrial Relations

The joint consultation model of industrial relations formulated by the Labour Department turned out to be unacceptable to the Tanganyikan trade unionists since it precluded their confrontation with employers. Adherence to the model would have excluded union leaders permanently from involvement, in the primary stages, in the settlement of disputes. The unions sought to establish direct relationships with employers at various levels to solve the problems of their constituents.

Union-Party Relations

TANU and the unions developed not only simultaneously but symbiotically, each depending on the other for support to provide outlets for action and mobilization of the African population. Initially the degree of cooperation was strong, although the Labour Department's model of autonomy was maintained and there was little direct participation by the unions in political activities. As Tanganyika approached independence, divisive tendencies developed as unions of government employees found themselves in conflict with the political movement. It was this conflict that led ultimately to the formal affiliation of the unions with TANU. Subsequently, as the unions continued their normal activities, conflicts with TANU and the TANU government became sharper and deeper. After independence, the unionists, fearful of losing their power, came to support the Labour Department's model of autonomous

142

unions which they had wanted to reject in colonial days. The growing hostility was ultimately resolved by the legal abolition of the unions and the creation of a new organization dominated by the political leadership.

Relations with International Organizations

The Tanganyikan unionists had no clear-cut models of international relationships. Rapid growth and staggering social and political change forced the unions to work out in their own way relations with international trade union bodies in order to obtain the necessary organizational help in terms of expertise, money, and models for the solutions of new problems. The necessary support was forthcoming because of the interest of various international organizations in Africa, particularly in light of the cold war. The proffered assistance supported but at the same time undermined the autonomy of the unions, for the ready availability of help conditioned the unions to expect it and to neglect the building of an internal base. Thus the relations between the unions and the international trade union groups were far more significant than were similar relationships between British unions and the international groups.

SOURCES OF ORGANIZATIONAL CHANGE

Core Functions of Unionism

The Labour Department's model for trade unions in Tanganyika failed to take hold because it was inappropriate to the situation as perceived by the receivers and did not fulfill the functions of a trade union as the receivers understood them. After 1950, in the period in which protest had not yet begun to be meaningful to the mass of Tanganyika's workers, the joint consultation model failed because of the lack of understanding of such mechanisms by the Tanganyikans. Later, as Tanganyikans became more socially, economically, and politically aware, mechanisms were needed that facilitated a direct confrontation between representatives of workers and centers of power and decision making. The Labour Department model continued to have little meaning for the Tanganyikans who sought, instead, to develop mechanisms that would facilitate the expression of protest which was seen as the core function of unions.

In examining transfer institutions, analysis must center therefore on the core functions of the institution as seen by the receivers. Functions that are core for receivers will be most visible and most transferable, and can override conflicting social and cultural aspects of the receiving culture.

The Social Structure of the Receiving Society

The sharp differences between the social structure of underdeveloped Tanganyika and Britain at the time of the growth of British unionism were responsible for the total inappropriateness of the transfer model. Thus ideas about the heterogeneity of the labor force, gradual "organic" development of unions, and high levels of membership participation on a voluntary basis had little meaning in a society the labor force of which was barely differentiated, which was undergoing rapid political change, and in which the concept of voluntarism was only beginning to develop. Inevitably changes in many aspects of the model were made when it was taken over by the receivers.

The Influence of Tradition

The importation of traditional elements into the modern transfer institution is selective, in that traditionalism is found only in some areas. In particular and most importantly the decision-making process in Tanganyika was strongly influenced by traditionalism, although the formal structure of decision making largely followed the British model. Similarly, traditionalist components were found in the emergence of the new leadership role of consensus-molder, in the subsistence orientation of leaders, and in the concept of membership as an ascribed status. Traditionalism was often found in the patterns of deference used by members toward leaders, although this varied according to the individual's experience in the urban environment and the relative age of workers and leaders.

New Problems of Institutional Development

Since the British could not anticipate and specify all aspects of trade union development, their model contained many gaps which the receivers found necessary to fill. The sources from which the receivers could supplement the inadequacy of the model included the traditional patterns and the example of other modern institutions. TANU, for example, was an important influence, for it constituted a single national organization in contrast to the union structures proposed by the Labour Department. Similarly, parliamentary practices in the Legislative Council influenced trade union practices. As unanticipated situations arose in the day-to-day activities of the unionists, the gaps were filled by the use of guides other than the model, thus contributing to the evolution of the transfer institution.

Finally, in the absence of detailed guidance from existing sources, the unionists turned to innovative behavior in setting the pattern for their activities. It was perhaps inevitable that caucuses be invented by the unionists, since models of caucuses had not been provided either by the Labour Department or by the European trade unionists, as the unionists became involved in internal conflicts within the unions. The level of completely innovative behavior appears to this writer to have been relatively small, and this is understandable. Tanganyikan unions arrived on the scene after unionism was well advanced in many parts of the world, and the Tanganyikans naturally looked to their more advanced counterparts for models of development. They therefore rarely felt the need to resolve problems strictly by themselves, particularly because they knew the experimentation was a relatively costly and difficult process.[1]

FROM TRADITIONALISM TO MODERNISM: INTERPRETATIONS OF CHANGE

Anthropological concepts of acculturation and culture contact as formulated by Malinowski, Redfield, Herskovits, and others have been shown to be somewhat inappropriate to situations in which modern institutions are transferred to traditional or modernizing societies. It has yet to be proven that contact between traditional societies and societies with superior technologies and more complex social organization produces entirely new cultural forms. The present study indicates that the complex forms will in fact be adopted almost entirely, although substantial change will occur within the form. The influence of traditionalism and of traditional society on the new social forms will be limited.

The static view of the development of unionism in Africa is illustrated by the anthropologist Charles, who argued that unions would be unsuccessful because they introduced into Africa ideas that were foreign to African culture.

> In Africa, in places where the tribal influences are strong, there have been obstacles to trade unionism which are easily blamed on the Africans . . . Yet the idea behind trade unionism is extremely simple and the African grasps matters more complex . . . Solidarity is an essential element of Bantu culture. Why is it so difficult for solidarity among workers to be expressed in trade union form?
>
> Anthropology, I think, will give an unhesitating answer . . . Trade unionism . . . comes up against a major cultural characteristic of tribal society, which has no institution based on the idea of conflicting forces or organized resistance to or defense against the chieftain. In the Bantu culture, such a notion would seem as unnatural and ridiculous as a defensive alliance of children against their parents. Authority is indivisible. For workers to combine against their employer would be anarchistic, a kind of open declaration of mistrust against the *smbwana* or guardian chief who is there to take the place of the clan, with the same power and responsibilities. A trade union is an instrument of protest. Except in cases where the African worker has been greatly influenced by European propaganda he never dreams of protest, any more than of sabotage. He only wants a chance to air his grievances in all their detail . . .[2]

From this analysis, another anthropologist, Beaglehole, argued for the development of institutions that would accord with the cultural expectations of African workers.

> For the Bantu, not a trade union but a Labour Council is the form of labour organization that fits more closely his traditional way of

acting and thinking—a Labour Council where the worker can state his grievances and difficulties before reasonably sympathetic associates and make suggestions for improving the joint enterprise.[3]

Views such as these became an intellectual justification for the formation of joint consultative structures and, ultimately, for the reluctance to accept the development of unions as protest organizations in Tanganyika. This approach proved not to be viable.

The relatively insignificant role played by traditionalism in the development of Tanganyikan unionism can be understood within an anthropological framework if a dynamic theory is employed. For such purposes, the work of Max Gluckman and his colleagues is relevant, for they have emphasized the appropriateness of different forms of behavior and institutions for different situations. Mitchell, for example, has shown how Africans in the urban areas do not behave in traditional fashion but rather emphasize forms of behavior appropriate to modern urban life.[4] Similarly, Epstein has shown how tribal "elders," whose authority was accepted for certain purposes outside but in the same area as the Rhodesian copper mines, were thoroughly rejected by African copper miners who preferred trade unionism. At the same time, the miners accepted traditional practices in the living situation existing in most rural areas.[5] Gluckman has pointed out the irrelevancy of tribal ways of life in modern contexts:

> It seems essential to start analyses of town life by saying that the moment an African crossed his tribal boundary, he was "detribalised," outside the tribe, though not outside the influence of tribe. Correspondingly, when a man returns from the towns into the political area of his tribe he is tribalised—de-urbanised—, though not outside the influence of the town . . . Hence the African in rural area and in town is two different men; for the social situation of tribal home and of urban employment determine his actions and associations, within the major politico-economic system covering both areas.[6]

Africans as individuals may suffer anguish to have to function in a milieu in which they have not been socialized.[7] This writer, however, must express some skepticism as to the extent to which the suffering of these marginal men can be generalized. The question of whether marginal personalities actually suffer more than nonmarginal men is an empirical one which, to my knowledge, has never been answered.

The present study has shown that institutional change does not take place on a random basis but that systematic sources of change can be found when new institutions are transferred from one society to another. When institutions are transferred under conditions in which they are given by a donor to a receiving society and in which the circumstances that brought about the institution differ substantially from the conditions obtaining in the donor

146

society, the transferred institution will evolve to fit the local sociocultural, economic, and political circumstances.

Social change in developing areas has been of concern to a great many social scientists since the massive changes that have taken place following World War II. The purpose of formulating the conceptual approach in this work has been to indicate a systematic strategy for the study of institutional transfer. Institutions other than trade unions are now developing under similar conditions of transfer throughout Africa and Asia, and to some degree now in Latin America, and it is hoped that the strategy proposed here may be useful in examining the processes of institutional change and development.

XIII   Epilogue[1]

The lengthy struggle between the trade unions and the TANU government during the period after 1960 culminated with the January 1964 army mutiny. When the mutiny was put down through the assistance of British troops, the TANU government also struck at the trade unions, and approximately 200 trade unionists including many of the TFL Executive Committee were detained. The basis for this detention, according to the government, was that the unions had had suspicious dealings with the mutineers. While no evidence was ever made public to this effect, there is some likelihood of contact between the mutinous soldiers and some union officials.[2]

With the majority of the union leadership in jail, the government took the opportunity the following month of introducing legislation that effected a total restructuring of the unions. Under the new National Union of Tanganyika Workers (Establishment) Act, the Tanganyika Federation of Labour and its affiliates were dissolved. In their place was created a new organization, the National Union of Tanganyika Workers (NUTA), to which members would belong directly. Instead of having affiliated unions, NUTA was composed of nine sections, each concerned with grouping workers in industrial areas: transport, agriculture, central government, local government, domestic and hotel, docks, teachers, mines, and the East African Common Services. Geographically, ten regional offices and 41 branch offices were established to carry out organization and administration at the local level. The two top officials (the general secretary and his deputy) were to be appointed by the President of the Republic and subject to removal by him. The remaining administrative ranks were appointed by the general secretary. The sole remaining elected group was to be the general council, chosen by delegates to the annual conference.

NUTA's relations to TANU were to be organic, with affiliation to exist mutually between the two organizations. In addition, the act provided that NUTA would promote the policies of TANU and the government and encourage union members to join TANU. The union was guaranteed a union shop in cases where more than half the workers belonged to the new union.

No provision was made in the act as to whom the President of the Republic might appoint as general secretary. The designation, shortly thereafter, of Michael Kamaliza to this post showed that the TANU leaders were proposing to maintain a tight control over the new union. Nor was Kamaliza required to surrender his position as Minister of Labour; until June 1967, he occupied both posts concurrently.

Although a single trade union structure had been discussed by the Tanganyikans when the TFL was still very young, there are indications that the new structure had non-Tanganyikan origins, and earlier events and discussions suggest the influence of Ghanaian, Soviet, and Israeli models.

Beginning in 1963, Labour Minister Kamaliza initiated private discussions with the TFL leaders on a proposal to integrate the unions into the Ministry of Labour. There are some indications that conversations in Tanganyika with John Tettegah, then secretary-general of the Ghana Trades Union Congress, provided some stimulus to the proposal. Tettegah's views on trade unionism were well known in Tanganyika; indeed, as early as January 1962 he expounded in *Spearhead*, a magazine published briefly in Dar es Salaam, on the Ghanaian view of union-party relations, calling for close collaboration of the unions with the government. Also by 1963, the unionists and various TANU and government leaders had had extensive contacts with Soviet Russia and Israel where highly centralized trade union organizations articulated closely with the ruling political parties. Thus notions about centralized union structures were in the air even though strongly opposed by most of the unionists.

Whatever the origins of the new model, the unions were not involved in the creation of the new structure. It was imposed through legislative action, and as the unionists began to be released from detention they were confronted, in effect, with a structural fait accompli from which many of them were now excluded.

One significant responsibility assigned to NUTA by the NUTA Act was that of participating in the development of the national economy. To this end, savings plans were developed and the Tanganyika Workers Development Corporation, a revised version of the Workers Investment Corporation, was formed. These savings plans were to encourage capital accumulation and investment by workers. In addition, because NUTA was expected to have ample funds from the checkoff of union dues, it was required that the new organization devote only 50 percent of its income to administrative costs, leaving the residue for development activities.

The period following the creation of NUTA was one of considerable uncertainty. While it was not clear how far the TANU government would permit the new organization to exercise its strength, the emphasis placed on impeding consumptionist activities and encouraging productionist activities was manifest. In December 1964, the government reemphasized the significance of productionism through the passage of the Security of Employment Act, 1964. The act was intended to establish workers' committees in enterprises in Tanganyika where ten or more trade union members were employed, to limit the power of dismissal of workers by employers, and regulate the procedures for the settlement of disputes between workers and employers. Recognizing that disputes might not be settled in discussions between the workers' committees and employers, a conciliation mechanism was established to deal with deadlocked issues. The main power in the conciliation boards would rest with the chairman, who was to be the regional officer of the Ministry of Labour. The boards were tripartite and included a representative of NUTA and the employers, but authority to dismiss the workers' committees was given to the Minister of Labour. Training courses were organized for the members of the committees in April 1965.

During 1965 and the beginning of 1966, little information was available on the character of union activities or the success of NUTA in carrying out its development work, but there are some indications that the performance was somewhat less than satisfactory.[3] NUTA had inherited debts from the former unions and was unable to support the Workers Development Corporation to the extent proposed by the Five Year Development Plan.[4] That the union was not operating to the full satisfaction either of workers or the government became manifest when in May 1966 President Nyerere appointed a commission to examine NUTA and its operations. A reading of the commission's report[5] provides evidence of widespread dissatisfaction. The report places heavy emphasis on complaints by workers about NUTA although it deals with some of the dissatisfactions of government and employers. Many of the grievances cited by workers to the commission are reflections of dissatisfaction with NUTA's failure to carry on traditional trade union activities. There were, for example, complaints about the rise in the cost of living and the failure of NUTA to take action to raise workers' wages. The work tasks of some workers, particularly in the sisal industry where tasks had been a standing complaint in the 1960-196 period, were said to be too heavy. Substantial complaints existed against NUTA officials, some of whom were said to be inefficient, overly friendly to employer and unwilling or unable to defend or assist the workers' committees in dealing with employers. Nor could workers see any justification for the existence of two separate and distinct administrative bodies—NUTA and the Ministry of Labour—carrying on similar functions in industrial relations.

From an administrative point of view, the commission also heard a number of complaints. The method of designation of the two top officers and their being representative of the President of the Republic rather than of the union membership was criticized as was the specific appointment of the Minister of Labour to the top position in NUTA. The argument was made that in carrying out two capacities the general secretary of NUTA was unable to fulfill his responsibilities to that organization satisfactorily. Although the formation of NUTA had been expected to establish financial order, the change had apparently not brought about any significant new method of handling the administration of finances. NUTA's financial structure continued to be unsatisfactory and too highly concentrated on administrative expenditures.

The commission's report substantiated the feeling of many persons that NUTA was not fulfilling its functions of representing workers' interests satisfactorily. Moving cautiously, the commission proposed a slight restructuring of NUTA to permit a greater degree of organizational autonomy. The major recommendation called for an end to the designation of the key posts by the President of the Republic and for their election by the NUTA Annual Conference. To avoid the development of potentially hostile situations, the Commission recommended that the Minister of Labour be given power to reject a candidate elected to the two top positions.

The response of the government to the commission's recommendations was delayed by the lengthy internal discussion within TANU about the implementation of socialist policies in Tanzania. This discussion, embodied in the Arusha Declaration of February 1967, provided the context against which any restructuring of NUTA had to be considered. Since the government contemplated nationalization of all major sectors of the economy, most of Tanganyika's workers would become employees of the government. Thus the government would be dealing with NUTA in the future as the employer of most of NUTA's members. The government's response to the commission's proposal therefore reemphasized the productionist functions of trade unionism. Rejecting any revision of the work tasks of sisal workers, the government also argued that, far from raising wages of employees, the gap between the incomes of employed persons and the great mass of Tanganyika's peasantry had to be reduced. Nor did the government accept the view that the two top officials of NUTA should now be elected; the existing system of appointment by the President was retained. To remedy some of the internal problems of NUTA, the government called for a training program that would make NUTA officials more effective in dealing with branches of the union and in cutting its administrative costs.

To implement the original division of union finances, half of which were to go to the Workers Development Corporation and welfare and social benefits, the government refined and extended the regulations over union expenditures.

In July 1967, in a restructuring of the government, Michael Kamaliza was dismissed from his position as Minister of Labour although he retained his post as general secretary of NUTA. While no explanations were made for this change, there are some indications that Kamaliza had continually found himself in an untenable position in representing both the interests of workers to the TANU government and the interests of the government to NUTA's members. The continued dissatisfaction of the unionists with their situation was made manifest at the annual congress of NUTA in mid-1967 when the unionists again asked the government to raise the monthly minimum wage from Shs. 180/- to 330/-. Thus while the unionists endorsed the sentiments of the Arusha Declaration, they continued to press for traditional trade union demands.

On the other hand, the government continued to press for controls. In October 1967, in a speech dealing with the implications of the Arusha Declaration, Nyerere stated: "Our trade union movement must shake off its British heritage, where it found its justification for existence by quarreling with the employers. The largest employer in Tanzania now is the people —their government and their public institutions. NUTA must learn something from the Soviet trade unions or the Swedish ones. Both of these, in their different ways, are chiefly concerned with ensuring that the wage earners get a fair share of an increased value of output. Thus, they first work to encourage and to help improve productivity, and then argue about its fair distribution."[6] The day following this speech, the National Assembly passed a bill limiting the total value of wage increases to 5 percent a year, stipulating further that all increases should be related to productivity. Later the same month, the Permanent Labour Tribunal was established to mediate agreements and enforce the government wage policy. Acting now in his sole role as general secretary of NUTA, Kamaliza asked that, in return for support of the strike ban, the government prohibit layoffs and allow for workers' participation in the management of industry.

An assessment of the situation of the unions since the formation of NUTA is difficult without first-hand information available directly on the scene; the effective elimination of strike activities since 1964 has removed one source of information about the unions. Relatively little documentary material is now emerging that provides data about the functioning of NUTA. A tentative assessment, however, is that the restructuring of the unions has not had the consequence of removing the sources of economic and social tension that have existed in employment relationships in Tanganyika for some time. Indeed, the need to designate an investigatory commission and the removal of Kamaliza from his post as Minister of Labour argue that tension continues to exist but is buried by the pressures created by the TANU government.

Tanganyikan workers had, by 1964, institutionalized to a considerable degree the consumptionist activities of the unions and they probably continue to bring pressures to bear, particularly at the lower levels of the union officialdom, to induce the union to defend their interests against employers. In a period in which the political leadership is under great stress to produce major changes in the development of the national economy, continuing demands of workers doubtless serve as a constant source of tension. The mechanism for the resolution of these tensions is now somewhat less than adequate; certainly, the mechanism is less adequate today than it was in the final years of British control. The unions can therefore be expected to remain as a significant source of political instability. This does not necessarily mean that NUTA will emerge as an open spokesman of workers' interests against the government; more likely, it means that a quiet battle will be carried out day by day on many fronts, with little dramatic impact. The political leadership may be able to substitute national goals as a mobilizing device for Tanganyika's workers, but it is equally likely that these goals will not resolve the day-to-day issues that arise on the shop floor in every employment relationship.

Appendix I   Methodology

This study was conducted in field conditions in a developing area that presented a number of problems entailing the use of a variety of research approaches. One of the major problems in such areas is that the researcher has considerable difficulty in delineating his role, which is strange to most of the people with whom he establishes contact. The colonial governments, for example, had experience with demographers and social anthropologists operating largely on applied problems that the governments themselves identified, but they had relatively little experience with free-lance researchers investigating problems of rapid social change. Almost by definition, the idea of someone investigating modern political, social, and economic movements represented a form of threat to those concerned with maintaining stability.

I found that the concept of an autonomous researcher was conveyed with great difficulty to members of government agencies, in particular the Labour Department. The department was willing, for example, to permit a number of formal interviews with its officers and access to its library, but a request for access to noncurrent files, particularly those relating to the early period of trade unionism, was rejected, so that the main repository of documentation of the early development of trade unionism was not available.

A similar problem of role delineation existed with the trade unionists themselves. The African unionists were accustomed to meeting Europeans as employers, as representatives of the government, or, occasionally, as trade union advisers. My presence raised special problems because, although I had satisfactory credentials from international trade union circles, I went around asking a great many questions. It took considerable time to establish that I was neither a trade union adviser nor a police spy. Over a period of months I was accepted, but continually had to reject the role of trade union adviser with which the unionists sought to identify me. Acceptance was facilitated by my having been previously prohibited in Northern Rhodesia by the Federal Government of the Central African Federation; I was thus

154

able to cite my genuine fear, well understood by the Tanganyikan Africans, of being expelled from Tanganyika for becoming involved in union affairs.

Other special problems developed because of the paucity and unreliability of documentary materials. Trade union files were in especially poor condition, but even those of the modernized bureaucratic organizations were astonishingly inadequate. Examining records of a large scale semigovernment organization, I found, for example, that employment forms were undated, so that it was not possible to obtain the ages of employees; what ages were given were estimates, but these often revealed surprising anomalies. In most cases, forms gave education as "nil," but a check of some of the workers revealed two who claimed Standard VIII education: although the claim may have been exaggerated, the ability of these two to speak English moderately well indicated that both had had substantial formal education. Even the names of employees proved to be unreliable since there were some who had changed their name when they converted from Christianity to Islam; the official records, however, were never changed. Nor did the records make provision for plural marriage although I encountered workers with several wives. Even newspaper documentation was not completely reliable; this in part was due in the early period to lack of interest in the unions, and in part to incomplete or biased reporting.

The documentary records of the unions were extremely useful in a variety of ways but they required careful interpretation. This was not so great a problem as was the incompleteness of the union records—gaps in minutes, missing copies of constitutions, inadequate or lost reports of officers, and other such difficulties. Records were used with discretion therefore, and normally were authenticated either through interviews or from accounts in some locally published source.

Because of the problems cited, the research approach included a number of methods:

1. *Ethnographic observation.* Much of the observational data was collected by establishing contact with trade unionists and following them through their day's activities—listening to their conversations, attending meetings, and observing them closely. The main product of this approach was a detailed daily diary totaling close to 600 pages and 350,000 words. The diary was coded in terms of qualitative events.

2. *Use of documentary materials.* These included official Labour Department materials, newspaper accounts, summaries of the Swahili press and, most important, minutes and other documents, and records of the TFL and affiliated organizations. The last-mentioned included constitutions, financial records, and correspondence between headquarters and field officers.

3. *Unstructured interviews.* Whenever conditions permitted lengthy and detailed discussion, the unstructured interview was used, sometimes in

addition to a structured interview, occasionally in lieu of it. Of necessity, the
of these interviews dwelt heavily on union history and the personal experienc
respondents in the unions. Such interviews were written up following the inte
either from brief notes or from memory, depending upon reactions of respon
to the presence of a notebook.

4. *The leadership survey.* The survey involved the development of an i
view schedule which was pretested in late December 1959 and in early Januar
1960. In its final form, it was used from mid-January 1960 for the remainder
the field period.

No attempt was made to use the schedule with a systematic sample o
full-time leaders. Limitations of time and finances precluded a search throu
Tanganyika's towns for full-time unionists, and even those noted on union re
usually did not correspond to the officers actually found in the field. Accordi
most interviews were conducted with leaders I met in Dar es Salaam and in th
various towns visited. The first upcountry tour in February 1960 took me to
towns between Tanga and Arusha; the second, in May, to Mwanza, Shinyanga
Mwadui, and Tabora. In July, during several short trips I reached union office
in Morogoro and Dodoma. Thus, with the exception of Iringa, Mbeya, Lindi-
Mtwara, and Kimamba, all major trade union centers in Tanganyika were visit
Upcountry leaders were interviewed whenever possible during these visits and
while attending four conferences of unions in July and August 1960.

Interviews were conducted in a wide variety of circumstances, not all o
them conducive to establishing rapport. In a number of cases, circumstances
made it necessary to focus only on sociodemographic questions. In other case
the presence of one or more onlookers changed the entire interview situation.
was impossible, for example, to interview officers of the Domestic and Hotel
Workers Union individually. Each interview involved more than a half dozen
persons; in such circumstances, the schedule was abandoned and group intervi
techniques were utilized to obtain some idea of the work being carried on.

The records of the time required to conduct the structured interviews
showed that 44 percent of the interviews lasted less than 30 minutes, 41 perc
were over 30 minutes; no record was kept for 16 percent. Records were also
maintained of a subjective estimate by the writer of the ability of 62 respond
ents to understand and speak English. The abilities were ranked as follows:
"excellent"—in which comprehension was perfect and no reformulation of qu
tions was necessary, 0; "good"—occasional reformulations, 23 percent; "fair"
frequent reformulations, 32 percent; "poor"—each question had to be reform
lated once or possibly several times, 32 percent; "hardly"—understanding of
English was so minimal that questions could deal only with a few basic facts,
percent; "none"—the interview was conducted through an interpreter, 2 perc

Completed schedules were brought back to the United States where the
were coded, punched, and tabulated.

Appendix II

Registered Trade Unions of Africans in Tanganyika, 1950-1963[1]

Year	Name of Union	Number of Members
1950	Lake Province African Tailors Association	33
1951	None	None
1952	Tabora Tailors Association	85
	Kilimanjaro Drivers Association	216
	Total Members, 1952	301
1953	African Commercial Employees Association	40
	Tanga and District Clerical Workers Union[2]	53
	Tabora Tailors Association	85
	Kigoma-Ujiji Tailors Association	88
	Kilimanjaro Drivers Association	421
	Total Members, 1953	687
1954	Tabora Tailors Association	Not known
	Kigoma-Ujiji African Tailors Association	Not known
	African Commercial Employees Association, Dar es Salaam	30
	African Staff Association of the Landing and Shipping Company, (E.A.), Dar es Salaam	50
	Dodoma District Masons Association	65
	Kilimanjaro Drivers Association	146
	Total Members, 1954	291
1955	Tabora Tailors Association	None
	Tanganyika African Railway Union	Not known
	Kigoma-Ujiji Tailors Association	5
	Mwanza Mechanics and Fitters Union	10
	Mwanza General Office Workers and Clerks Union	22

Year	Name of Union	Number of Members
1955	Mwanza Masons and Bricklayers Union	36
(Con't.)	Dodoma District Masons Association	42
	Mwanza African Carpenters Union	44
	Domestic and Hotel Workers Union	73
	Mwanza African Tailoring Union	75
	Mwanza African Road Transport Workers Union	85
	Dar es Salaam Dockworkers and Stevedores Union	101
	Musoma African Drivers Association	118
	Local Government Workers Union	135
	African Staff Association of the Landing and Shipping Co., Dar es Salaam	153
	Kilimanjaro Drivers Association	154
	Mwanza Hotel Workers and Domestic Servants Union	202
	Tanga Port Stevedores and Dockworkers Union	484
	African Commercial Employees Association	610
	Total Members, 1955	2,349
1956	Kigoma-Ujiji African Tailors Association	None
	Mwanza Mechanics and Fitters Union	15
	Mwanza Masons and Bricklayers Association	25
	Kilimanjaro Drivers Association	25
	Mwanza General Office Workers and Clerks Union	29
	Mwanza African Carpenters Association	35
	Mwanza African Road Transport Workers Union	35
	Dodoma and District Masons Association	36
	Nzega Tailors Association	39
	Mwanza African Tailoring Union	70
	Mwanza Hotel Workers and Domestic Servants Union	90
	Musoma African Drivers Association	100
	Tanga Province Building and Construction Workers Union	136
	African Tailors and Garment Workers Union	146
	Tanganyika Railway African Union	368
	Tanga Motor Drivers Union	480
	Local Government Workers Union	777
	Tanga Port Stevedores and Dockworkers Union	939
	Transport and Allied Workers Union	1,230
	Eastern Province Building and Construction Workers Union	1,716
	Dar es Salaam Dockworkers and Stevedores Union	1,800

Year	Name of Union	Number of Members
1956 (Con't.)	Domestic and Hotel Workers Union	2,000
	Commercial and Industrial Workers Union	2,800
	Total Members, 1956	12,891
1957	Tanganyika Public Road Transport and Maintenance Workers Union	200
	Eastern Province Plantation Workers Union	300
	Tanganyika Tailors, Shoemakers and Garment Workers Union	512
	Tanganyika P.W.D. Workers Union	753
	Tanga Motor Drivers Union	855
	Dockworkers and Stevedores Union	1,000
	Tanganyika Local Government Workers Union	1,000
	Tanga Port Stevedores and Dockworkers Union	1,039
	Tanganyika African Government Workers Union	2,000
	Tanga Province Plantation Workers Union	2,818
	Building and Construction Workers Union	3,000
	Tanganyika Transport and Allied Workers Union	4,109
	Tanganyika Commercial and Industrial Workers Union	5,000
	Tanganyika Domestic and Hotel Workers Union	5,500
	Tanganyika Railway African Union	5,900
	Total Members, 1957	33,986
1958[3]	Tanganyika African Customs Union	50
	Tanga Province Building and Construction Workers Union	200
	Tanganyika African Postal Union	300
	African Medical Workers Union	400
	Tanganyika Tailors, Shoemakers and Garment Workers Union	500
	Tanganyika Mine Workers Union	800
	Tanganyika Union of African Teachers	800
	Tanganyika P.W.D. Workers Union	1,000
	Tanga Port Stevedores and Dockworkers Union	1,100
	Dockworkers and Stevedores Union	1,200
	Tanganyika African Government Workers Union	2,500
	Building and Construction Workers Union	3,000
	Tanganyika Local Government Workers Union	3,000
	Tanganyika Domestic and Hotel Workers Union	5,000

Year	Name of Union	Number of Members
1958 (Con't.)	Tanganyika Transport and Allied Workers Union	5,000
	Tanganyika Railway African Union	6,000
	Tanganyika Commercial and Industrial Workers Union	6,000
	Tanganyika Sisal and Plantation Workers Union	8,000
	Total Members, 1958	44,850
1959	Tanganyika African Customs Union	100
	Buhaya Native Authority Employees Association	217
	Tanganyika Tailors, Shoemakers and Garment Workers Union	387
	Dockworkers and Stevedores Union	579
	Tanga Port Stevedores and Dockworkers Union	594
	Tanganyika Union of African Teachers	678
	Tanganyika African Postal Union	1,115
	African Medical Workers Union	1,468
	Tanganyika African Local Government Workers Union	1,847
	Tanganyika Mine Workers Union	3,000
	Tanganyika P.W.D. Workers Union	3,500
	Building Construction and Woodworkers Union	3,900
	Tanganyika Domestic and Hotel Workers Union	4,418
	Tanga Province Building Construction and Industrial Workers Union	4,629
	Transport and General Workers Union	5,900
	Tanganyika African Government Workers Union	6,961
	Tanganyika Railway African Union	13,698
	Tanganyika Sisal and Plantation Workers Union	25,326
	Total Members, 1959	78,317
1960	Tanganyika High Commission African Staff Union	70
	Tanganyika African Customs Union	100
	West Lake Native Authorities Employees Union	250
	Tanga Port Stevedores and Dockworkers Union	600
	Tanganyika Union of African Teachers	1,000
	National Union of Post Office and Telecommunications Employees	1,000
	African Medical Workers Union	1,500
	Dockworkers and Stevedores Union	2,500
	Tanganyika Mine Workers Union	3,000

Year	Name of Union	Number of Members
1960 (Con't.)	Tanganyika Domestic and Hotel Workers Union	4,000
	Building, Construction, Woodworking and Industrial Workers Union	4,500
	Tanganyika African Local Government Workers Union	8,000
	Transport and General Workers Union	10,000
	Tanganyika Union of Public Employees	14,000
	Tanganyika Railway African Union	16,250
	Tanganyika Plantation Workers Union	25,000
	Total Members, 1960	91,770
1961	Tanganyika High Commission African Staff Union	91
	Tanganyika African Customs Union	124
	Tanga Port Stevedores and Dockworkers Union	700
	National Union of Post Office and Telecommunications Employees	1,000
	African Medical Workers Union	1,500
	Tanganyika Union of African Teachers	2,000
	Dockworkers and Stevedores Union	2,500
	Tanganyika Mine Workers Union	5,000
	Tanganyika Union of Public Employees	7,000
	Tanganyika African Local Government Workers Union	8,000
	Tanganyika Domestic and Hotel Workers Union	8,000
	Tanganyika Railway African Union	9,000
	Transport and General Workers Union	19,000
	Tanganyika Plantation Workers Union	136,000
	Total Members, 1961	199,915
1962	Tanganyika Union of Customs and Common Services Employees	416
	Tanga Port Stevedores and Dockworkers Union	700
	National Union of Post Office and Telecommunications Employees	1,039
	Dockworkers and Stevedores Union	2,500
	Tanganyika National Union of Teachers	5,006
	Tanganyika African Local Government Workers Union	5,230
	Tanganyika Mine Workers Union	5,300
	Tanganyika Union of Public Employees	7,000

Year	Name of Union	Number of Members
1962 (Con't.)	Tanganyika Railway African Union	9,000
	Tanganyika Domestic and Hotel Workers Union	15,484
	Transport and General Workers Union	22,353
	Tanganyika Plantation Workers Union	108,125
	Total Members, 1962	182,153
1963	Tanganyika Union of Customs and Common Services Employees	416
	National Union of Post Office and Telecommunications Employees	1,050
	Tanga Port Stevedores and Dockworkers Union	1,063
	Tanganyika Mine Workers Union	2,400
	Dockworkers and Stevedores Union	2,758
	Tanganyika National Union of Teachers	6,761
	Tanganyika Union of Public Employees	8,112
	Tanganyika Domestic and Hotel Workers Union	8,866
	Tanganyika African Local Government Workers Union	10,000
	Tanganyika Railway African Union	10,386
	Transport and General Workers Union	18,732
	Tanganyika Plantation Workers Union	76,633
	Total Members, 1963	147,177

Appendix III

Interview Data on Tanganyikan Full-time Union Leaders

A copy of the schedule for interviewing leaders mentioned in Appendix I is appended here so that readers may see the approximate wording of the questions. Wording had to be varied frequently, especially when used with respondents whose understanding of the English language was limited.

Because field conditions did not always permit systematic application of the full questionnaire, the number of respondents varies from table to table. The total number of interviews conducted was 64.

At the top of each table, next to the title, the number in parentheses refers to the relevant question in the schedule. Below each title, the number of respondents for the particular question is given.

Interview Schedule—Tanganyikan Union Leaders

1. (Date)
2. (Time begun)
3. Full name
4. Address
5. (Location where administered)
6. (Code number)
7. How old are you? (Probe for birth date.)
8. What position do you hold in the union?
   a. Full-time or not full-time?
   b. Were you appointed or elected to this position?
   c. What body/group/person appointed/elected you?
9. What did your father do for a living?
10. What is your father's tribe?
11. What is your mother's tribe?
12. What is your tribe?
13. Where were you born? (Village, district, province, country)
14. Please give me the history of your education.
   a. Years attending each school
   b. Name of school

163

    c. Location of school

    d. Mission or government operated

    e. Standard completed

15. Have you ever had any correspondence courses?

    a. How many?

    b. Did you complete any?

    c. Did you take and/or pass an examination in completed courses?

16. Employment history (not including trade union)

    a. Name of employer(s)

    b. Location

    c. Type of work performed

    d. Employment period(s)

    e. Reasons for leaving (Probe)

17. When did you first join a union?

18. Which union did you join?

19. Was there any specific incident that led you to join the union?

20. Were there any general reasons why you joined?

21. To which union do you belong now (if any)?

22. What positions have you held in the union?

    a. Name of post

    b. Appointed or elected

    c. Name of union

    d. During which years

    e. Reasons for leaving

23. Have you ever participated in a strike?

24. If "yes," under what circumstances? (As a striker, as a leader?)

25. Are you now a member of any organization, association, club? (Probe for TANU)

    a. Name

    b. Type (sports, music, cultural, etc.)

    c. Participation (officer, member)

    d. When did you join?

26. To what organizations, clubs, etc., have you belonged in the past?

27. Where do you consider your "home" to be?

28. When was the last time you visited home?

29. How long were you at home during that visit?

30. When was the time before that that you visited home?

31. Length of visit?

32. Do you often have visitors from home?

33. Who are they; how often do they come; how long do they stay?

34. Are you married?

35. What is the tribe of your wife?

6. Through what standard was your wife educated?
7. When and where did you meet your wife?
8. When did you get married?
9. Is your wife now with you or is she somewhere else? Where?
0. How often does your wife go to her home? How long does she stay?
1. When you got married, was *mahari* [bride wealth] paid?
2. (If "yes") Who paid it?
3. Do you have any children? (Number?)
   a. Age
   b. Sex
   c. Education at present
4. Do your children belong to your tribe or your wife's?
5. Are your children all staying with you or are they somewhere else? Where?
6. What is your religion?
7. What is your wife's religion?
8. How often do you go to church?
9. (a or b, asked alternatively) Suppose:
   a. A worker came to you and told you that he had just been unjustly discharged. He wanted assistance. What would you do?
   b. A group of about 25 workers came to you and told you that they had just gone on strike because one of them had been unjustly discharged. What would you do?
0. What kind of jobs do you do as a union officer? (Types of activities engaged in: clerical, dues-collecting, correspondence, meetings, etc.)
1. What hours do you normally work?
2. Are you interested in work other than what you are doing at the present (non-trade union work only)?
3. (If "yes") What sort of work?
4. If a private employer came to you and offered you a job doing some job similar to one you have worked at in the past and offered to pay you Shs. 100/- more each month than you presently receive, would you be interested in such a job?
5. (If "no") Suppose someone offered you a job teaching students about unions, let's say, at Makerere [the University College in Uganda] at the same salary you get at present. Would you be interested?
6. What do you think would be the best age for you to retire from your present work?
7. Where would you like to retire when the time comes?
8. What sorts of things would you like to do when you retire?
9. How do you expect to earn a living after retirement?
0. What age do you think workers in your industry should retire at?

61. Do you have any questions or comments about my questions?
62. (Estimate of degree of command of English: excellent, good, fair, poor, hardly any at all, none).
63. (Time completed)
64. (Time elapsed)

Table AIII-1
Age of Respondent (7)
(N=64)

	Percent
Under 21	4.7
21 - 23	17.2
24 - 26	20.3
27 - 29	18.8
30 - 32	20.3
33 - 35	9.4
36 - 39	7.8
40 plus	1.6

Table AIII-2
Standard of Education Completed (14e)
(N=53)

	Percent
Standard 5 or lower	3.8
Standards 6 and 7	11.3
Standard 8	34.0
Standard 9	18.9
Standard 10	28.3
More than Standard 10	3.8

Table AIII-3
Type of School Attended (14d)
(N=50)

	Percent
Government or Native Authority only	46.0
Roman Catholic Mission only	8.0
Non-Catholic Mission only	8.0
Mission — (denomination unclear) — only	12.0
Combination of government and mission	26.0

Table AIII-4
Correspondence Courses Taken (15)
(N=43)

	Percent
Never taken any	48.8
Taken one or more — never completed any one	41.9
Taken one or more — completed at least one with examination	9.3

Table AIII-5
Tribal Origin of Father (10)
(N=64)

	Percent
Tanga Coastal: Digo, Bondei, Sambaa, Zigua	20.3
Pare	15.6
Mountain, Northern: Chagga, Meru	7.8
Nyasa Complex: Rungwe District, Songea, excludes Nyasalanders	15.6
South and West Lake: Nyamwezi, Sukuma, Haya	10.9
Luo or Kenya	1.6
Nyasalander	3.1
Other	25.0

Table AIII-6
Tribal Origin of Mother (11)
(N=62)

	Percent
Tanga Coastal: Digo, Bondei, Sambaa, Zigua	22.6
Pare	14.5
Mountain, Northern: Chagga, Meru	8.1
Nyasa Complex: Rungwe District, Songea (excludes Nyasalanders)	12.9
South and West Lake: Nyamwezi, Sukuma, Haya	11.3
Luo and Kenya	1.6
Nyasalander	3.2
Other	25.8

Table AIII-7
Marital Status (34)
(N=61)

	Percent
Single	29.5
Married	70.5

Table AIII-8
Level of Education of Wife (36)
(N=33)

	Percent
Standards 1 - 4 inclusive	24.2
Standards 5 - 6	36.4
Standards 7 - 8	18.2
None at all	18.2
Literate only	3.0

Table AIII-9
Length of Marriage (38)
(N=34)

	Percent
Less than one year	11.8
1 - 2 years inclusive	14.7
3 - 4 years inclusive	17.6
5 - 7 years	23.5
8 - 9 years	14.7
10 years or more	17.7

Table AIII-10
Number of Living Children (43a)
(N=42)

	Percent
None	9.5
One	26.2
Two	19.0
Three	23.8
Four	4.8
Five or more	16.7

168

Table AIII-11
Religion (46)
(N=60)

	Percent
Roman Catholic	26.7
Protestant	28.4
Seventh Day Adventist	6.7
"Christian"	3.3
Muslim	35.0

Table AIII-12
Religion of Wife (47)
(N=42)

	Percent
Roman Catholic	28.6
Protestant	26.2
"Christian"	2.4
Muslim	42.9

Table AIII-13
Frequency of Church Attendance (48)
(N=43)

	Percent
Never	2.3
Less than once a month	14.0
About once a month or so	2.3
About twice a month	11.6
About once a week	51.2
Active Muslim, daily attendance at mosque	18.6

Table AIII-14
Occupational Background (16c)
(N=54)

	Percent
Clerical: clerk, bookkeeper, typist, etc.	83.3
Technical: mechanic, artisan, electrician, etc.	14.8
Manual: unskilled worker, laborer, etc.	1.9

169

Table AIII-15
Self-employment (16)
(N=63)

	Percent
Never has been self-employed	88.9
Has been self-employed for less than one year	6.4
Has been self-employed for between 1 - 2 years inclusive	1.6
Has been self-employed for three or more years	3.2

Table AIII-16
Type of Employers (16a)
(Does not Include Employment by Unions)
(N=64)

	Percent
Never has been employed	1.6
Government agencies	26.6
Nongovernment only	20.3
Combination but predominantly in government	29.7
Combination but predominantly in nongovernment	17.2
Combination, predomination indeterminable	4.7

Table AIII-17
Mobility in Employment (16)
(N=63)

	Percent
One employer only	30.2
Two-three employers	28.6
Four-five employers	30.2
Six or more employers	11.1

Table AIII-18
Geographical Mobility in Employment (16)
(N=61)

	Percent
In one town or area only	32.8
In 2 - 3 towns or areas	42.6
In 4 - 5 towns or areas	16.4
In 6 - 7 towns or areas	4.9
In 8 or more towns or areas	3.3

Table AIII-19
Years in Employment (16d)
(N=64)

	Percent
None—entered union employment directly	1.6
Less than one year	6.3
1 - 2 years inclusive	17.2
3 - 4 years inclusive	17.2
5 - 6 years inclusive	18.8
7 - 9 years inclusive	10.9
10 or more years	28.1

Table AIII-20
Occupation of Father (9)
(N=60)

	Percent
Traditional: farmer, herdsman, headman, fisherman	60.0
Educated modern: clerk, teacher	21.7
Noneducated unskilled: askari, warden, laborer	10.0
Noneducated skilled: artisan	3.3
Other	5.0

Table AIII-21
Knowledge of Birth Date (7)
(N=59)

	Percent
Knows exactly	55.9
Knows month	6.8
Knows year	15.3
Very vague	22.0

Table AIII-22
Place of Birth (13)
(N=64)

	Percent
Rural	79.7
Urban	14.0
Not clear	6.3

171

Table AIII-23
Location of "Home" (27)
(N=50)

	Percent
Place of birth	88.0
At father's home — if different from place of birth	4.0
At place of longest adult residence	4.0
At place of current residence if other than longest adult residence	2.0
Ambivalent	2.0

Table AIII-24
Tribe of Wife (35)
(N=38)

	Percent
Same as respondent	63.2
Geographically or culturally close to respondent's	13.2
Different from respondent's	23.7

Table AIII-25
Place of Meeting of Wife (37)
(N=37)

	Percent
Same village or area	62.2
At school — away from area	2.7
In Town	32.4
Other	2.7

Table AIII-26
Location of Wife (39)
(N=30)

	Percent
Preponderantly with respondent wherever he is	63.3
Preponderantly at "home" away from respondent	10.0
Shifts back and forth, cannot establish preponderance	26.7

Table AIII-27
Source of *Mahari* [Bride wealth] Paid for Wife (41, 42)
(N=32)

	Percent
None paid	0.0
Paid by respondent alone	43.8
Paid by respondent's father alone	25.0
Paid by respondent's kin	31.3

Table AIII-28
Location of Children (45)
(N=25)

	Percent
All with respondent at present location	48.0
All children elsewhere	32.0
Some children with respondent and some elsewhere	20.0

Table AIII-29
Expected Age of Retirement (56)
(N=47)

	Percent
Under 43 years of age	8.5
43 - 47	14.9
48 - 52	25.5
53 - 57	6.4
58 - 62	14.9
63 - 68	6.4
69 or over	10.6
Rejects, unclear, unclassifiable	12.8

Table AIII-30
Expected Place of Retirement (57)
(N=40)

	Percent
"Home"	85.0
Place of lengthiest residence	2.5
Other	7.5
"Haven't yet decided" or don't know	5.0

Table AIII-31
Expected Activities During Retirement (58)
(N=37)

	Percent
Traditional (farm, fish, etc.)	67.6
Self-employment (shop owner, etc.)	10.8
Altruistic ("give advice," "help brothers")	8.1
Combination of activities	10.8
Don't know, unanswered	2.7

Table AIII-32
Level of Post Currently Held in Union (8)
(N=63)

	Percent
Branch	38.1
Regional or provincial	38.1
National	23.8

Table AIII-33
Type of Post Currently Held in Union (8)
(N=64)

	Percent
Secretary	76.6
Treasurer or financial secretary	6.3
Organizer	6.3
Lower level than secretary: assistant secretary, assistant treasurer, collector	9.4
Other	1.6

Table AIII-34
Method of Accession to Office (8b)
(N=59)

	Percent
Elected	40.7
Appointed	52.6
Appointed subject to approval of some official body	6.8

174

Table AIII-35
Year of Joining Union (17)
(N=63)

	Percent
1955 or earlier	12.7
1956 or 1957	38.1
1958	33.3
1959 or after	12.7
Never joined	3.2

Table AIII-36
Union First Joined (18)
(N=63)

	Percent
T&GWU and/or predecessor organization	23.8
Plantations and/or predecessor	25.4
Dockworkers	3.2
Government worker unions	3.2
Local Government Workers Union	11.1
Railway Workers Union	9.5
Other	20.6
Never joined	3.2

Table AIII-37
Reasons for Joining Union (19,20)
(N=54)

	Percent
Altruistic	29.6
Self-interest	38.9
Other	1.9
Unclassifiable	7.4
Joined when began working for a union	22.2

175

Table AIII-38
Number of Union Positions Previously Held (22)
(N=63)

	Percent
Currently holding first post	17.5
One	30.2
Two	27.0
Three	4.8
Four or more	20.6

Table AIII-39
Mobility in Union (8,22)
(N=48)

	Percent
Stable	8.3
Upward	72.9
Downward	6.3
Pattern uneven — rise and fall	12.5

Table AIII-40
Strike Participation (23,24)
(N=52)

	Percent
Never involved	38.5
Involved as a striker	9.6
Involved as a leader	51.9

Table AIII-41
Willingness to Accept Alternative Employment if Offered (52,53)
(N=40)

	Percent
Unwilling, no explanation given	47.5
Unwilling, for altruistic reasons	32.5
Willing, in career pattern as originally in non-union employment	5.0
Willing, in self-employment	5.0
Other, vague, unclassifiable	10.0

176

Table AIII-42
TANU Participation (25)
(N=62)

	Percent
Ordinary member at present	67.7
Ordinary member but once an officer	16.1
Currently an officer	16.1
Not a member	0.0

Table AIII-43
Work Experience in Industry of Same Union (8,16,21)
(N=64)

	Percent
With work experience in same industry	70.0
Without work experience in same industry	30.0

Appendix IV

Formal Change: The Case of a Union's Constitution

A delineation of specific manifestations of organizational change in a single union illustrates the operation of social forces within the unions more microscopically. Most unions (the main exception being the Plantation Workers Union) had constitutions based entirely on the Labour Department's Model Constitution[1] prepared in 1957. Indeed, it was found that all unions continued to utilize their original constitutions. The sole exception was the Transport and General Workers Union (TGWU) which had undertaken a constitutional revision while the union was being formed through amalgamation. The constitution prepared for the TGWU contains many concrete indications of the character of organizational change, and comparison of it with the Labour Department's Model permits the elucidation of factors producing change.

Concerned as the Labour Department's officers were with controlling a burgeoning movement, the Model Constitution stresses the development of decentralized structures, particularly in the form of substantial branch autonomy. The Model reflects the concern of the British that the unions not be taken over by the political movement; emphasis on the importance of elections and the preservation of internal democracy in the unions is evidence of this concern. The need for regular administrative procedures and financial regularity is emphasized in the Model. Built into it are definite expectations of the British about membership participation in the development of union policies. Altogether, the Model Constitution reflects the British concern with social control as well as their cultural and political preoccupations and conceptions based on British social experience.

Most of Tanganyika's unions adhered strictly to the language of the Model Constitution. Indeed, in some cases, the Model was copied word for word to the extent of reproducing spelling errors.[2] The unions that were the predecessors of the TGWU, the Transport and Allied Workers Union (TAWU), and the Commercial and Industrial Workers Union (CIWU), had constitutions that closely followed the Model Constitution.

The amalgamation in 1959 of TAWU and CIWU (along with elements of two other unions) permitted considerable constitutional change as the now-experienced unionists created a new organization, the TGWU. Although many aspects of the Model were incorporated into the new TGWU constitution, particularly those relating to the election and duty of officers and procedures to be followed in handling trades disputes, there was substantial constitutional evolution, some of which is relatively unimportant for our purposes. Three significant types of change, however, can be noted, and an analysis of them provides some indication for the reasons underlying the constitutional revision. After illustrating the character of constitutional change, an examination will be undertaken of the sources of constitutional change. The illustrations cited are not intended to be exhaustive but simply indicative of the kinds of change introduced.

MODEL RULES OMITTED FROM TGWU CONSTITUTION

Among the Model's rules omitted in the TGWU constitution, the most striking are those concerning branch organization. Rule I of the Model provides that "the Membership of the Union may be further divided into Branches in which case, to one of which each member must belong" [sic]. (1,6)* Subsequent elaboration provided for relatively autonomous branch structures: "Branches shall conduct their own affairs and make their own decisions in regard thereto . . . ." (16,2) The TGWU constitution, in contrast, omits reference to branch structure in the initial section. Although including a section on branches later, it omits those rules providing for relatively autonomous and strong branches. In the Model Constitution, rules pertaining to branch elections of officers, duties of branch treasurers, and provision for a branch imprest account are included, but are missing from the TGWU constitution. Also omitted are rules relating to the composition of a general executive committee and provisions for its election from various representative groups, minimum age requirements for officers, and the requirements for the maintenance of books by the branches and the head office.

RULES ADDED

The most significant rules added to the TGWU constitution but not found in the Model are the regulations for a regional structure. "For the purpose of locally administering the general business of the union there shall be a regional committee for such regions as shall be specified by the General Executive Council. (6,1) . . . The powers and duties of the Regional Committee shall be to carry out within the Region all the policies and decisions made by the GEC and the Annual Conference. It will be responsible for the establishment

*Numbers refer to sections and subsections in the Model Constitution and the TGWU constitution. Some of these are given in Chart AIV-1.

179

of branches, their proper administration and conduct." (6,5) Also provided for were the composition of the regional committee, its officers, and the frequency of meetings. A second major committee added by the TGWU was the Emergency Committee which was to be "the supreme authority in between the meetings of the General Executive Council." (7,1) The TGWU rules also provided for the establishment of specific union departments to carry out organizational, social, and educational activities. There was no similar provision in the Model aside from a vague reference in the "Objects" to "stimulate an incentive and sense of responsibility in members that they may become more efficient workers, and to seek the provision of all possible facilities . . . to improve the efficiency of members by means of organized training or otherwise." (2,2,c) Most of the other additions in the TGWU constitution extended the power of its General Executive Council.

RULES CHANGED

Most changes in the TGWU constitution were expansions and revisions of rules found in the original Model. The following chart summarizes a few of the more significant rule changes.

Chart AIV-1
Rule Changes in the Labour Department Model Constitution
and the TGWU Constitution*

Labour Department Model	TGWU Constitution
One object is generally to promote the welfare of members. (2,2e)	Generally to promote the welfare of members in such manner as the General Executive Council shall deem expedient. (2,2c)
The Executive Committee shall be empowered to fill any vacancy occurring in any office but only until the appropriate election has been taken. (7,5)	The General Executive Council shall appoint all permanent and full-time officers[3] of the union. It shall fix the salaries attached to each official position. It shall have powers to suspend and/or dismiss any officer. (8,7g)
The branch secretary shall conduct the business of the branch in accordance with the rules and shall carry	The branch secretary shall keep the branch register and accounts. He shall supervise the working of the

*Wording in the chart is either actual language from the original constitution or a close paraphrase; those parts of the rules that are unchanged or irrelevant for delineating the changes have been omitted. The numbers in parentheses after each rule identify the rule and the subsection numbers in the originals.

out the instructions of the branch committee. He shall be responsible for the notification of all meetings of the branch or the branch committee and shall attend all such meetings and maintain records of such meetings. (16,12)

branch and all its officers. He shall, at every meeting, read aloud the receipts for all monies forwarded to the central office since the last meeting. He shall collect all union monies from members and collectors and remit such monies to the regional or central office within 7 days of collection irrespective of any resolution passed to the contrary by any branch or committee. (5,11)

The formal TGWU constitution was different from the Labour Department Model for three basic reasons: One, there were marked differences in the views of the functions of the union between the Labour Department and the unionists. Two, the Model Constitution was inadequate for the social and organizational conditions of an underdeveloped economy and society. Three, the great differences of social backgrounds and experiences between the Labour Department personnel and the trade unionists resulted in substantial cultural and social reinterpretation of the Labour Department rules by the trade unionists.

CONFLICTS IN INTENDED FUNCTIONS

To the Labour Department, the manifest function of trade unionism was social control. Concerned with managing the dissatisfaction that was developing among urban workers as a concomitant of political change, the department was primarily interested in keeping unions, as a movement, from getting out of departmental control. For the labor officers, therefore, constitutional language provided an organizational structure that was weak and decentralized. To the unionists, the intent of trade unionism was to express dissatisfaction. This discrepancy in intent was reflected throughout the revised TGWU constitution—in changes in the formal goals (i.e., "objects") of the union, and in the creation of a structure that was more centralized and that specified the powers of the central authority more explicitly.

The differences in the intent of the two constitutions became apparent in the sections dealing with objects. Although most of the objects of the Model Constitution were incorporated into the TGWU constitution, those dealing with increasing efficiency of the members were omitted. More significantly, the TGWU constitution added the object of endeavoring "to control the industries in which the members are engaged." It also departed from the vague injunction "generally to do all such things as are conducive to the above objects . . ." by specifying that "the union shall have power . . . to impose such restraints upon the labour of its members or generally to interfere,

181

whether such interference is in restraint of trade or conduct of such industries, business, and occupation as [it] may deem expedient." (2,4)

The TGWU deleted the Model's specification that union members could not belong to "any organization which opposes the democratic principles to which the trade union movement is dedicated." The Model's language was regarded by the unionists as an infringement on their right to hold membership in political parties—more specifically, in TANU. TANU's structure was essentially democratic, yet many Britons in Tanganyika felt the party to be monolithic and authoritarian.

As for structural considerations, the unionists favored a much stronger central authority than was envisioned in the Model. This difference in conception is obvious in the considerable and careful specification of powers given to the General Executive Council in the TGWU constitution. For example, the unions' objects relating to welfare were essentially unchanged, but the TGWU constitution made the General Executive Council rather than the Annual Conference the allocating body. The Model left open the ultimate authority on the enforcement of the rules, whereas the TGWU constitution specified the General Executive Council as the source of authority and control.

The emphasis on centralized power by the unionists is also evident in the rules for representation at annual conferences. The Model provided that the number of delegates was to vary according to the size of the branches (one delegate per 100 members of each branch). In the TGWU constitution, provision was made for only one delegate for each branch unless the branch had over 3000 members, in which case there were to be two delegates. By effectively restricting the influence and power of any individual branch in this way, the larger branches were prevented from utilizing their greater representation to divide and weaken the union.

THE INADEQUACY OF THE MODEL

Many of the changes made by the TGWU in the new constitution reflected the inadequacies of the Labour Department Model to sustain trade union growth in the circumstances of an inexperienced leadership and a largely inert membership. Full-time leadership developed in Tanganyika because the union members were unable to carry out voluntary activities, and centralization of union power was necessary to permit the unions to deal with the central structure of decision making in Tanganyika.

The rapidity of growth of the membership combined with its inexperience precluded the development of a broadly based branch leadership. Branch autonomy, taken for granted by the Labour Department's Model, is contingent not only on the development of strong branch-level leaders but also on extensi

*Emphasis added, W.H.F.

membership participation. In this respect, therefore, the Model was inadequate for the prevailing social conditions under which unionism developed in Tanganyika. In constitutional language, the recognition of these problems by the unionists is evident in the TGWU constitution in the extensive changes and additions to the rules relating to branch organization. There were more changes made in this section of the rules than in most of the other sections, and they included a far more detailed enumeration of the duties and responsibilities of branch officers.

To compensate for the weakness experienced at the branch level, the TGWU provided for the appointment of branch officers in contrast to the provision for their election in the Model Constitution. The TGWU constitution also recognized the general weakness of branch leadership by allocating control over branch officers and their duties to the General Executive Council.

One major change in the structure of the TGWU reflected its rapidly increasing size and the difficulties experienced by headquarters officials in maintaining control over activities at the branch level. An intermediate regional structure was formed to create a level that would be staffed by competent leaders who could supervise quite closely the activities of the full-time branch secretaries. In addition, many activities, previously the responsibility of the branches, were shifted to the regional officers.

Incompetence in keeping books at the branch level led to changes in the Model Constitution. The Model specified that each branch should maintain a membership register "of each and every member of the branch . . ." (14,1) A similar register was to be maintained by the head office of the union which would be kept up to date by monthly statements from each branch. (14,3) The maintenance of these registers was, in fact, impossible not only because of the inadequate administrative skills and responsibilities of branch officers, but also because of the ambiguous concept of membership. The lack of properly trained treasurers at the branch level dictated the shift of the control over branch financial activities to the regional offices.

The TGWU constitution also recognized the general shortage of competent leaders by reducing, in almost every case, the number of officers specified by the Model Constitution for given offices. Where, for example, the Model specified a general secretary, general treasurer, and assistants to both, at the national level, the TGWU constitution provided only for a general secretary and assistant and a financial secretary, thereby reducing this group of four officers to three. There were similar reductions at the branch level.

The Model Constitution included as members "all workers, irrespective of race, creed or sex . . ." (1,4) The three predecessor unions of the TGWU had memberships composed essentially of African workers, and this composition of membership was retained by TGWU. Contrary to the practice of many of Tanganyikan unions, the word "African" did not appear in the union's name,[4] but the TGWU constitution in effect recognized the predominantly African character of the labor force and the constituency of the union by omitting any reference to race or creed. It also specifically stated that both men and women could belong to the union.[5]

DIFFERENCES IN SOCIAL CONCEPTS

Many of the rules of the Model Constitution which embodied British social conceptions were either removed or amended by the TGWU to make the new document conform to the social experiences of the Tanganyikans. For example, in spite of a full-time union leadership in Britain, British unions could not be sustained without voluntary leadership and fairly extensive participation by rank and file members. In the Model Constitution, extensive volunteer participation by the members was taken for granted, for example, in the autonomy given to the branches, in the lack of provision of full-time leadership, and in the assumption of a relatively extensive leadership.

Although the language of the Model was taken over by the Tanganyikans in most of the early constitutions, conceptions of voluntarism were not well developed even under the westernized leadership and, perhaps more significantly, it was soon learned that the rank and file could not be depended on to carry any significant portion of the work of the union. Accordingly, the TGWU constitution expressed the need for full-time leaders, reduced wherever possible the number of leaders, removed autonomy at the branch level, and concentrated powers of decision making at the center. Where the model constitution made no references to full-time leaders, the TGWU constitution made provision for a network of full-time officials.

Similarly, where the Model Constitution made extensive provision for membership participation at the branch level, many such specifications were removed in the TGWU constitution. Tanganyikan experience had shown that elections of branch officers were honored more in theory than in reality and were meaningless in the case of full-time branch officials; meetings were held irregularly and were "mass meetings" rather than business meetings of the branch. Thus, the Model's detail concerning an annual general meeting, quarterly general meetings, monthly branch committee meetings, and rules for conducting meetings were not included in the TGWU constitution.

The British traditions of representative democracy were manifested in the Model in the form of increased representation at conferences for larger branches. The TGWU constitution disregarded this concept and made no distinction in representation at the annual conference between a branch of 20 and one of 3000. This change in part reflected the desire to avoid possible domination of the conference by several large branches, but it also illustrated different concepts of the principle of representation. The Tanganyikans could see little purpose in multiple representation because delegates were expected to reflect the consensus already achieved within their branches. It was considered wasteful, therefore, to have two, three, or more delegates presenting the same point of view. Only a minimal concession was made to the larger branches by permitting two representatives for branches exceeding 3000 members.

Appendix V

Estimate of Full-time Unionists in Tanganyika, 1960

Any estimate of the number of full-time officials of trade unions must be speculative because it is doubtful that any agencies, including the Labour Department or the trade unions themselves, had accurate figures for the numbers of full-time personnel at the time. This was owing, first, to the considerable and rapid movement of personnel; second, to discrepancies between the table of organization of unions and the realities found in the field; and third, to the unsatisfactory data on the number of branches of some unions. Although the statistics for some unions, such as the Domestic and Hotel Workers Union, are almost completely unreliable, estimates can be made with some reasonable assurance for a number of other unions, such as the Plantation Workers Union.

Despite the problems, the attempt to estimate the size of the full-time leadership has been made on the basis of internal evidence, interviews, personal contacts, and other available evidence (see Table A V-1). In the case of each union, minimum and maximum estimates are given. Full-time leaders are defined here as the equivalent of a business agent or a representative in an American trade union. Included for Tanganyika are officers such as branch secretaries, regional or provincial secretaries and treasurers, and national officers (general secretaries and treasurers, but not presidents who were not full-time).

There were other categories of union employees who functioned in leadership capacities from time to time but who have been omitted from these estimates. These include two broad categories then found in many unions:

1. *"Union Collectors" or "Union Agents."* These were frequently but not always full-time officials. Persons occupying these positions collected dues and initiation fees from members and received a percentage of their collections but no wages. In some circumstances they operated as "leaders" although their formal responsibilities excluded activities normally associated with full-time leadership. They rarely dealt with employers or spoke to members at meetings. These offices were frequently preliminary to full-time employment. Many full-time branch secretaries, for example, began their union careers as collectors.

In this sense, collectors could have been included in the "leadership" category, but the margin of error in the estimates would have been increased, since no one had any idea as to the number of collectors actually working.

2. *"Lady Clerks."* Each union usually employed a number of women as clerical assistants. Normally these women worked in a purely clerical capacity but occasionally one of them might engage in educational or propagandistic activity with the wives of workers. A few were beginning to move into positions of branch secretary, and the lady clerks, like the collectors, represented a preliminary occupation to full-time employment in a leadership capacity. Women clerks have also been excluded from the estimates.

There were probably also a few individual entrepreneurs still functioning in 1960 as "union leaders" on an independent basis but it is doubtful that they would exceed half a dozen for the entire country; they have not been included in the estimates, since there was no information available on them.

Table A V-1

Estimates, by Union, of Numbers of Full-time Leaders, 1960

Union	Minimum	Maximum
Plantation Workers Union	73	125
Transport and General Workers	42	80
Tanga Port Dockworkers	1	2
Mine Workers Union	3	5
Customs Workers Union	0	1
Dar es Salaam Dockworkers	2	4
Postal Workers	1	2
Railway African Union	5	8
Public Employees	3	6
Local Government Workers	7	10
Domestic and Hotel Workers	30	200
Tanganyika Federation of Labor	4	5
T. F. L. Trades Council	0	0
Totals	171	448

Appendix VI

Informal Joint Consultative Bodies in Tanganyika and Their Significance

The Labour Department first formally noted the existence of informal bodies of joint consultation in 1952 only after it had established policies encouraging the development of consultation.

> . . . there are some fifty known bodies of less formal nature, covering some 50,000 employees, which may in some cases be called Domestic Councils or in others Headmen's Councils. The majority of these are in agricultural enterprises such as the Overseas Food Corporation's farms and on sisal estates, and there are others on mines.[1]

The department continued to take note of these informal councils until 1958. Table AVI-1 gives the department's estimates of the number of workers covered by such arrangements. In 1958 no further mention was made of these councils and they disappeared from further consideration by the Labour Department as instrumentalities for consultation.

Little is actually known of the councils, their composition, functions, or activities. Guillebaud referred to them in very general terms when discussing industrial relations in the sisal industry following his study conducted in 1957-58.

> For many years past the relations between employers and their African employees in the Sisal Industry have been in general good and harmonious on most estates. Each tribal community had its elders and headmen to whom matters concerning the welfare of the individual or community were brought. Many of these issues arose out of disputes over women, petty thefts, brawls, etc. and were dealt with by the headmen or elders, sometimes being referred for a decision to the manager of the estate or the local African Authority. But issues could also arise out of the working of the Estate and they were dealt with in discussions between the manager and the headmen and elders.[2]

Table AVI-1
Estimated Number of Workers Covered by Elders'
Councils in Tanganyika, 1952-1957

1952	50,000
1953	80,000
1954	80,000
1955	80,000
1956	100,000
1957	100,000

Source: ARLD, 1952-1957.

Nor were many details forthcoming from Jack, who studied the sisal industry in 1959.

> On most estates a considerable amount of joint consultation was normally practiced. In many cases the estate manager would hold frequent meetings with the tribal headmen, or Council of *Wazee* for the purpose of dealing with individual, tribal or other difficulties which might arise . . . These estate meetings provided a regular means of dealing with the problems which arose and appear to have been firmly established. They had the further advantage that they gave full recognition to tribal authorities.[3]

No other documentary evidence is available about these councils of elders in Tanganyika, and interviews indicated that their existence was extremely precarious. I was unable to find evidence that the councils met frequently with estate managers. On the contrary, indications are that meetings were called only when substantial pressures were built up or when managers had news they wished to communicate to the workers. Jack's statement that the councils gave "full recognition to tribal authorities" is unsatisfactory in light of two pieces of evidence: one, the "disappearance" of the councils as trade unions developed; and, two, the experience of such councils on the Rhodesian Copperbelt.

The disappearance of the councils in the 1958 *Report* of the Labour Department is significant. Either their existence had been exaggerated by the department in previous years or they had collapsed under the impact of trade unionism. No satisfactory data exist, but it is likely that the councils followed an evolution similar to that followed in Northern Rhodesia where the councils were more highly organized, and information on their existence has been documented by Epstein and others.[4]

Tribal elders were organized as groups in the early 1930s at mines on the Rhodesian Copperbelt. Although the elders were elected, the basis for success in election appears to have been their closeness to chiefs or councilors in tribal society. The foundation of their authority was therefore traditional.

The tribal elders, in the urban context, became instruments of control for the management of the mines to settle internal tribal conflicts at the mines. Later, however, in two strikes on the Copperbelt in 1935 and 1940, the authority of the elders was rejected by the African strikers who, in one case, drove them to seek refuge in the mines' offices. After the 1940 strike, attempts were made by the government and management to reinforce the tribal leadership, but the trade union leaders in the mines and the educated Africans who formed themselves into welfare societies in the townships had developed new leadership which challenged and overwhelmed the tribal elders. In 1953 the African Mineworkers Union demanded the abolition of the elders, or tribal representatives, and in an election by secret ballot their abolition was supported by 95 percent of those voting.

Epstein explained these developments in terms of the failure of the tribal representatives to deal with the realities of urban life and the problems of workers at the mines. Because the tribal representatives had been supported by the mines' management they had been regarded and, indeed, had regarded themselves as employees of the management. For certain kinds of problems, the authority of the tribal representatives was unquestioned. As intermediaries between workers and employers, however, their authority was replaced by a new and more appropriate authority whose functions related better to the problems of African workers in an urban environment.

Unlike the councils of elders in the Rhodesian Copperbelt, those in Tanganyika were less elaborately organized. Rhodesian mine management made conscious attempts to support the authority of the tribal elders. In Tanganyika, the councils were more loosely organized and structured, and no coherent organization supported their existence. Apparently the elders' councils were mainly ad hoc bodies created by employers and managers and there was no evidence that the elders' councils were independent and continuing bodies or had an established basis for representation. Indications are that, when a problem presented itself, the estate manager would call together a meeting of representatives. The meeting might be convened because of a specific complaint, or a general sensing of dissatisfaction in the work force; or the manager might have some message or orders he wished to convey to his workers. These councils do not appear to have had any "rights" but existed, in effect, at the pleasure of the employer. In such circumstances, it can be seen that their authority might easily be challenged.

In addition, the authority of tribal elders was more subject to question in Tanganyika than in Rhodesia. Many Rhodesian Africans came from tribes having centralized political systems, but, in Tanganyika, most tribes had attenuated political systems that bordered on anarchy. Since authority in many Tanganyika tribes rested with clan or lineage heads, it is doubtful that lineage heads of one tribe could have maintained the allegiance of members of other tribes.

On the sisal estates and in the mines, where most of the councils of elders were found, tribal organization was undermined by housing and working arrangements. In Tanganyika and most of the other African territories except South Africa, the tribal basis of social organization was ignored in the organization of work gangs, or housing of labor. Attention was occasionally paid to various groups of tribes or affinities of tribes, but most employers were concerned with such problems only insofar as they might affect working relations.[5] This tendency of most European supervisors to lump Africans together as a single group and, with a few noticeable exceptions (such as the Masai), to consider them simply as Africans accelerated the breakdown of the tribe as a basis for social organization, particularly among those workers who remained in employment for periods in excess of several years. Thus the evidence about the councils of elders uncertain as it is, implies that this form of joint consultation had little significance and no long-standing impact upon the development of industrial relations in Tanganyika.

Appendix VII   Case Studies in Tanganyikan Unionism

The case studies have been included in this appendix to permit the reader to develop a better qualitative grasp of various aspects of Tanganyikan unionism. In all the studies, except 9 and 10, names and minor details not essential to the case have been changed to protect the anonymity of individuals and unions involved.

CASE 1: MARTIN: BIOGRAPHY OF A UNION LEADER

A qualitative picture of a Tanganyikan union leader can be seen in this short biography of one of Tanganyika's early unionists. Although the name has been changed and a few insignificant details have been varied to protect anonymity, Martin is a real person and not a composite. He was typical of many Tanganyikan full-time union leaders in that he manifested many attitudes commonly found among them; but he was unique in that he was older, more experienced by virtue of his long personal history in the unions, more efficient, and better organized in his work. As one of the early unionists, he occupied a prominent position in the Tanganyikan unions.

Martin grew up at his place of birth in southwestern Tanganyika near Lake Malawi. His father engaged in traditional pursuits of cultivation and fishing. The traditional character of Martin's early life is reflected in a story he once told about his early childhood. The adults would occasionally soak a piece of bark from a tree in gravy and give it to him as a substitute for a piece of meat. The child would chew on the bark until he realized he was chewing wood. The elders would laugh and scoff at his disappointment and send him away hungry. Martin always accompanied this tale with gales of laughter, indicating that he believed that such experiences were good for children since it taught them to endure the hunger that frequently occurs in Africa.

At the age of six, Martin was sent to a nearby Roman Catholic mission school which, after completing the first four standards, he left to go to another mission school where he had a "misunderstanding" with a teacher (a nun) who began to punish him by hitting him with a ruler. When Martin grabbed the ruler, he was ordered to go to the principal who intended to give Martin some strokes as punishment, but Martin refused to accept them and he was sent home. He then went successively to a government school and a Protestant mission school, eventually completing Standard VII. To continue his education, Martin was sent to school at Iringa, over 200 miles from his home, which involved, among other forms of travel, a walk alone or with other students through 90 miles of lion-infested bush. Later, when he went on to Standard IX, he had to travel to Tabora, which added a bus ride and a train ride to his complicated transportation. At the close of each school year, Martin returned to his family by the same long route. Of these trips he had many memories, not all unpleasant.

While at Tabora, Martin helped to organize a students' strike to protest the quality of the food. Again he was sent home, and his formal education ended. In Dar es Salaam, he obtained his first job as a train guard with the Tanganyika Railways in 1947 and was sent to Dodoma which became his home base. In September 1947, while his train was at Morogoro, the strike which had begun on the Dar es Salaam docks spread upcountry. Martin remembered comparatively little about the strike except that African workers were delighted to stop work, that messengers were sent out on bicycles to spread the word and call other Africans out on strike, and that during the evening of the strike, he and some of his fellow workers went on a monumental binge.

Martin later became a clerk for the railways. After two and a half years with them, he went through a variety of jobs with government agencies in Tabora, and later moved to Dar es Salaam. In 1951 he was employed for ten months by a large commercial firm in Dar es Salaam but he was discharged, as he had been from the previous job, because of arguments. While with a commercial firm in Dar es Salaam, where he was relatively happy despite a number of grievances, he took a correspondence course in accounting and eventually passed the examination. He was proud of his certificate, which hung in the living room of his house in Dar es Salaam. It was also during this time that Martin became interested in trade unions.

Martin joined one of the early unions in 1952-53 because an Asian bookkeeper who was doing the same work as Martin was being paid four times as much. Martin promoted the union, largely a "paper" organization, in his spare time, and soon became one of its leaders. Martin contends that it grew from 30 members to 300 over a period of two years but he probably exaggerated. His rise to the top in his organization was due primarily to his perseverance, for many leaders left the organization because of quarrels or discouragement.

Martin did not become discouraged. Along with a handful of others, he plugged away at organizational activities, calling meetings, recruiting members.

He was involved in the preparation for the visit of Tom Mboya in 1955 and became one of the organizers of the future Tanganyika Federation of Labour.

Martin realized that the organization process would be slow as long as no one worked full-time for the union. He therefore proposed to his executive committee that he devote himself entirely to union work. Since there was no money with which to pay him, each of the seven members of the committe agreed to contribute Shs. 25/- monthly ($3.50) for Martin's salary. Martin resigned from his job to become an early full-time union officer, and began a period of financial hardship since the promised payments were not always forthcoming.

Martin, however, stuck to his work and helped to organize a number of unions, which made him known nationally. During this time he experienced physical danger on a number of occasions, and his tension over such incidents was evident when he related them.

What characterized Martin and his work were three things:

1. He was technically qualified. His training in accounting permitted him to perform a number of jobs required by the unions to comply with the law.

2. He had a bureaucratic orientation. Compared with many of his colleagues, Martin was well organized and efficient even though his files were in poor shape. His organizational bent showed in his story telling for, unlike many other Tanganyikans who rambled on with little respect for the chronology of events, Martin consulted his old diaries. He could tell who had been active on various committees that organized the TFL and the dates on which the committees met. Martin's bureaucratic orientations were important because they provided the technical abilities that enabled him to function as a union leader.

3. He was persistent. Martin was not easily discouraged by pressures from government officers, employers, or even his own colleagues. Although at times he showed weariness with his colleagues and the pressures to which they subjected him, he stuck to his job. He was not a powerful or brilliant speaker as were many other leaders, but in spite of this, he outlasted many colleagues who became discouraged easily. Nor was he a good politician in a trade union sense. He had, however, made himself relatively indispensable to the unions.

Martin, because of his union activities, had married late. His relations with his wife and children had the same ambiguity that he experienced as a person raised in a tribal society but functioning in a modern society. Although he was closely attached to his family, when he invited my wife and me to dinner, his wife served the three of us and then went elsewhere for her own meal with the children. Yet he brought his wife and children (the children more frequently than his wife) to visit us.

Also, because of his union activities, he was rarely at home. Most evenings, as well as many weekends, were taken up with lengthy meetings. He traveled in Tanganyika a great deal and had made a number of trips abroad. During these times, his wife remained at home with the children, usually visited by one or more of his or his wife's relatives.

Martin, like many of his trade union counterparts in the Western world, was very argumentative. Because of this and because of his relative lack of political or social skills in assessing situations, he had a serious break in relations with one of the Labour Department officers. He was equally argumentative with his colleagues and visitors to the unions from outside Tanganyika. His technique was to hold tenaciously to a single point about which he felt his opponent was weak; he would return to it even after some concession had been made to him. One felt often that Martin was seeking to develop his argumentative skills; to engage in the game was more important than to win. But his arguments frequently were tiresomely naive.

In spite of his argumentativeness, Martin was a devoted trade unionist. Surrounded by many incompetent leaders, many of whom engaged in petty peculation, he worked hard at his job and appeared to be completely honest. His devotion to unionism helped carry him through many crises and was to continue to sustain him when he felt great frustration with the failure of his colleagues to recognize his services and contributions to Tanganyikan unionism. After many years of union activities he found it impossible to continue and became an industrial relations officer with a prominent Tanganyikan employer.

CASE 2: HERMAN: A 1960 TRADE UNION ENTREPRENEUR

Herman was nineteen when he started working for a government unit, and he joined the union soon afterward. About three months later, he resigned his post to become full-time branch secretary. He had been earning Shs. 300/- ($42.00) a month but felt that "helping my poor fellows would be more helpful than getting Shs. 300/-."

The branch committee had promised to pay Herman Shs. 200/- ($28.00) a month. He had not collected this sum, however, during any of the four months in which he held office. He indicated that if he collected more dues he would probably get a salary increase. He was somewhat discouraged by the prospects and did not seem enthusiastic about his future opportunities with the union.

CASE 3: A SEARCH FOR CONSENSUS

The executive council of the union consisted of over 20 people but, with a number of full-time officers and staff present, about 30 people attended the council meeting. The problem to be resolved was the action to be taken against the assistant to a top officer of the union. He had been suspended by the other officers at headquarters because he had accepted a drink from an employer.

The meeting began with a detailed report on the case, after which the council members began discussion; this continued for well over an hour until the session was adjourned for the day. No resolutions were proposed; the case was simply discussed. The chairman indicated his belief that resolutions would be forthcoming the following morning.

Discussion began again at 9:05 a.m. A resolution was proposed by a council member. The chairman surveyed the group and by some visual process assessed that the resolution was not satisfactory to the group. Discussion was therefore continued. Other resolutions were forthcoming but, by the same process, the chairman noted that they were unsatisfactory.

After further discussion, a resolution was proposed which appeared satisfactory. The chairman asked that the resolution be reread and, when this was done, asked if there was any objection. There being none, he was handed the written resolution and he passed it to the secretary. The time was 11:05 a.m.

Serious conflict existed between various officers of this union. The president was at odds with the headquarters officers, but there is no indication that he was in a bloc with the suspended officer. The headquarters officials unquestionably had the support of the bulk of the council members. No attempt was made by the majority, however, to remove the assistant from office or to push through a decision counter to the wishes of the minority. The resolution finally adopted represented a compromise. It criticized the assistant for having accepted a drink from an employer and warned him and others not to do so in the future. The assistant was instructed to show proper respect to his superior officer; the superior was instructed to provide proper guidance to his subordinate. Lower ranking officers were instructed to show proper respect for higher ranks. Finally, action would be taken against officers acting dictatorially.

CASE 4: A RATIFICATION MEETING TO ACCEPT AN AGREEMENT

In March 1960, an agreement was reached in the Central Joint Council (CJC) of the sisal industry which provided for a substantial percentage increase in monthly wages of sisal workers and a much lower percentage increase in work load for most workers. The CJC consisted of representatives of employers (Tanganyika Sisal Growers Association) and employees.

No provision had been made in the CJC's constitution for ratification of decisions by the workers themselves. Yet the union, as spokesman for the employees, felt the need to seek ratification of workers' decisions in some form. The broad changes envisioned in the agreement required that its possibly controversial terms be explained to the workers, and so a series of ratification meetings were held on the various estates.

One such meeting, comprising 1000-1500 people, was held in the social hall of "X" estate—an open-sided building with metal roof. After some introductory remarks, the regional secretary of the union began to work his way through the lengthy and detailed agreement. As he completed each point, he would explain what it meant. When he felt that he had explained sufficiently, he would ask the audience, "Mmesikia?" ("Have you heard?") and would receive the standard response, "Tumesikia." ("We have heard.") He would then continue to the next point.

When he was explaining the new wage increases, the "tumesikia" responses numbered in the hundreds. When he was explaining the increases in tasks, the responses came from half a dozen to a dozen members of the audience.

When the meeting was over—and, indeed, during the secretary's speech— a representative of the management complained to the secretary that the workers did not understand the production increases. He was reassured by the regional secretary that the workers had accepted the task increases.

The ratification of an extremely complex wage agreement involving a great many job classifications and wage rates meant that several hundred figures were read to the assembled multitude of illiterate workers. The resulting lack of comprehension, added to the ability of a small segment of the group to accept an unpopular decision in the name of the entire meeting, increased considerably the probabilities of internal conflict.

It might have been expected that the most traditional members would have participated more, as would be characteristic in tribal society. In all likelihood there are two reasons why they did not. One, the sheer number of people involved precluded the kind of participation found in small scale traditional societies. Second, and possibly more important, the character of the membership was distinctly different from that found in tribal society. Union members came from a variety of tribal backgrounds and spoke many languages (although Swahili served as a lingua franca). Customs are different among the many tribes. Decision making as it is found in tribal society probably works only when strong ties to local units exist, usually based on kinship. Among workers in the towns and estates, no such basis for cohesion exists. This traditional form of decision making may be satisfactory in relatively uncomplex societies; in modern situations, it leads to breakdowns of communication or misunderstandings.

CASE 5: AN ANNUAL CONFERENCE

In this case, the union was suffering the consequences of a rapid extension of branches and a shortage of full-time secretaries to cope with its growth.

197

The general secretary at headquarters was moderately competent; other officers were less effective. The general treasurer, for example, was totally ignorant of the mysteries of bookkeeping. The result of these deficiencies was a lack of internal coherence in the union.

First Day

The annual conference began inauspiciously. Although it was not held at the headquarters in Dar es Salaam, numerous delegates arrived there first and consequently had to be moved. Some branches had sent more delegates than they were entitled to; most delegates arrived expecting their expenses and return travel to their homes to be paid by the union. On the morning of the day the conference was to begin, the executive council met to consider various points prior to their being submitted to delegates. The ten-point agenda was impossible for the executive council to get through in the five hours allowed. Thus only part of the agenda could be digested before the public meeting which preceded the opening of the conference in the afternoon.

The public session,[1] occupying about two hours, consisted mainly of speeches by the union's president, by TFL president Rashidi Kawawa, and by an international trade union visitor who spoke in English and whose speech was translated into Swahili—the language of the conference. All emphasized the importance of the conference for resolving union problems.

In addition to the usual amenities the union president gave a brief preview of the general secretary's report, informing the audience of the number of meetings held by the cabinet (the executive officers in Dar es Salaam), the problem of recruiting members, the failure of members to pay dues, and the weaknesses of the leadership. In discussing the work of the leadership, the president said:

> The delegation of authority to the leadership has been like a long road the end of which we have now approached. Our work is like road-building; we have only constructed about a quarter and now the conference must reflect on how we may come to the end of the road where all men will be equal and where there will be no difference between a white man and an African. We have to think about the holes and the rocks in the road so that we can consider how we can build a smooth road. (Delegate: "Well said.") If anyone thinks that the progress of this union can be hindered, he is wrong: this conference will benefit not only our children but our children's children. I will ask you to always pray for this union.

When the speeches were over, the general public departed and the delegates got down to business. First, reports prepared by the officers were distributed, among them the mimeographed text of the president's address which, since it had not been collated and stapled, was passed out sheet by sheet to the delegates. Other reports, also prepared by the officers had been incorrectly

198

collated at headquarters. These therefore were spread out on the head table and officers and delegates began to pull them apart and to search through the increasingly jumbled mess for proper sheets. While various delegates shouted that they were missing specific pages, thereby abetting the chaotic search at the head table, the president vainly tried to keep the meeting going. Nothing could be accomplished and, after some time, the conference was adjourned.

Second Day

The meeting convened half an hour late. Facing three parallel tables of delegates was the head table where the officers sat. To the side and near one wall was the "government bench."[2] Farther down the hall were the tables for observers. These physical arrangements, maintained for the rest of the conference, indicated that the working sessions had begun.

After stating that minutes of the past annual conference were not to be read because they had been circulated to the branches, the president made some introductory remarks and the conference then passed to a consideration of the general secretary's report with a discussion concerning its presentation. It was suggested that the report be considered paragraph by paragraph while the delegates read it for themselves. Before this suggestion could be considered, however, the question of who was eligible to vote was raised and consequently it was found that delegates and observers were mixed up at all the tables. After five minutes of rearranging, the president called the meeting to order again.

An immediate vote by show of hands on whether the report should be read to the delegates was overwhelmingly defeated. Meanwhile, the president and the organizing secretary were busily conferring (a feature that continued throughout the conference to the irritation of the delegates). Before the treasurer, who was taking minutes and had failed to get the vote count, could get a revote, he was requested to read the names of the delegates. It now became clear that the credentials committee, during the night, had designated some people as observers who had expected to be classified as delegates. The vote on the proposal to read the general secretary's report was then taken, followed by an announcement by the general secretary that delegates should give their branch names before speaking. Discussion then resumed on credentials for 18 minutes of protests, responses, and argument. It was agreed finally that those protesting would meet with the credentials committee.

The general secretary's report was now considered paragraph by paragraph. After obtaining no comments on the first two paragraphs, one of the full-time officers at the government bench interrupted the president to request that each paragraph be read aloud. The president referred to the vote which had just been taken and explained that time would be given for each person to read the paragraph for himself.

199

An observer asked how the paragraphs were numbered, since no numbers were given. The president attempted to explain that the order was obvious. When a government-bencher pointed out the dividing spaces between each paragraph, the president grew visibly angry at the interruption, and the observer who had raised the issue complained that the president was "too rough. You may be intimidating us." All laughed and applauded, including the president. Another observer irritated the president by asking whether the titles and subtitles were considered paragraphs. The president reminded the conference that "we are all grownups and we all understand." An hour after convening the conference, actual discussion of the report got under way.

After 50 minutes of discussion, one delegate announced that the president had told the conference the day before that the report would be read in the morning and discussed in the afternoon. Amid the resulting confusion and turmoil at the head table, officers blamed the president *sotto voce* for having forgotten what he had said. It took several minutes to agree to continue the present system of discussion which was resumed, except for a lunch recess, paragraph by paragraph throughout the report. It was impeded by the raising of many irrelevant points or ones scheduled for later discussion as well as by the necessity to resolve procedural questions owing to the lack of standing orders (by-laws).

Shortly after lunch the full-time secretaries of the government bench suddenly withdrew from the meeting to organize themselves because they did not like some of the proposals in the officers' reports. The conference, it now became clear, was constituted of three groups: the full-time headquarters officers (elected by the annual conference), the full-time field staff (appointed, generally, by headquarters), and the delegates.

The report having been considered, the president announced that a motion to accept it was in order. One delegate complained that the report was too long; another stated that, since it contained few errors, it should be adopted. A scattering of applause from the delegates followed the latter's statement, and the president moved to the next item on the agenda. Thus there was no formal vote on the general secretary's report; the president and everyone else interpreted the applause to indicate its acceptance.

Next a mimeographed four-page history of the union required 75 minutes of discussion of details, including membership figures and which of two possible founding dates of branches were to be used. Consideration of the organizer's report then began, during which a delegate pointed out that the total membership figure in the history was added incorrectly. A re-addition of the figures revealed that the report was indeed wrong. The organizer's report was again taken up and, after less than an hour of discussion, was adopted, when there was thin applause from the delegates for a statement by one of them that the report was "satisfying."

At 5:15 p.m., discussion of the treasurer's report began with a question of presentation which was debated for over ten minutes. Finally, the paragraph-by-paragraph consideration started, and the lengthy discussion which followed revealed the financial chaos of the organization as well as the many conflicts existing between the union leaders. When the conference recessed at 8:00 p.m., some of the report remained to be discussed.

Third Day

The credentials committee opened the conference with the announcement that 11 branches had been raised from observer status to full delegate status, thus raising the total number of participating delegates to 34. Because of the absence of two delegates, the total number voting would be 32.

Meanwhile, the other officials at the head table were busy conferring on proposals to consolidate the agenda. This consultation continued for some minutes after the completion of the credential committee's report until, finally, the president called the meeting to order to resume the treasurer's report. The opening prayer having been forgotten, the discussion was interrupted, and delegates stood for 30 seconds in prayerful attitude.

The flavor of the detailed and occasionally acrimonious discussion is provided in the following extract.

Delegate 1: Did headquarters maintain an overall membership register?

Organizing Secretary: Yes.

Delegate 2: How many membership cards have been printed?

Treasurer: 6000 were originally distributed and all have been accounted for except 35.

Delegate 2 is dissatisfied with the report because it indicates that the treasurer has had things printed for which no use has been planned.

The president blames the branches for not sending in proper information about their needs for printed material.

Delegate 3: You, the president, have no right to convince us to these matters (e.g., this is the province of the treasurer). Anyhow, this should not be discussed here but when we receive the balance sheet.

Observer 1: What procedure does the headquarters use in ordering stationery?

General Secretary: The difficulty exists because of the discrepancy between the number of members and the number of cards printed. There is a discrepancy because the branches have not submitted their returns in full.

Delegate 4 complains because he had originally received two cards. He was instructed by headquarters to return both.

Treasurer: The cards you received were not numbered; they therefore have to be returned for numbered cards.

Discussion continued concerning all aspects of the printing and distribution of membership cards, and the illegal printing by some branches of receipt books. The treasurer apologized for the lack of detail on expenditures and ascribed it to lack of time to prepare the full report. Recriminations were leveled against the treasurer for not having the balance sheet prepared and against the chairman for permitting delegates to ask irrelevant questions.

Complaints about the misuse of funds by the organizer started a major dispute about the procedure used by him to take funds from a branch. Apparently the general secretary also took money in an incorrect manner from a branch. After over 45 minutes of debate, a vote was taken which favored the formation of a committee to investigate the charges. The total vote, however, was not in accord with the number of delegates eligible to vote and additional time was spent unsuccessfully trying to locate the discrepancy.

The conference concluded with a paragraph-by-paragraph discussion of the treasurer's report at 12:10 p.m. One delegate expressed regret that there was no report on the solidarity and vehicle funds. Another criticized the treasurer for presenting a report for the fiscal year ending in 1959; where had the treasurer been since that time? The treasurer excused himself on the grounds of sickness, an important TFL mission, and the departure of his clerk. The president then accused the critical delegate of an attitude ruinous to the conference because it showed distrust of the treasurer.

The president then turned to a consideration of the balance sheet, which had not been mimeographed. The request from a delegate that it be placed on a blackboard was honored, during the process of which the designation of the investigations committee was discussed. The size of the committee and the principle involved in its selection took 15 minutes to settle, after which the delegates took nine minutes to nominate the committee. No formal decision about the distribution of committee members had been made, but the delegates nominated one person from each province represented and one member from the executive committee. When some delegates objected to a particular delegate, his name was withdrawn and another substituted.

The foreign union visitor suggested that the investigations committee be given "terms of reference," an idea which puzzled most of the delegates. The visitor would not himself provide the terms of reference but proposed that the committee be instructed to investigate the financial situation in the branches where money was apparently mishandled. Finally, the terms of reference were written and read to the conference which, after a short debate, accepted them.

By this time, the general secretary had returned with the balance sheet written on the blackboard, which he placed in front of the head table thereby obscuring the officers. It was now well past the lunch hour and a recess was called.

The session, scheduled to resume at 2:30, opened at 2:55 with a lecture by the president on the lack of progress. The balance sheet on the blackboard was examined until 3:45 during which time difficulties in understanding were expressed. One delegate suggested that the balance sheet was too complex for anyone except a treasurer or a station master. Another, also commenting on its obscurity, suggested that the treasurer be thanked. The president quickly arose and thanked the delegates for having accepted the report.

The president, moving to new business, suggested that the conference designate a constitution committee, and a quick vote indicated agreement on a committee of six. The remainder of the session was devoted to designating the committee. The conference recessed at 4:20 p.m. because a public meeting had been called by the union.

The Final Day

The conference convened exactly on time, but minus a number of delegates because of an all-night meeting of the constitution committee. The proceedings of the final day started with a long discussion at the head table about a proposal by the TFL representative to consolidate the agenda into a more manageable schedule. The proposal was accepted by the delegates, and the constitution committee began its report.

The first proposal of the committee to retain the word "African" in the title of the union was opposed by the TFL and the international trade secretariat with which the union was affiliated. After half an hour of discussion, however, the proposal was accepted by an overwhelming vote. Many constitutional changes discussed throughout the morning were accepted simply by a number of delegates saying in unison, "Tumekubali" (We accept).

As a result of the foreign visitor's shock at the lack of financial organization, the delegates considered a proposed budget for the next nine months. They briefly discussed also the newly proposed checkoff, joint staff councils, and eligibility for membership in the union.

The conference then returned to a reiteration of the weaknesses of the branches and their leadership and devoted fifteen minutes to the discussion and defeat of a proposal to "forgive" the branches for not having paid dues. Proposals for combining branches to make them larger and more viable consumed fifteen additional minutes during which the government benchers returned from meeting elsewhere most of the day. They immediately withdrew again to discuss additional points that had not been settled.

At 6:30 p.m., despite serious pressures for adjournment, discussion began on an agenda point titled "change of office bearers." The problem, as it slowly unfolded to the delegates, was that the treasurer was totally unfit for his post, yet the leadership generally respected him, particularly for his abilities as a public speaker and consensus-molder. His inability to manage the financial records of the organization had forced additional work on the general secretary. During discussion of the problem, chaos in the conference increased as delegates, hoping to catch an evening train, grew irritable. The proposal to change officers received a "yes" voice response each of the three times the president asked, "Do you accept?" After a frantic 14-minute discussion, a vote, from which over a third of the delegates abstained, placed the treasurer in the post of the organizer. The conference agreed to refer the matter of what to do with the former organizer to the incoming executive committee.

The committee to investigate financial irregularities next reported briefly that there was insufficient evidence upon which to make any decisions. The president thanked the committee and said that an investigatory delegation would visit the branches in question.

The conference had now completed its agenda except for the election of president, vice president, trustees, and executive committee, all of whom were elected annually. The president, thanking the delegates and requesting that he not be considered for reelection, ceremoniously withdrew from the head table accompanied by the vice president. A vocally prominent delegate from one of the larger branches was now spontaneously shouted into the acting chairmanship of the election, which proceeded after the outgoing president and vice president had left the room.

The acting chairman was a man with a sense of humor who introduced cooperative congeniality into the confusion of the conference and, utilizing the pressure for adjournment, moved events along with considerable speed and hilarity. The president and vice president, reelected by acclamation, were led back into the room where the acting chairman formally "enstooled" them by pressing, with his hands on their shoulders, first the president and then the vice president into their respective chairs. As the vice president was being "enstooled," he turned to the acting chairman and asked why he had been chosen. The response, "Kwa sababu" (Because), almost broke up the conference.

The president made a five minute speech in which he expressed his dismay over his reelection. He had requested not to be reelected not because he did not wish to help his brothers; he did and he had worked hard for the union. Democracy was a hard thing, however, and he did not know what to do now. But it would be a disgrace if he did not accept the action of the delegates and therefore he would do his best to build the union. The delegates applauded this statement and turned to the election of the other officers after granting the president's request to permit those who had to catch the evening train to leave. The foreign visitor left to arrange with the driver of the vehicle, which had been loaned by his organization, to ferry the delegates to their hotels.

The president then tried to get the remaining elections under way. Matters were complicated by the fact that the departing delegates had to be given their allowances by the treasurer (now organizer) in order to pay for their return journeys. The chaos at the front table became formidable when one-fourth of the delegates clustered around the treasurer at the head table while he counted money and insisted that the departing delegates sign receipts. The cacaphony of a car horn steadily blown irritated everyone; the driver of the vehicle had disappeared with the keys and the visitor was attempting to summon him.

The trustees were reelected en bloc and the assistant general secretary was quickly returned to office. The election of the executive committee required only four minutes but proved to be the most hilarious portion of the proceedings, since it was handled in a joyous chant-and-response between the president and the delegates as follows. When the assistant general secretary named the "Eastern Province," for example, delegates searched the room until they spotted a delegate from that area. As soon as several fingers were pointing at the delegate, the "nominating" group began to chant his name or, in many cases not knowing his name, his branch. The president then began a call:

President: Any other nominations?
Delegates: Hapana! (No!)
President: Any other nominations?
Delegates: Hapana!
President: Any other nominations?
Delegates: Hapana!
President: Do you accept him?
Delegates: Ndeyo! (Yes!)
President: Do you accept him?
Delegates: Ndeyo!
President: Do you accept him?
Delegates: Ndeyo!
President: Uhuru! (Freedom—independence—the general political slogan current at the time.)
Delegates: Uhuru!
President: Uhuru!
Delegates: Uhuru!

The process was repeated for eight provinces. There were no contests although on occasion different groups pointed to several delegates. Then, by some process, fingers would not remain fixed but would begin to converge on a single delegate. It was not clear what forces were at work producing consensus; it was clear that consensus was desirable and was quickly achieved. Once there was consensus, the chant-and-response directed by the president constituted the only formal affirmation.

Meanwhile, delegates trying to depart continued to mill around the treasurer and the horn continued to blow. The elections concluded, there remained the issue of the boycott by the government bench. The hilarity immediately ceased and, although proposals were made as to what to do with the boycotters, discussion soon revealed the complexity of the problem. It was finally agreed to refer this and all unsettled business to the incoming executive committee, and the conference adjourned *sine die.*

Comment

This conference marked an extreme in disorganization among the many meetings witnessed. The inability of the leadership to organize the preparation or reports prior to the opening of the conference, the waste of time in getting the reports distributed, the chalking of the balance sheet on the board, and the many irrelevancies and procedural points, all might have been avoided with some coherent organization. Had standing orders controlling the procedures of the conference been prepared, considerable time and confusion could have been saved.

Although the annual conference of this union was the worst of any visited, the disarray shown was a matter of degree and not of kind. That is, this union's disorganization was typical if extreme for Tanganyikan unions at the time.

CASE 6: AN EXECUTIVE COMMITTEE MEETING

The union in this case had had a strong leadership for many years and was actively involved in TFL affairs. Although the union had experienced considerable growth and organizational difficulties, it was affluent and well organized compared with the union in Case 5. Its national leadership was highly competent and its local leadership was strong in a number of branches.

This union was also unusual in the number of volunteers who had contributed to its growth and who occupied important leadership positions as chairmen and trustees. Largely debarred from full-time leadership because of their inability to speak English, these leaders, who will be referred to as "old-timers," were available for travel assignments, organizational work, and speech-making. In this respect, the union was almost unique in Tanganyika since very few unions had either the number or the quality of personnel for voluntary activities.

The executive committee meeting prior to the union's annual conference spent two and a half days at work. A brief mimeographed agenda devoted largely to organizational matters was prepared for its first session at which a steering committee was elected to prepare the agenda for the remainder of the meeting. This agenda was mimeographed for the executive committee members by the next morning, and the committee adhered to its scheduled hours with seriousness; every session began late but the chairman struggled to keep to a schedule by intervening to keep the members on an issue, or to produce consensus, or to bring questions to a vote. Rather than lose time through recesses for refreshments, the leadership arranged for tea and soda pop to be brought in during the mid-morning and mid-afternoon, which limited the time lost for each recess to only fifteen minutes, yet gave the participants a welcome break from their deliberations.

Despite these contrasts to Case 5, this union also had difficulty organizing and handling both finances and conflicts of interests between national officers, regional officers, the old-timers, and the volunteers (e.g., volunteer members of the executive committee who did not occupy positions of organizational prominence as did the old-timers).

First Day

The meeting of the executive committee began with a confusion reminiscent of the annual conference in Case 5. The meeting time was changed at the last minute from 9:00 a.m. to 2:30 p.m., and the truck rented to move the participants brought them to the wrong building. Sometime after 3:00 p.m., however, most participants were assembled in a good meeting place set up with the usual arrangement of tables.

The session opened with the president's 35-minute review of the year's work in which he concentrated on the internal difficulties that had preoccupied the union's officials and on the successful growth in membership. With independence soon to come, the president cautioned the executive committee that the union must not be allowed to rest on its accomplishments but its members must work even harder to prevent the union's decline.

The president then introduced the general secretary who explained that the purpose of the executive committee was to prepare for the annual conference. He also discussed the critical shortage of trained and competent leaders and the seriousness of the limited participation by members in union affairs except at times of contract negotiations. In his report, one of the proposals for remedying the critical situations was for an education program with a full-time education director who would help educate leaders and members. Finally he, too, encouraged the participants to work hard to prepare for the annual conference.

After the roll call of the delegates, a consideration of the question of the eligibility of some of those who had been elected as executive committee members began and occupied the next hour and a half. A substantial number of full-time regional secretaries of the union had unconstitutionally had themselves elected as executive committee delegates by the regional committees,3 notice of which, according to the general secretary, had been sent to the regional committees. The full-time officials who were present as delegates protested that notices had not been sent and objected that headquarters officials had not notified them earlier than this meeting. In the intense discussion that followed the finding and reading of a copy of the notice, the full-time regional officials admitted their guilt. Rigorous interpretation of the rules meant, however, that the executive committee would not have a quorum and it was therefore agreed to try to round up new members from nearby regions.

A steering committee, including three top full-time officials as ex-officio members was then quickly elected, and the meeting was adjourned to permit the committee to begin its deliberations.

Second Day

The meeting began 20 minutes late after a brief rearrangement of the seating pattern so that the executive committee members faced the head table of officers, now including the secretary of the steering committee, and the government bench of full-time officers other than the national officers was clearly identified. The government benchers were active, but nonvoting, participants.

The secretary of the steering committee read the list of nine voting delegates and appropriate sections of the constitution dealing with meetings of the executive committee. The eight-point agenda was distributed and the executive committee moved immediately to Point I, the registration of branches, and a consideration of the number of members necessary for full branch status. The general secretary proposed 700 as the minimum number for a branch and argued against the proliferation of small branches, which would not be viable. Participants in the discussion were torn between a desire to provide the proper recognition to small branches and the necessity for a sufficient number of fully paid members to support a number of full-time officials.

Regional Secretary 1 agrees with the steering committee that the figure should be high, but 700 was too many--let it be 300. Executive Committee Member 1 opposed 300 as insufficient to yield enough income for wages, rent, and other expenses.

Old-timer 1 agrees with the steering committee: not all members pay their subscriptions so that even with 700 members there are financial problems. A branch should have a minimum of 700 members.

Regional Secretary 2: Does this mean 700 recruited members or paid-up members?

General Secretary: 700 recruited members; there should be at least 500 paid-up members.

The chairman quickly surveyed the room and asked if everyone was convinced. There was silence and he then asked three times: "Do we accept this?" to which he received an affirmative "Ndeyo" (yes) from the executive committee members.

The president and the general secretary then explained the composite nature of the agenda and the work of the steering committee in answer to a regional secretary's persistent complaint that the branches that had forwarded proposals now incorporated into the agenda had not been identified. The chairman ruled the protesting regional secretary out of order and the conference proceeded to a consideration of visits of national officers to the branches. The discussion revealed the conflicting interests of different groups in the executive committee. On the whole, the old-timers criticized the national leadership for not visiting branches and regional offices to encourage officers and members; the national officers defensively argued that they had in fact made visits concomitant with their duties at headquarters and responsibilities to the TFL. The full-time regional officers were generally not in favor of visits unless specifically requested by the regional offices. An old-timer pointed out that TANU was strong because its president continually traveled the country; he disagreed strongly with the regional full-time officials that they were competent to build the union by themselves. A trustee who endorsed these sentiments said: "Power is a matter of respect (heshima); if a person has respect, he has great power and can accomplish many things. But some branches do not respect the headquarters and take things into their own hands. As a result of visits by headquarters officials, Shs. 30,000/- ($4,200) have been collected in the past six months. I have myself visited branches to find that they are using illegal receipts." He then proposed a regular schedule of branch visits by headquarter officials. After various tangential procedures which the chairman stopped, a resolution embodying the essence of the trustee's remarks "as a guide only" was adopted.

After a short break, the conference members considered the handling of correspondence, office supplies (especially receipt books), and equipment, which involved the role of regional officials in the routing of correspondence and supplies between the national office and the branches. The regional officers usually objected to direct relationships between headquarters and the branches and wanted everything to be routed through them in both directions. The national officers, aware of the financial drain often created by regional officers, wanted the dues and entrance fees to be sent directly from the branch to the financial secretary, as provided in the constitution. The customary procedure of cash being sent to the regional offices first had made it possible for the regional officers to pay their own and other employees' salaries, as well as rent and other miscellaneous expenses before forwarding the residue to the headquarters. After a half hour of heated discussion an agreement was reached through consensus whereby actual cash would be sent directly from the branches to headquarters but correspondence and equipment (e.g., receipt books) would be channeled through the regional offices.

A lengthy discussion then followed as to whether vehicles should be bought or public transport used for the transportation of union officers. Forty minutes of discussion produced agreement that the type of vehicle should depend upon the income of the branch or region and should be determined by headquarters.

Since lunch was overdue, the chairman proposed that the next two points on the agenda which would take much time be skipped and that the final two points relating to administration which could be dealt with briefly be considered. These two points, determination of the venue of the next meeting of the executive committee and of a cable address, required the better part of an hour to solve, after which the president thanked the participants for a fruitful session and recessed the meeting for lunch.

The afternoon session began fifteen minutes late and returned to the order of the agenda with a discussion of problems of education in the union. The opening comment by a member of the executive committee thanked the TFL for its current educational program. The secretary of the steering committee, himself a full-time regional secretary, contended that education was basic to the success of the union; the speaker continued that he had to substitute common sense for his lack of experience and knowledge and wanted a program that would help to educate leaders. These comments irritated an executive committee member representing the same region who took the secretary to task for being ignorant. Waving a book at the delegates, he indicated that he studied on his own and questioned how the previous speaker had become a regional secretary if he had no knowledge. A point of order interrupted his proposal to inform his members, on his return home, not to recognize their regional secretary. In the brief remainder of the discussion it was decided to employ as soon as possible a person with proper training to begin an educational program.

After almost an hour of discussion of the next agenda item dealing with the table of organization of the union, it became obvious that it was an extremely complex question involving the size and salaries of staffs at every level of the union. The president proposed that a four-man committee be nominated to consider the question and report the next morning; this was done, with the understanding that no member of the committee could already be a member of the steering committee.

Again at the initiative of the chairman, because it was already after 5:00 p.m., the next point on the agenda was passed over for organizational problems that were expected to be easily disposed of. The first question concerned the eligibility of non-Africans for membership in the union. Although there existed no bar to non-Africans, consideration of their eligibility was included on the agenda because of a current TFL drive to persuade the unions to remove racial restrictions. To support opening membership to all races, the general secretary pointed to the American trade unions, which admitted Negroes, and to Kwame Nkrumah's membership in the seamen's union. He also pointed out how expatriates had acted as strike breakers in recent strikes which they could not have done if they had been union members. An old-timer objected to the entire discussion since, in his region, Asians already belonged to the union. The reluctance of some of the executive committee members to accept the proposal led the president to explain that the committee could recommend, but the annual conference had to legislate. After wrangling over four resolutions, including one offered by the general secretary, to open the unions to all workers irrespective of race, creed, or sex, the conference agreed that the union should be open to all races.

In a half hour discussion of recommendations to raise the entrance fees and dues—the usual arguments heard whenever dues increases are proposed in any organization—were repeated. The main variation came from those opposed to the increase who argued that workers were not now paying their dues; and increasing the dues would mean only that fewer would pay in the future. The discussion was not long and the committee voted overwhelmingly to recommend the increases.

After a short break, the financial secretary reported that regional officers had not yet turned over to him the records and money that had been given them before they left for the conference. The chairman, after instructing all regional officers to do so, and announcing that the matter would be discussed the next day, adjourned the session by reiterating the purpose of the executive committee. He warned participants against discussing publicly any action taken within the committee and called for unity and harmony outside the meeting, which was the only place where it was appropriate for disagreements to occur.

Third Day

The entire final day of the executive committee meeting was devoted to organization problems on the basis of proposals formulated by the committee on salaries and allowances for all levels of the union. The committee's report began with a discussion of allowances to sub-branch collectors (who received a percentage of funds collected) and to secretaries, and dealt as well with the salaries and table of organization for branches, regions, and headquarters. The unusually large Dar es Salaam branch received special consideration. The report also included a proposal that larger travel allowances be given to old-timers than to full-time officials.

A highly detailed discussion of the report involved a number of votes and, in most cases, fairly close decisions. The results are summarized in Chart A VII-1. The salary recommendation made by the committee for an organizing and educational secretary was rejected by the executive committee which believed that the salary proposed was inadequate. As one delegate put it, the low salary would attract only "takataka" (junk, rubbish). The long discussion of the salaries of the index clerk and the driver at headquarters stemmed from the fact that the salaries were being paid to specific persons rather than being set for an occupational role. The index clerk would normally have received a much lower salary than that paid to the incumbent old-timer; the executive committee recognized the services of the particular man but did not want a salary pattern to be established

Debate on Salaries and Table of Organization

Shillings per Month	Position	Minutes Required to Reach a Decision	Votes*
		9	7-2-1
500	General Secretary	1	Unanimous
400	Assistant General Secretary	2	8-2
	Financial Secretary	7	9-1
350	Organizing and Educational Secretary	1	Unanimous
300	Regional Secretary		
	Organizing and Educational Secretary		
		3	Unanimous
250	Administrative Clerk, HQ		
	Driver at HQ		
		9	7-2-1
240	Index Clerk at HQ	20	6-4
230	Driver at HQ	3	Unanimous
200	Branch Secretary	22	9-1
	Office Assistant, Regional Office	27	5-4
150	Office Assistant, Branch	10	Unanimous
	Lady Index Clerk, HQ	5	Unanimous
	Office Boy, HQ		
	Office Boy-Dar es Salaam Branch Sub-branch Secretary		
		1	Unanimous
130	Office Boy, Regional Office	9	5-4-1
	Office Boy, Dar es Salaam Branch	22	5-2-2
125	Sub-branch Secretary		

*Votes invariably were between two or more proposals; the first number given is the vote for the winning proposal; the other number(s) for the other proposals. Boxed titles represent recommendations of salary levels proposed by the committee but not accepted by the executive committee.

for his successor. The headquarters officers felt that the driver should not receive the recommended Shs. 250/- because of his surliness and lack of "proper respect," a view which aroused the ire of a former driver, an old-timer, who contended that the driver should be paid for his driving and not for his behavior with passengers. No clear definition emerged from the considerable discussion of the position of office assistant. Some participants considered office assistants to be high-grade office boys and others viewed the post as a preliminary to full-time secretaryships. Nor could the executive committee members accept the argument that the office boy in the Dar es Salaam branch should receive more than the office boy at regional offices.

Discussion of the table of organization and allowances was not completed until after 5:30 p.m. when the conference moved to consider the final point of travel allowances and leave, and concluded late in the evening. This final day was relatively subdued although occasional differences could be seen between the old-timers and the full-time officials. The only other major dispute resulted from the request on the previous day that regional officers turn over money and records to the financial secretary. The full-time regional secretaries had taken regional funds for use during the conference; headquarters officers had made arrangements, however, for housing, feeding, and pocket money for all participants and therefore wanted the regional officers to turn over all funds and records to them. The regional officers' hesitation in doing so indicated their deep suspicion, which was mutual, of the national officers. Almost all of them eventually complied, but one stubborn holdout had to be publicly threatened before he cooperated. It was discovered that delegates to the annual conference would also have received funds from their branches or regions. The executive committee was persuaded by these developments to adopt a rule that delegates would turn in all funds and would use the facilities arranged by the headquarters officers.

Comment

Unlike other Tanganyikan unions, because this union had been able to develop its leadership at a pace concomitant with membership, it was able to provide an intermediate level of officer between the branch and national levels. This did not resolve all the organizational problems, however, because considerable suspicion existed between different strata in the organization. The battle for control between the national leadership and the regional officers is evident in the fight over dues collections.

CASE 7: SECRET BALLOT IN THE ELECTION OF OFFICERS

The union involved in this case had experienced a long and serious internal split. Its annual conference was marked by intensive fighting between the general secretary and a large group of officers on the one hand and the president and the assistant general secretary, on the other, until it became necessary for a delegation of TFL officers to be present to ensure the continuation of the conference. The conference eventually reached the final point on the agenda: the election of officers. After the incumbent officers had ceremoniously surrendered their offices by leaving the head table, the chief TFL delegate occupied the chair for the elections.

Most of the delegates were illiterate, which necessitated the use of symbols for the candidates; the fear of a split necessitated vigilance to ensure that no delegates were influenced while they cast their ballots. The nominees stood outside the conference hall holding individual symbols, and each delegate, on being called, left the hall, studied the candidates and their symbols, and then retired to the ballot box about thirty feet from the entrance to the hall. The keeper of the ballot box on the first evening of the elections was one of the TFL delegates but he was aided the following day by one of the regional secretaries of the union.

The president opened the nominations, and he and the incumbent vice-president were both nominated for president. Both left the room and were positioned prominently en route to the ballot box, one with the symbol "O" on his chest and the other with "X". Delegates were now permitted to leave the room, one at a time; the ballot box keeper would give the delegate an "X" or "O" as requested, and this would be deposited by the delegate in the ballot box. The procedure, necessary because of the illiteracy of the delegates, meant that the ballot box keeper knew how each delegate voted.

In the election for president, candidate "O" received 24 votes to 18 for "X." The acting chairman thereupon declared "O" president and "X" vice-president. Thus, the main position and the assistant position were elected simultaneously. In the election for general secretary, the incumbent received 36 votes; the incumbent assistant general secretary (in opposition to the general secretary) four votes, and the third person (the nominee of the general secretary's group for assistant general secretary) received two votes. The two incumbents were therefore declared reelected to their respective positions.

The defects in the system are fairly obvious. Not only was it possible to identify how each delegate voted but the election of two officers simultaneously meant that the will of the overwhelming majority of the delegates could not be effected. In the election of the general secretary and his assistant, for example, the supporters of the general secretary voted for him to a man because they feared he might not be reelected if they did not. Indeed, even the group's candidate for assistant general secretary cast his ballot for the general secretary rather than for himself. (This was discovered through subsequent interviews with one of the ballot keepers.) Thus elements of the election procedure were well suited to the capacities of the delegates and to the situation of internal dispute, but the will of the delegates was frustrated by the dual elections.

CASE 8: SECRET BALLOT IN STRIKE VOTE

In this case a strike vote was called in a large branch of a large union. The meeting was held at a place familiar to most of the members, and over 500 workers (out of a possible membership of over 1000) assembled, crowding the hall.

The meeting began with a hostile statement by the branch secretary that there were people present who did not belong. Whether this was directed at ostensible employer spies or nonpayers of dues was not clear; in any case, no one left the hall. Mounting the table for his address, the branch secretary gave the *"uhuru* (freedom) salute" then current to which the workers responded, the exchange being repeated three times. The procedure served as an introduction used by all speakers and as a means of maintaining order.

For about fifteen minutes the branch secretary reviewed the events leading up to a recent wildcat strike and the subsequent breakdown in discussions between the union and the management; he concluded with: "You must tell us if you want a strike or not." He did not actually propose a strike. Throughout his speech, the audience was absolutely quiet. The chairman of the branch who followed the secretary covered the same ground and also concluded that the workers now should instruct their officers.

Discussion did not materialize, and the assistant branch secretary spoke, breaking the embarrassed silence; he was followed by a visiting officer of the TFL. When the floor was again thrown open for discussion, there was the same silence, shuffling, and looking around among the workers sitting on the benches. Finally, a few workers stood, were recognized, and generally assured the officers that the workers supported a strike. The third speaker, commenting along the same lines, asked those who favored a strike to raise their hands and every hand that could be seen was raised.

The branch secretary then announced that there would have to be a secret ballot and that as only members in good standing were permitted to vote workers would have to show membership credentials. There was an enormous shuffling in the hall as workers reached into their clothing and pulled out sheafs of dog-eared papers to search for membership records and dues receipts. Some workers waved these at the officers while others protested that the officers knew that everyone present was a member of the union.

As the branch secretary talked and explained the formalities of the legal requirements of the secret ballot, the noise in the hall increased as workers continued to search for the necessary papers and to talk among themselves. It became clear that the branch officers were not certain how to proceed, and the TFL officer suggested that two differently shaped boxes be placed in a small room off the main hall. After a conversation at the head table, the secretary again mounted the table to tell the workers that they would have to put their ballots--hastily torn from a pad by officers at the head table--either into the large box which he named "Ghana" for votes favoring a strike, or into a small box which he labeled "South Africa" for votes against the strike. The voters would have to show dues receipts to obtain a ballot and go into a small room at the front to vote. The procedure was reviewed several times by the branch secretary and he emphasized the fact that the workers had a choice of voting for "Ghana" where there was independence or "South Africa" where Africans had to work on farms for two shillings a day.

The voting began as hundreds of workers descended upon the head table waving receipts and papers, and the officers began to distribute the ballots. Any check of receipts to determine voter eligibility was impossible; indeed, it was quite likely that some workers received a number of ballots. Because of the smallness of the door and the press of bodies trying to get from the main hall into the small room, those who had entered first to vote were unable to get out. Within seconds, the small room filled and movement was paralyzed, a situation to which the branch officers, now standing on the head table passing out ballots, paid no attention. Eventually, the TFL official drove himself through the mob, wedged himself in the doorway, and began to empty the room by blocking the door with one arm at shoulder level while using the other arm to push those inside under his arm and into the mass outside. Slowly he emptied the room and then began to allow single individuals in to vote, with which process the officers, by this time cognizant of the problem, helped him. But no attempt was made to queue up the workers and the mob remained clustered at the door so that the doorkeeper had to push each man out under his arm.

Inside the room, two union officials guarded the boxes and, of course, could see how the workers cast their ballots. The vote was serious business to the workers who streamed slowly by casting their votes in a steady stream into "Ghana," so that the count was overwhelmingly in favor of the strike.

CASE 9: JOINT CONSULTATION IN THE SISAL INDUSTRY[4]

The Background

The sisal industry, highly organized from the start, consisted, in 1956, of 169 estates owned by a variety of national, ethnic, or racial groups, almost all of whom were expatriate. The Tanganyika Sisal Growers Association (TSGA), an advisory association supported by a compulsory levy on each ton of sisal produced, advised growers on many questions including those relating to labor and wages, and, in 1951, on its recommendation, a new wage structure was set for the industry.

Despite the autonomy enjoyed by individual growers, the TSGA and the industry generally were significantly influenced by a small elite of employers, and for a long time TSGA was dominated by Sir Eldred Hitchcock, the resident manager of a large British-owned firm, who sought to minimize the influence of the developing Plantation Workers Union on the industry.

Prior to the middle 1950s, the direction and control of labor was not a major problem to estate managers, for Africans did not normally think it was their right to protest. Because the estate managers dealt with workers from vastly different cultural milieux, they occasionally utilized informal organs of communication such as councils of elders.

Interest in union organization began to develop on the plantations, as elsewhere, after 1954, and in February 1957, sisal workers on four estates in the Kilosa area struck in response to the general strike call made earlier and then canceled by the TFL in Dar es Salaam.[5] Later in 1957, plantation workers' unions were organized in Tanga, and in the Eastern, Southern, and Northern Provinces.

As early as 1956, these stirrings prompted discussions in the industry on

. . . the desirability of introducing more formal arrangements (than the councils of elders) which would be in line with procedures in other countries. At first there was a widely held view that the

216

traditional arrangements should not be disturbed, but it is clear that opinion among estate owners subsequently moved in the direction of support of a more modern type of arrangement.[6]

As the unions became more active, the sisal employers felt the need for machinery to solve workers' grievances, which would also obviate the need for trade unionism and they invited C. W. Guillebaud early in 1957 to make an economic survey of the industry. As a result of Guillebaud's recommendations, [7] TSGA created an elaborate machinery of joint consultation which consisted of four levels.[8] At the top was the Central Joint Council (CJC) of 42 members, half of whom represented management and half the employees. The members of the council were elected according to a specified formula by the four regional consultative councils, which constituted the second level of the machinery and were "subject to the jurisdiction and control" of the Central Joint Council. At the third level were seven area consultative committees which were "under the direction and control" of the regional councils,[9] and at the last level were estate committees composed of "one or more representatives of management and employees representative as far as possible of all categories of work."

The functions of the Central Joint Council and the dependent machinery were formally defined in seven articles which were very general and intended to cover all employee and employer interests throughout the industry. The first article is typical:

(1) To secure the largest possible cooperation between Management and Employees for the development of the Sisal Industry and for the improvement of the conditions and prosperity of all engaged in that Industry.

The constitution also provided that, were a trade union to be recognized in the future, it would be represented in CJC by three members designated by the union who would be matched by three from TSGA. Representatives at the three top levels of the machinery were to be elected; the union later fought for and finally won agreement that members of estate committees also had to be elected in the presence of representatives of the union, employers, and of an impartial third party.

This elaborate and ponderous structure was inherently incapable of fulfilling its assigned functions. The African employee representatives to the estate committees were unprepared to challenge the authority of the estate managers. In addition, the manner in which the CJC was introduced gave it little meaning to African workers, since there had been no organic growth or experimentation at the bottom. Instead, in a single step, TSGA had created a massive machinery of consultation that was intended to function at a variety of levels for a national industry.[10] If it became necessary to include a union at some later date, the intention was to hamstring it by fitting it

217

into an established machinery without direct access to employers rather than to permit it to participate in the structuring of the industrial relations.

The Union and Its Fight for Recognition

The Tanganyika Federation of Labour established contact in 1957 with various entrepreneurs who were organizing skeletal unions in different parts of Tanganyika and urged a merger conference of the four provincial unions in February 1958. The new National Plantation Workers Union began to function immediately as a relatively coherent, central organization, although it was not registered for several months.

Two major and connected problems of industrial relations facing the union's inexperienced leadership were those involving recognition by the employers and access to the estates. Because the estates were unfenced but private property, they were open to African union organizers on foot but they could be prosecuted for trespass. One union demand, therefore, was the right of access to the estates for union personnel.

Union recognition was first sought through strikes on estates and, between December 1957 and mid-February 1958, they occurred on at least four[11] estates to demonstrate to the employers that the unions represented the workers. As TSGA completed the formation of CJC and as pressures by the unionists built up, it became clear that some modus vivendi would have to be developed with the union. Between February and April 1958, the employers sought agreement with the union while retaining the CJC structure intact.

The conditions that TSGA set for union recognition included: (1) a change in the union's name to indicate a membership limited to sisal workers; (2) union headquarters to be in Tanga, the center of the sisal industry and the location of TSGA. The union rejected these demands as unwarranted interference in its internal affairs,[12] but after informal meetings between representatives of TFL and TSGA and after pressure had been brought on the officers of the Plantation Workers Union, it was agreed that: (1) the name of the union would be changed to Tanganyika Sisal and PlantationWorkers Union; (2) the union would have its headquarters in Tanga; (3) officials appointed to negotiate with sisal employers would come from the sisal industry; (4) ninety percent of the executive board of the union would come from the sisal industry. On its part, TSGA agreed: (5) to recognize the union; (6) to recommend to its members that accredited union officials be permitted access to the estates; (7) that the union could nominate three representatives to the employees' side of the CJC.

While these arrangements were worked out, a preliminary organization meeting of the CJC was held in Tanga on April 10, 1958, at which representatives of the union were present, and agreement was reached on the functions and structure of the CJC. But union recognition and the seating of its three representatives in CJC represented only a temporary solution to the industrial disputes in the industry; the problem of direct confrontation between the union and the employers continued to block the achievement of industrial peace.

The Central Joint Council: Its Operation and Its Consequences

Although six meetings of the CJC took place up to mid-1960, the main business was carried on in smaller private committees, and the council meetings became semipublic sessions at which decisions were ratified. The timing and nature of the six meetings divide the history of relations between the union and employers into convenient blocks.

First meeting, June 26, 1958: Primarily concerned with adoption of the constitution.

Second meeting, August 14, 1958: Wage demand presented by employees; an offer made by employers but rejected by employees.

Third meeting, November 13, 1958: Revised wage offer made by the employers, accepted by the employee representatives, but rejected by the three union representatives.

Fourth and fifth meetings, May 29, 1959, and November 26-28 1959: Discussion of specific demands with respect to pensions, housing, conditions of service, and other matters.

Sixth meeting, March 10, 1960: Acceptance of a complex agreement on wage and task increases.

The first meeting of the council was praised by the employers, the Labour Department, and the *Tanganyika Standard.* Hopes spread for the dawn of a new era in labor relations. Sir Barclay Nihill, the impartial chairman of the CJC, wrote an enthusiastic article titled "Wind of Cooperation Blows Lustily on Sisal Estates."[13]

In the second meeting, also relatively harmonious, the chairman of the employees' side submitted a carefully prepared and reasoned demand for a wage increase justified on the basis of ability to pay, increase in the cost of living since 1951, and rates of pay in comparable industries. The employers, having been warned earlier by Guillebaud of the dangers to the future of the council if they were to reject the wage demand, made an offer approximating a 5 percent increase, which was rejected by the employee's side. They agreed, however, to discuss it with the workers.

The period up to the third meeting, although generally harmonious at the top level, was not peaceful on the estates. Upon obtaining access to the estates, the union organization had grown phenomenally and began to experience a serious shortage of leaders. The majority of the incompetent and barely literate clerks who were hastily recruited to act as full-time branch

secretaries had only the vaguest idea of trade unionism. The general secretary of the union, V. M. Mkello, sought to control this mushrooming apparatus, but it was clear that his control was at best tenuous. Some of the new secretaries appeard on estates and issued ultimata and threats to managers in an extravagant fashion; some meetings held on estates turned into small riots, and in July, an uncontrolled strike took place near Korogwe. At the end of October in a strike at Mjesani estate near Tanga the police were called in and when strikers refused to disperse fired on the crowd killing one person. As the strikers ran down to a nearby river, three were drowned.[14]

The third meeting of the CJC took place against this background of deteriorating relations at the estate level. A revised offer for a wage increase from the employers was accepted by the employees but rejected by the three union representatives, a split which brought to a head the question of who legitimately represented the sisal workers. The unionists needed proof of their backing.

No official strike call was made by the committee, yet strikes began on many estates within three days of the meeting, and in the period until December 12, twenty-four work stoppages of 15,000 workers involved a loss of about 105,000 man-days.[15] The union leaders became sufficiently concerned that the situation might get out of hand that on November 28, Rashidi Kawawa, the TFL general secretary, in a radio broadcast, called for an immediate return to work, to which the strikers responded almost immediately, except at the Mazinde estate. By the strikes and the response to the call to return to work, the union leaders demonstrated their leadership of the workers to the employers.

The continuing Mazinde strike soon became the center of political and economic tensions in the country because the owner-manager of Mazinde estate, David Lead, was a leading supporter of the United Tanganyika party (UTP), the political organization created to counter TANU. Reports conflict as to the origin of the Mazinde strike. According to the owner of Mazinde estate the strike was organized by the union; this union officials denied—they claimed it was a spontaneous action by the workers. When the strike began on November 25, no demands were formally presented to management. There were indications that one of the informal demands of the strikers was the discharge of the two members of the CJC from the Mazinde estate who had voted for the employers' wage offer. Jack describes the events as follows:[16]

> On 28th November (three days after the strike began), Mr. Lead was visited by Mr. Salehe, an official of the union. Mr. Salehe informed Mr. Lead that the union was not responsible for the strike and was told that in the circumstances his help would not be required. Mr. Salehe then held a public meeting at which he called for representatives who would put the case before the management.

Mr. Lead later agreed to see these representatives but not in the presence of Mr. Salehe and when Mr. Salehe attempted to join the discussion he was told to leave and eventually did so, after ordering the three representatives to leave with him. From this date up to 6th December no meetings were held. Later there was a mass meeting at which a demand was made for the dismissal of an estate manager and two other employees. This was refused. The management then decided to dismiss eight ringleaders. It was also announced that as from 8th December if there should not be a complete return to work 100 employees would have their services terminated each day. Following this announcement the union, which on 5th December had given its full support to the strike, began to remove workpeople from the estate with the result that while 300 employees had their services terminated by the management some 800 were withdrawn by the union.

It is probable that the local secretary of the union had some responsibility for the organization of the strike, but his exclusion from attempts to obtain a settlement only intensified the conflict. When the situation became grave, Michael Kamaliza, president of the TFL and full-time general secretary of the Commercial and Industrial Workers Union, went to Mazinde but was unable to achieve a settlement. It was agreed at the mass meeting of the workers on December 6, 1958, that no one would go back to work until the discharged workers were reinstated, and, on December 8, 1958, when management's ultimatum took effect, the union, using rented buses and trucks, within several days moved a large number of strikers from the estate to nearby towns. On December 17, the same day that the Tanganyika Federation of Labour called for a three-year boycott of the Mazinde estate, Julius Nyerere, the leader of TANU, pointed out that the conflict was limited to the Mazinde estate and was not a battle between all plantation workers and all employers. He backed the boycott of the estate and called upon African workers to support the strikers with food and housing.

Meanwhile TSGA and the union attempted to bring the Mazinde situation under control and agreed in a meeting on December 22 to the election of an estate committee at Mazinde; this was held on December 29 under the supervision of the Senior Labour Officer. When the committee met that afternoon and agreed unanimously that the dismissed workers should not be reinstated because they were responsible for the troubles of the estate,[17] the union repudiated the election of the estate committee on the grounds that it was not representative. Since the striking workers were no longer on the estate they had been unable to participate in the election of the committee, which left only "loyal" workers to do the voting. The union also contended that a union representative should have been present.

While the Mazinde strike continued week after week, the center of conflict between the union and the employers shifted to estate committee elections. Early in January 1959, the TSGA executive committee suggested

221

privately to estate owners that new representatives be elected to the estate committees and on January 23 issued a circular letter to its members setting out the procedure for the election.[18]

When the union discovered that elections to the estate committees were being prepared, it warned that these would not be acceptable unless representatives of the union and the Labour Department were also present.[19] From mid-January to mid-April, TSGA persisted in conducting its elections for the estate committees, which produced sporadic strikes from time to time, and the state of the industry continued unsettled.

Professor D. T. Jack of Durham University was appointed to make an inquiry into labor relations in the industry on March 12, 1959. Working with astonishing speed (for the colonies), Professor Jack, on April 7, presented his report which took both sides to task for inadequacies, and recommended the amendment of the constitution of the CJC. One amendment, that employee representatives should be elected whenever feasible, did not satisfy the union, and it called for a boycott of the proposed fourth meeting of the CJC scheduled for May 29. On May 19 at an informal meeting between representatives of TSGA and the union, a number of Professor Jack's recommendations were accepted and a set of rules for elections to estate committees was adopted. Its most significant section on elections provided that:

> The three observers whose duty it shall be to conduct the election shall consist of one representative of the management and one representative of the union, together with an independent observer elected from a panel of names drawn up in agreement between the association and the union.[20]

The parties to the agreement became involved in implementing the elections agreement, and a period of quiet descended so that the fourth meeting of the CJC was relatively harmonious. At this meeting, the general secretary of the union, Victor Mkello, was elected chairman of the employees' side which put that side from then on effectively under union control.

During the fifth meeting, however, harmony disappeared as pressure built up within the estate committees in which the union had no direct representation. Two issues called attention to the union's dissatisfaction with the system of representation.

1. *The infrequency of meetings of the CJC.* Mkello proposed a constitutional amendment that the council meet every four months instead of six. Lead's response for the employers was that the meetings of the council cost between £ 2000 and 3000; if the employees' side wanted more frequent meetings they could pay some of the expenses. The president of the union, Lawrence Gondwe, retorted that the lengthy period between meetings delayed decisions and the solutions of problems, and this the workers could not understand. The workers could not afford to pay any of the expenses of

the meetings but, Mr. Gondwe suggested, the employees' side would be willing to cut down on the number of representatives to the council by having union officials alone represent the workers.

The union, recognizing that the work of the council increasingly was accomplished by smaller committees, indicated its desire for a direct confrontation with the employers without recourse to the elaborate consultative machinery. The union leaders believed, in any case, that they were responsible to their own executive committee and annual conference and not to any other body.[21]

2. *The issue of the Corona workers.* The question of union representation at the estate level culminated in a discussion of work tasks for Corona workers on the estates. The Coronas were machines to break down the sisal leaf and wash away everything but the sisal fibre. The issue of work tasks was highly complex, since the means by which the leaves were brought to the Corona were not standardized in the industry. The chairman, because agreement within CJC was unlikely, framed a resolution referring the matter to the estate committees for recommendations. Mkello, speaking for his side, indicated that he could agree to the resolution except that the union was not represented on the estate committees. He suggested that a union official should be invited to attend estate committee meetings while the Corona issue was discussed.

The employers' rejoinder was still another proposal that, after the estate committee investigations, a representative of the Corona workers would attend the next meeting of the area committee which included union representatives. Mkello remained dissatisfied because this proposal indicated that the management did not favor having the union represented at the estate level. Discussion became acrimonious and no agreement could be reached on this issue.

The fourth and fifth meetings of the CJC produced a number of concessions to the workers but demonstrated that representation of the union at the estate level continued to be a source of tension. The issue of wage increases also remained unsettled so that a 14-man committee was organized at the fifth meeting to examine the intricate wage and task systems of the industry and to prepare a unified wage proposal applicable throughout the industry. The employers insisted that any wage increase had to be accompanied by a productivity increase and, over a period of months, a detailed proposal was worked out which gave workers substantial wage increases and also, by a much smaller percentage, increased the work loads. These proposals were formally adopted at the sixth meeting of the CJC which turned out to be a "love feast" even though the issue of union representation at the estate level remained an irritant, this time enflamed by a "Guide to Estate Consultative Committees" prepared by Leechman for the TSGA and by Mkello for the employees. The paragraph in the "Guide" which was the subject of contention read:

> In cases in which the Employees' side of the Committee think
> that there is good reason. . . to believe that some employee has
> been dismissed unfairly, they can bring the matter up for discus-
> sion in the Committee. As a result of the discussion it may be that
> the Management may get further information which may cause it
> to change its mind. On the other hand, the Employees' side may
> come to realize from the Management's explanation that, in fact,
> there was no injustice.
>
> While the final decision must rest with the Management, it is
> important that such decisions should be reached in the light of
> the discussions in the Committee, and after full consideration of
> the views that have been expressed.[22]

The chairman indicated as possible alternatives in this kind of situation
that the dismissed person could sue the employer if he felt he had been discharged unjustly or he might go to the Labour Department or the union. The
weaknesses of the consultative machinery lay in the fact that, since no procedures existed for appeal against a decision of an estate manager, the aggrieved
worker had to go outside of the machinery. But recourse to the law was
unrealistic since most workers had neither the money nor the knowledge to
initiate a law suit. Had the employee gone to the Labour Department, he
would have been referred back to the existing consultative machinery; it was
a firm policy of the department not to become involved in disputes for which
consultative machinery existed. The only real alternative, then, was the union.
Branch secretaries found themselves inundated by grievances, unresolved by
the estate committees for which they, the branch secretaries, as representatives
of the workers were responsible. They forwarded many of the problems to the
national headquarters of the union so that the national officers also felt the
pressure to obtain union participation in the estate committees, pressures
which continued after the sixth meeting of the CJC.

Between mid-1960, when this account of industrial relations in the sisal
industry ends, and February 1964, the state of industrial relations continued
to remain unsettled for basically the same reasons. Many of the problems the
industry experienced undoubtedly can be traced to the startling growth of the
union, the rapid expansion of its leadership, and problems of internal organization and inexperienced leadership. Many of the disputes might, however,
have been avoided if direct confrontation between union and management at
all levels of the industry had been made possible and the joint consultation
apparatus had been dropped.

CASE 10: THE RAILWAY STRIKE: COLONIAL ATTITUDES PERPETUATED[23]

The case of industrial relations in Tanganyika's railways shows far less
adaptation to political, social, and economic changes than did joint consultation

in the sisal industry. Indeed, managerial attitudes in the East African Railways and Harbours Administration reflected unchanging colonialist attitudes toward the labor force and an almost total insensitivity to the revolution taking place. These attitudes led inevitably to serious breakdowns in the relations between employers and employees, in part because of the charismatic and somewhat irresponsible leadership which the conditions helped to engender. The inadequacies of colonial attitudes in industrial relations are most clearly evident in the examination of the 82-day strike of Tanganyika's railway workers.

The Background: The Industry and the Unions

The East African Railways and Harbours Administration was one of the principal services of the East Africa High Commission,[24] an interterritorial agency created in 1948 to administer common services of the British-controlled territories of Kenya, Uganda, and Tanganyika. Set up as a central agency in order to economize on the high cost of administering railways and harbors, customs, posts and telecommunications, currency, and other services of a scientific nature, the High Commission consisted of an executive, made up of the governors of Kenya, Uganda, and Tanganyika, and of an advisory legislative assembly, representatives to which were designated by the legislative councils of the three territories.

The largest of the High Commission services was the East African Railways and Harbours Administration (hereafter referred to as the "railway administration") which was directed by a general manager based in Nairobi, Kenya, the headquarters city of this administration. A regional representative in each of the three territories was, theoretically, the head of administration in that territory although, in fact, as the railway administration was highly centralized, the regional representatives were mainly concerned with public relations functions. As the railways were functionally organized as well as centralized, the district mechanical engineer in each territory was responsible not to the regional representative but to the chief mechanical engineer in Nairobi. Most orders originated in Nairobi with the general manager and his staff, and minor problems at the bottom levels were invariably channeled upward. The parallel consequences for industrial relations were that, because lower level management personnel were permitted little discretion in resolving problems, they were invariably referred to Nairobi.

Union organization developed early among railway workers and by 1955 there was a functioning organization which, for the most part, acted as a petitioning organization. In 1957, as political changes became manifest, the railway administration instituted organs of joint consultation which reflected the ideas then current in the territorial labor departments to avoid direct negotiations with the African unions in the All-Line Joint Staff Advisory Council (JSAC). JSAC was a top-heavy body concentrating union participation

225

only at the interterritorial level and leaving lower level bodies without formal trade union representation. JSAC consisted of an employees' and an employers side with the general manager of the railways as chairman.[25] The employees' side, reflecting the racial division of labor in East Africa, consisted of three Africans, three Asians, and three Europeans—one in each category from Kenya, Uganda, and Tanganyika. Thus, although African workers constituted the overwhelming majority of employees, they had fewer representatives than the much smaller racial groups combined, a situation further complicated by the fact that many of the Asian staff and all of the Europeans were supervisory employees. The presence of these supervisory employees on the JSAC emphasized its functions as a staff advisory organization rather than as an industrial relations mechanism in which representatives of workers on the one hand confront representatives of management on the other.

At lower levels, following procedures established in the British railways, local department committees (LDC) were organized[26] in which the basic problems of inexperienced African representation and unsatisfactory appeals procedure that existed in the sisal industry were found. In 1959 various factors contributed to a change of leadership in the Tanganyikan union as a result of which a militant young firebrand, C.S.K. Tumbo, was elected general secretary of the Tanganyika Railway African Union (TRAU), and things began to change.

In July 1959, Tumbo made his first move by withdrawing TRAU from the JSAC for which he gave three reasons: (1) Europeans and Asians had a majority in the council, and they supported management; (2) the machinery was purely advisory; (3) the chairman of the council should not be the general manager of the railways but some independent person. This action was followed in August by a TRAU conference where the possibility of a strike was broached, and the feelings expressed were that a strike was inevitable.

On September 17, the general secretaries of the three territorial African unions met and agreed that, as there was no confidence in the railway's general manager, they should all withdraw from the JSAC. An interterritorial union was created in name but was not given independent administrative reality. The general secretaries privately agreed to a unified wage demand which became public several weeks later when the Uganda union filed a wage claim.

Unresolved grievances continued to aggravate the situation, so that in October 1959 a spontaneous strike took place in the mechanical workshops in Dar es Salaam[27] over an old demand for "regrading" (that is, upgrading) of Africans. The union became officially involved only after the strike started and was active in getting the strikers to return to work on the understanding that negotiations would begin as soon as the strike ended. After the return to work, however, this situation remained unsolved for months.

Another issue was the nonrecognition of the district and regional secretaries of the union. One of Tumbo's first actions as general secretary was to appoint a number of full-time district and regional secretaries whom the administration would not recognize because these representatives had not been elected. Tumbo's position was that he had been authorized to appoint representatives by the union's executive committee and that this was an internal union matter over which the employer had no authority.

In November 1959, a major railway strike erupted in Kenya followed immediately by another in Uganda, in both of which about 95 percent of the African labor force joined. In neither case, however, did the strike have much effect upon the operation of the railways: the trains were kept running by the European and Asian staff with, in Kenya, considerable assistance from enthusiastic European volunteer strikebreakers. These strikes did not end until an official of the International Transport Workers Federation came to Africa to help make a settlement.

Management, seeing these strikes solely as the work of the irresponsible leadership of the two unions, did not seek to come to grips with the issues that had produced the African support for the strike: matters of wages and of involvement of the unions in the settlement of low-level disputes. Between November 1959 and February 1960 in Tanganyika, irresponsibilities of management were compounded by those of the union leaders as successive strike threats were issued and retracted, and management and the unions engaged in a series of maneuvers which actually sought to avoid a solution to the dispute. When a negotiations session was finally organized in Dar es Salaam in mid-December, the union forced its breakdown over a minor issue concerning the dismissal of two firemen and never began a discussion of the more significant wage question. It was apparent that management did not want a thorough discussion of the wage issue in any case. Both sides tended, in an irresponsible way, to conduct negotiations via the daily press, a practice of which Tumbo was particularly guilty. Indeed, more negotiation took place via public letters than at the bargaining table.

The general manager, Sir James Farquarson, demonstrated his insensitivity to the deteriorating situation when he reported the strikes in Kenya and Uganda to the December meeting of the Central Legislative Assembly of the High Commission and stated that services had continued without inconvenience to the public. He noted that the demands issued in Kenya had been formulated at the conference of the three unions at which the interterritorial union had been set up, and this union was neither registered as a trade union nor was formally authorized by the three unions to act on their behalf. The general secretaries of the three unions who attended the conference he described as former members of the railway staff whose "records can be best described as undistinguished."28

When negotiations broke down in Dar es Salaam in mid-December, TRAU planned a meeting of officers of the three railway unions to be followed by a discussion with the general manager on December 30. On December 29, the railway administration, acting unilaterally, announced a four shilling (56 cents) per month increase for Grade C workers[29] to take effect on January 1, 1960. This action doomed the negotiations which began the following day during which the unions demanded a minimum wage of Shs. 7/75 ($1.08) per day as well as a commission of inquiry into conditions in the railways and the problems of upgrading. After several days of quiet negotiations the talks broke down on January 5 when the administration announced that it would raise the minimum monthly wage for workers in Grade C another three shillings (42 cents) effective February 1. This offer was rejected by the unionists, and plans were announced for a general strike of all East African railwaymen.

All was not harmonious, however, within and between the three railway unions. On January 23 the Kenya RAU general secretary gave the 21-day notice of strike action required by Kenya law,[30] which action ultimately resulted in the repudiation of the general secretary's action because the Kenya union would not join any interterritorial railway strike.

Within Tanganyika most of the TFL affiliated unions were opposed to a railway strike. A strike of postal workers which had begun December 24, 1959, had already strained the slender resources of the Tanganyikan organizations. Tumbo was subjected to open criticism in the newspapers by his union colleagues as well as to considerable private pressures. As January came to an end, Tumbo was clearly determined to adhere to the strike deadline agreed on by the leaders of the three territorial unions on the basis that he could no longer control his members. It is equally likely that he was determined to have a showdown with the railways even if he had to act alone against the advice of his Tanganyikan colleagues. Tumbo announced on February 6 in a letter to the general manager, also sent to the press, that a strike would begin on February 9.

The 82-day Railway Strike

The success of the strike was in terms of African participation for, although Tanganyikan railway management contended that the strike was unsuccessful, more than 90 percent of the African personnel responded, and most nonstriking Africans were not Tanganyikans. The strike was almost a complete failure in terms of affecting railway services. Except for a number of bus services, trains continued to run throughout the entire strike, even if schedules were not rigorously maintained; this was owing, as in Kenya, to the willingness of European and Asian staff to keep the railway functioning. The successful stoppage of the bus services prompted the regional representative of the railways to propose that, since the union had proved its strength, the bus strike be regarded as successful, and that the men should return to work in their own interests. This proposal was rejected by Tumbo.

In spite of the bitterness of the situation, a meeting was arranged for February 11 at which each side made clear its position and thereby produced the impasse that prolonged the strike. Management would not undertake discussion of substantive questions under the pressure of the strike; they saw the purpose of meeting while the strike was in progress solely to discuss the conditions under which a resumption of work would take place. Tumbo made clear that no resumption of work could take place until negotiation on substantive issues had shown that management was making some move to settle the outstanding problems. As no serious negotiation had taken place before the strike, management would have to show willingness to negotiate seriously before the strike could end.

When the general manager came to Dar es Salaam on February 13, the talks immediately broke down. The Labour Commissioner, Kenneth Sanders, then convened a session with the trade unionists at which the union officially reported to the commissioner the existence of a dispute, thus permitting the Labour Commissioner to initiate conciliation. In a statement to the newspapers following his meeting with the union, Mr. Sanders acknowledged that he had of course known that there was a dispute between the union and the railways, but this had never been declared to him officially. "The gravamen of my advice was that in view of the circumstances, they ought to consider reporting to me officially the existence of a dispute in order for me to appoint a conciliator. I am very pleased to say they took that advice."[31]

The tone of the statement and the subsequent conciliation process could hardly be reconciled with the new political spirit abroad in the country. Sanders named as conciliator, C.W. Howard, the Deputy Labour Commissioner, who was unable from the beginning to assume an independent role and remained officially responsible to the Labour Commissioner. The conciliation process was long, involved, and unproductive. The conciliator permitted a situation to exist in which the two parties were unequally matched, for Tumbo was empowered to make commitments on behalf of his union but the representatives of the railway administration had to consult with and await replies from Nairobi. Any agreements tentatively reached in Dar es Salaam were generally overturned in Nairobi. Thus the process did not produce agreement, but permitted the slow draining of union strength. Conciliation continued throughout the strike but, though it served as a source of hope for the union leaders, it was basically fraudulent.

The administration sought to end the strike by encouraging the split between the Tanganyikan and non-Tanganyikan Africans, and much was made in Tanga of an attack upon the TRAU branch leadership by some Kenyans.

229

Later, the Tanga critics announced their intention to organize a new trade union to "unite all black-legs." Of greater significance was the disaffection of some African Grade B employees who attempted unsuccessfully to organize still another competing union. The activities of this competing group indicated that many of the more highly skilled employees saw little benefit in the strike for themselves.

On March 1 the arrival of Jack Purvis representing the ICFTU and the International Transport Workers Federation (ITF), two powerful international trade union bodies, introduced a new force on the scene. After several meetings in Dar es Salaam with Tumbo, Purvis and Tumbo departed for Nairobi to meet with the other territorial railway unions. It was rumored that the Uganda union had reached an agreement with the railway administration, thereby setting a pattern for the entire system; it was important therefore that agreement be reached between the three territorial unions on the terms of the settlement. The new unified demands emerging from this meeting were a flat Shs. 10/– ($1.40) monthly increase for all grade C workers and the establishment of a commission of inquiry into industrial relations in the railways. The announcement of the unified demands created a furor in Uganda where the Uganda RAU had apparently agreed to the administration's "Uganda Offer," as it came to be known, which provided that the monthly wages for all workers earning less than Shs. 90/– ($12.60) monthly be increased to that amount. No increases were envisioned for workers earning more than that sum. The Uganda union—or perhaps its general secretary—had accepted the offer but it was repudiated after the agreement on unified demands was reached at Nairobi.

The Tanganyika Federation of Labour, increasingly concerned about the continuing strike, called a special meeting of its general council on March 22–23 at which it was resolved to urge Tanganyika's governor to intervene in the situation. It was also decided to convene a meeting of the three railway unions, the three central labor federations, and representatives of the international trade union bodies.

The possibility that the Tanganyika strike might become system-wide also alarmed the internationals, and Tumbo was requested to fly to Brussels for discussions, which were held between March 29 and April 4. Five days later Jack Purvis and two important international trade union figures, Charles Millard, the director of organization of ICFTU, and Pieter DeVries, the assistant general secretary of the ITF, followed him back to Dar es Salaam. This "outside interference" by the internationals was not welcome to the administration, which feared that the resistance of the union would be stiffened and the strike thereby lengthened.

After several days of meetings, Millard and DeVries made a public offer to mediate the dispute between the union and the administration. Mediation

230

was proposed to permit negotiations to go forward on substantive issues and at the same time to allow the administration to save face in view of its public commitment not to negotiate while the strike continued. Tumbo announced that he was retiring from the scene to permit the mediators to work, which they did in a series of informal meetings with Tanganyikan government officials whom they urged to intervene to end the strike. That the continuance of the strike, although not having substantial economic effects upon Tanganyika, would have political repercussions beyond the immediate parties involved and particularly upon the High Commission was emphasized at these informal meetings, and the Tanganyikan representatives of the railway administration found themselves under increased pressure to end the strike.

Pressure continued to build up during the week preceding the Easter weekend and a settlement seemed likely had discussion continued over the weekend. The Labour Department at this point showed its total lack of concern with the situation, for on the weekend the Labour Commissioner simply left the situation hanging and departed for his usual holiday pursuits. The pressure carefully built up by the international trade unionists was thus relieved, and they decided to move to Nairobi in order to deal directly with the general manager. At a meeting with him on April 19, the mediators argued for: (1) a Shs. 10/– increase for all workers in the C category; (2) a commission of inquiry to examine industrial relations in the industry; and (3) a prohibition of victimization of striking workers. There was little disagreement on the second and third points but the wage proposal was unsatisfactory because any decision reached with respect to Tanganyika had to be applied through all three territories; this, according to the general manager, was more than the system could bear. He reissued the offer that had originally been made to the Uganda union.

No agreement having been achieved in Nairobi, the international trade unionists moved back to Dar es Salaam and renewed their pressure on the Tanganyika government. By this time the political repercussions of the strike had become alarming and substantial pressures by the government were put on local representatives of the railway administration. As a result, agreement was finally reached on April 29.

According to the agreement: (1) a commission of inquiry was to be appointed to report within six months on the state of industrial relations in the industry; (2) neither strikers nor nonstrikers were to be victimized by the opposite side; (3) a complex wage formula provided for Shs. 10/– increase for those in the bottom grades and for raises all the way through Grade C, to Shs. 4/– per month for the top earners. It was estimated that this new agreement would cost the railways more than £130,000 a year.

It is perhaps a reflection of the lack of judgment of the administration that, having agreed to the wage offer to end the Tanganyika strike and that any agreement reached for Tanganyika would apply to Kenya and Uganda, no steps were taken to implement the offer immediately in Uganda and Kenya. By insisting, instead, that the processes of conciliation in both territories (which had been interrupted while the conflict in Tanganyika was resolved) should be resumed, the administration delayed the new wage increases for those areas.

Conclusion

The failure of the railway administration to recognize the changes taking place in Tanganyikan society and the growth of a union which unquestionably commanded the loyalties of Tanganyikan African railway workers had a number of ramifications. Not only were hostilities deepened and entrenched, but the behavior of the administration led the union to an increasingly political stand with respect to the establishment of political control over the High Commission and its agencies. Thus, characteristic of many underdeveloped countries, what began as an economic action took on an increasingly political complexion as the strike deepened and hostilities intensified. As Tanganyika was then on the brink of self-government and would soon be reaching independence, the question of making public agencies responsible to local political authority became a burning issue. The strike inspired bitter opposition in the unions of employees of High Commission services to the maintenance of the commission. The resulting split within the unions reflected the growing split between TANU and the unions.

The strike solved none of the basic problems of industrial relations, and the railway administration apparently learned little about the necessity of dealing realistically with a genuine trade union. Since a commission of inquiry had been appointed, the administration postponed any action until it could report. The delay and the consequent accumulation of grievances again provided Tumbo and the militant union leaders with a basis for agitation.

CASE 11: A NEGOTIATION

The inexperience of management and unions in dealing with each other across the bargaining table produced diffuse arguments filled with extraneous issues which showed little comprehension of negotiation principles. In the following summary of actual negotiations between the Local Company (a fictitious name) and the union over wages, the unions had been demanding a substantial wage increase to which the company had responded by making an offer. When the union issued a strike threat in the form of a letter, the company responded by withdrawing its offer. Two meetings then took place in an attempt to avert a strike and bring about a settlement.

Attending the two meetings—the first in mid-1960 and the second two days later—were the following (all names are fictional).

For the company: Mr. Rivers, the general manager, and Mr. Jones, his assistant.

For the union: Paul Maka, a prominent leader of the union, and Joseph Nangara, his assistant. These two were the spokesmen, but the meetings were also attended by the four members of the union's committee in the firm who entered the discussion only occasionally. The discussions between the company spokesmen and the union leaders were in English, but Maka and Nangara conferred with the committee members throughout in Swahili.

The Discussions

Rivers opened the discussion by noting a "misunderstanding" regarding the company's withdrawal of the wage offer which was in fact, Rivers said, a postponement as a result of an announced increase in diesel fuel costs which might affect the wage offer. Maka and Nangara, after insisting several times that they had heard that the offer was withdrawn, were willing to accept that there was a misunderstanding, but Nangara indicated sensitivity to the suggestion that the misunderstanding might have occurred because of any weakness in his knowledge of English.

The discussion then turned to the union's 21—day strike notice if the company was unwilling to negotiate. Rivers stated that the company was always prepared to negotiate and that the union, by giving a strike notice, forced the company to terminate a contract, previously agreed to, which provided for a board of referees to settle any dispute. Maka insisted that the union wished to negotiate a new wage structure in 21 days and refused to withdraw the strike notice letter. Rivers noted that the agreement required that three months notice be given before termination and that management was bound by this even if, for example, there was a slump in trade. "We want to have a clear understanding of the meaning of our agreement with which we must all live. It is for the good of Tanganyika." But Maka, though claiming no intention of dishonoring the agreement, refused to retreat and insisted that the issue be settled within 21 days for, he claimed, the discussions had been dragging on so long that the union was losing control of the workers who had wanted to strike two months previously. In addition, the rising cost of living in Dar es Salaam made it difficult for workers to exist there. Jones interrupted to ask how Yusuf, one of the committee members, had managed to gain weight, to which Maka seriously replied with a detailed description of Yusuf's personal financial arrangements.

A comparison of wages in similar firms led Rivers to claim that the Local Company paid higher wages on the average than were offered in other places and, in spite of the fact that the earnings of the company were decreasing, management would renew the offer of an all around Shs. 6/— (84 cents) raise plus Shs. 30/— ($4.20) assistance money for long leave. Rivers suggested

233

that the union accept this and make further demands later at a time when the company's receipts showed profit.

The union then wished the offer to become effective as of the time it was first made. Rivers claimed that the company did not have enough funds to pay the increase for the several months back to when the offer was made, but offered to "split the difference." Maka then claimed that, in any case, the offer of Shs. 6/– was inadequate because it would have a bad effect on other negotiations, which induced Rivers to return to the company's recent losses. Maka retorted that Africans were paid so little because some personnel were paid too much. Rivers, claiming that 95 percent of the wage bill went to Africans, noted the company policy to Africanize the staff, to which Maka replied that Africans who had taken over staff jobs were being paid less than Asians who had previously held the same job.

Discussion of the company's claim that it was unable to pay because of its recent losses soon produced an impasse in which Maka claimed that the company was indeed able to pay a reasonable increase since, in 1959, there had been a profit, and Rivers claimed that the circumstances in the industry were such that many of the running costs could not be calculated or predicted. Maka agreed enthusiastically with Rivers' comment that "frankly, I'd like to see the government take the company over." The difficulties for the union caused by the fact that the industry consisted of many small employers with which the unions must deal one at a time were also discussed, but the day's negotiations ended with a restatement by Rivers of the company's inability to change its offer; he backed his statement by an analysis of some of the technical details affecting the economic situation of the company and a demonstration to the unionists of various cost records in the industry. Maka responded, "I would suggest that you reconsider your offer. We all feel that you can go a little bit further."

The second meeting continued in the same vein with a statement by Rivers that the only way to increase wages more would be to cut services, which would mean a cut in staff. He suggested again that the union approach the matter after the company had time to assess some changes that would affect its income. He again presented further details on the cumulative losses of the company over a three-year period. Maka changed the subject to the discrepancy in wages which he claimed were based on racial differences. He was obviously irritated and suggested that the offer of Shs. 6/– indicated the contempt in which the company held Africans. Rivers denied this and claimed that there would still be a wide discrepancy between top and bottom ranks even if the staff was entirely European.

Since no agreement appeared feasible, Rivers suggested that the issue be arbitrated according to the agreement which called for the establishment of a board of referees in the case of a breakdown between the two parties.

Maka refused "because arbitrators here don't know how to arbitrate. . . we have no faith in arbitration," to which Rivers retorted: "Either we can go to arbitration or you can give three months' notice of termination of the agreement." Maka responded, "The workers may be prepared to do otherwise."

"If they do the company reserves the right to terminate the agreement and the individual contracts of the workers."

"Then we'll have a fight."

Rivers asked to be notified in writing of the union's intentions but did not want the unionists to announce the breakdown of negotiations to the press. He emphatically denied the company's responsibility for any work stoppage that might occur. Maka reaffirmed his distrust of arbitration and stated that, although aware of the terms of the agreement, negotiations were broken and the matter would be referred to the workers.

Analysis of the Negotiations

The diffuseness of the discussion, the tendency to skip around to a variety of issues rather than systematically to deal with the various problems, reflect the inexperience of both parties to the negotiations. Many principles of negotiation were violated. Rivers, for example, made an offer concerning the implementation date which was not even conditional upon acceptance of the main wage offer.

The union approached the negotiations with a "shotgun" technique: raising one issue, dropping it, raising another, dropping it, coming back to the first. The basic areas of argument however, can be summed up as follows:

1. The union was losing control of the workers because a solution to the dispute had been delayed for so long.

2. Other organizations were paying higher wages; assertions were made but no evidence was produced by the union.

3. Acceptance of the company's wage offer would establish an inadequate pattern affecting negotiations with other companies.

4. Racial arguments were also offered, but although the company had undoubtedly maintained such a policy earlier Rivers did show that substantial Africanization had occurred. Nevertheless, the failure to find significant numbers of Africans in higher levels of the company could be interpreted as discrimination.

5. In view of a profit the year before, the unionists were unable to understand why the company was unwilling to make a better offer. Rivers' response was that revenue in previous years had been continually rising, and even though the company still had lost money it had been prepared to take some risks to give wage increases. The company was not, however, prepared to take more risks in spite of the recent small profit.

6. The existence of unorganized competitors was an argument raised by the company but turned back on them by Maka who contended that the

employers had a responsibility to organize themselves into a single association with which the union could deal.

7. Maka's implied threat of nationalization was a weak argument, since Rivers originally proposed it, and Rivers added that, if the government took over the firm, it would be even more difficult for the unionists to gain benefits. This did not deter Maka from enthusiastically endorsing the idea.

Inability to pay is a standard argument of employers against raises, but there is always the danger in its use that the union will demand access to the details of financial records and will have someone able to interpret them. In this particular case, there was little likelihood that anyone from the union could understand the company's books so that, when Maka, who did not have the experience to understand them, demanded to see the books, Rivers showed them without hesitation.

Not only the unionists but Rivers as well showed inexperience in his inability to take advantage of several opportunities produced by the discussion. The union clearly violated the legal agreement by its strike threat, under which in similar circumstances in Great Britain, the threatened party would refuse to negotiate until the threat was withdrawn. Maka refused to withdraw the notice when requested, but Rivers continued the discussions and maintained his offer—a serious weakness by the employer and which the unionists took advantage of. Again, for unknown reasons, Rivers neglected the company's legitimate legal rights when he made no threat of legal action against the unions for their threatening to strike rather than, as required in the contract, being willing to arbitrate. By the same token, Maka's suspicion of arbitration was well founded, for the unions, to the extent that they had engaged in arbitration at this time, had generally lost their cases for three reasons. One, it was extremely difficult to find impartial arbitrators in East Africa. The number of people in a middle class whose income was not controlled by a company was extremely small; in any case, most such people were European and were therefore regarded with suspicion by Africans. Two, African demands were frequently astronomical and unrealistic. Although the unions were learning to accept from even the most sympathetic arbitrators figures that were much below their demands, the unionists continued to believe that their initial demands were fairly realistic and arbitration therefore was a threat to their fulfillment. Three, the unionists on the whole were unable to prepare satisfactory data for presentation to arbitrators.

The negotiations were also generally weakened by the introduction of a large number of irrelevant issues, many of which served to arouse hostility. Such were the issues of Yusuf's weight, the overinflated wage bill for Europeans and Asians, and the comments on nationalization. Other issues, such as the comparison of wages with other companies, could have become significant arguments had either side had hard facts but, as unsubstantiated statements, they were simply tangential to the main issues.

236

CASE 12: A JOINT CONSULTATION MEETING

This case describes a meeting of a joint staff council of a local government unit in Tanganyika which had been functioning for approximately two years and which was rather weak and undeveloped. By 1960, the Tanganyika African Local Government Workers Union (TALGWU) had become increasingly active and the changing situation in industrial relations in the country demanded that the committee be revitalized.

At a table at the front of the meeting room in the local authority building sat the secretary of the committee, the head of the local government ("the chief"), a priest ("Father Schmidt") who was to be elected chairman of the joint staff committee, the secretary of the local government, and a fifth person (unidentified). The employee representatives sat in a semicircle facing the table; behind them was the district officer ("Bwana DO") and myself.Bwana DO, the priest, and I were the only Europeans present. Also present was the full-time local secretary of TALGWU (Hubert Pallani).[32]

The purpose of the meeting was to make the existing constitution of the joint staff council (JCS) conform to a model constitution prepared by the Ministry of Provincial Affairs and TALGWU, which had recently been received from the ministry. The immediate question was the composition of a committee to do the work. The first consideration was the size of the committee but, confused with this, was the matter of representation, since some delegates were concerned about specific persons (such as the chief or Bwana DO) being on the committee, because they represented definite interests. Father Schmidt, the chairman, had spent years out in the tribal area behind the town and, in his inability to bring the meeting to a decision before some consensus was achieved, appeared to have gone native. Eventually, after considerable discussion and confusion between the topics of size and representation, it was agreed by consensus to proceed on the principle of representation. Nine nominations having been made, the other persons present, including Father Schmidt, withdrew leaving the nine as the committee but without a chairman. Nor was a chairman elected; the committee looked to the chief and Bwana DO for "traffic control" so that each exercised considerable power in pressing his point of view in the subsequent discussion.

During the proceedings, neither Pallani nor another leading union representative who was the local branch chairman played much of a role. Pallani seemed to expect the present author to represent his views. In the discussions, the chief and Bwana DO sought to keep the new constitution moving in directions which they either jointly or individually favored by playing two themes. When ideas came up that varied from the model but which they favored, their theme was that "minor variations were allowed"; when proposals were made that they opposed, the tune changed to the model "comes from Dar es Salaam." The chief and Bwana DO did not constitute a coherent or cooperative force. The chief was an African deeply involved in local and national politics, but not as a TANU supporter; Bwana DO was, of course, a British administrative officer with quite different concerns.

The committee began the constitutional review with a consideration of their old constitution, which was in Swahili, but shifted to a paragraph-by-paragraph consideration of the model in English to determine how they wanted it to fit their own situation. The first portion of the model, dealing with the name and objects of the JSC, was adopted by filling in the blanks left in the model. Significant discussion began on the method of choosing representatives. Under the old constitution, the union chose the employee representatives but whether they should be appointed or elected was not indicated. The model constitution provided that the employees' representatives be "elected by the employees themselves. . . If the employees so wish, the union may nominate one representative to the Employees' side who need not be an employee of the Local Authority." Discussion revealed that, in this respect, although both the chief and Bwana DO favored adherence to the model and had originally opposed the old constitution, the unionists were clearly reluctant to accept the model. During the discussion, the chief interrupted briefly but not discourteously to say that the model came from Dar es Salaam; Pallani, who appeared uncomfortable, kept looking back at the author; and the branch chairman muttered occasionally in Swahili. Pallani eventually told the meeting that he had been informed by one of the officers of TALGWU that the employees should elect their representatives. This ended the discussion, and the model clause was adopted.

The old constitution had provided for representation from various categories of employees, i.e., clerks, natural resources assistants, and others. The committee reached agreement rather quickly on a geographical basis of representation without insistence on representation from categories of employees, so that each working unit would be able to elect an available person rather than a person who happened to be a clerk, or whatever the category.

Bwana DO suggested next that, since Father Schmidt had indicated his willingness to serve as impartial chairman and would devote considerable time and energy to it, he be given ample time to learn his job. He thereupon proposed a three-year term of office for the chairman of JSC, which was quickly accepted with the proviso that some recall mechanism would later be incorporated into the constitution. As for the term of office for JSC members, the model constitution called for twelve months which Bwana DO suggested was too short and again proposed a three-year term. This apparently was considered a minor change by the committee members who adopted the proposal with little discussion. Since Bwana DO, supported by the chief, had generally been arguing for maximum flexibility in the adoption of the constitution, the suggestions and ready acceptance of a three-year term were surprising.

The model constitution provided that "The chairman. . .shall be appointed by the Local Authority Council from the Employers' side; the Vice Chairman shall be appointed by the Employees' side." The committee agreed that the model would not be followed in this respect because they had an impartial chairman available in Father Schmidt. The question arose, however, as to when the chairman should be elected since the model made no provision for this. Bwana DO thought that the outgoing council should elect the new chairman before the members' terms of office expired because they would be experienced and would know best who should be chairman, a plan seconded by the chief and several other committee members. But then Bwana DO had second thoughts and suggested that, although it was extremely unlikely, a revolution might take place resulting in a new JSC that would be confronted by a chairman it did not like. He proposed instead that the incoming JSC elect its chairman at its first meeting, which proposal was quickly adopted.

The model constitution provided that the "Chief Officers of the Authority shall not be appointed members of the Joint Staff Council, in view of their position as principal advisors to the Authority." The ministry wished in this way to insulate the chief officers of the local government unit from having to make decisions in discussions within the JSC. Instead, representatives of the employers' side would report to the officers of the authority who could accept or reject agreements reached tentatively in the JSC.

The chief, however, did not favor the model's provision because he felt that, in view of their intimate knowledge of its affairs, both he and the secretary to the authority should be members of the JSC. Bwana DO and the chief split courses in this case, with the former proposing to adhere to the model and the chief insisting upon membership. After considerable discussion, a compromise provided that the chief and secretary of the local authority on the one hand and the chairman and secretary of the union on the other be ex-officio members of the JSC.

No records were kept of the participation of the various members in meetings of the JSC and the committee, but in both cases the chief and Bwana DO dominated the scene. The two men occupied strong positions, not only by virtue of their formal offices, but also because of their superior knowledge of the operations of the JSC and their ability to manipulate the arguments. Most of the delegates spoke briefly, if at all, and much of their comment was devoted to endorsing statements made by others. The two unionists were ineffective; the full-time secretary's views were unclear and incoherent except in the case of establishing the principle of representation.

Notes

CHAPTER 1

1   All citations will refer, in the following order, to author, date of publi-
    cation of cited work, and page number (s). Authors are listed in the
    bibliography. Saint-Simon in Gouldner, 1959, 400-401; Spencer, 1958,
    Chapter XX; Weber, 1947, Part III; also see Bendix 1960, Chapters 11,
    12; Durkheim, 1947, Book I; Toennies, 1955.

2   Moore, 1951 and 1964; Smelser, 1959 and 1964; Hoselitz, 1960;
    Parsons, 1960.

3   See, for example, Apter, 1963; Almond and Coleman, 1960; and the
    series "Studies in Political Development," (Princeton, N. J.: Princeton
    University Press).

4   Toynbee, 1947; Teggart, 1918; Sorokin, 1957; MacIver, 1942;
    Parsons, 1964.

5   For example, Moore, 1964; Boskoff, 1957.

6   Merton, 1957, "Introduction," 5-10.

7   The term "institutional transfer" occurs initially, to my knowledge, in
    Apter, 1963. Apter refers to "political institutional transfer" but does
    not deal systematically with the phenomenon. In Hamilton, 1964,
    "The Transformation of Institutions," Daniel Lerner specifically rejects
    the concept of "institutional transfer" (although "exonerating" Apter
    for "this unfortunate phrase"). Lerner prefers his own formulation, the
    "transformation of institutions." Since I am concerned both with the
    transfer of institutions and their transformation as a result of transfer,
    I shall compound Apter's "unfortunate phrase" by attempting to stip-
    ulate the character of transfer.

8   For a discussion of the controversy see Lowie, 1937.

9   White, 1949; Steward, 1955. The recent interest of Parsons in evolu-
    tionary theory has given it a new impetus. See Parsons, 1964.

10 Malinowski, 1922.

11 For a summary of these studies, see Hoebel, 1949, 478-480.

12 Cf. as an example, Beaglehole, 1957.

13 See, for example, *American Anthropologist, 58,* April and December
    1956, in particular, Wallace, 1956.

14 Redfield, Linton, and Herskovits, 1936; International Institute of

African Languages and Cultures, 1938; Malinowski, 1945; Social Science Research Council, 1954; Herskovits, 1958.

15   For an overview of the literature see Etzioni, 1964; a systematic ordering of the large volume of material in this field will be found in James G. March, 1965.

16   There are some notable exceptions, the most significant of which is Crozier, 1964.

17   A subsuming of the variety of meanings of the concept of institution is undertaken by Smith, 1964. The lack of agreement on the concept can be seen in the critical evaluation of the literature by Znaniecki, 1954.

18   The functionalist view of institutions held here is not universally accepted. See, for example, Hanson, 1958.

19   For one example, see Redwar, 1909.

20   For example, Ericksen, 1964.

21   Rose, 1958, 21-22.

22   Merton, 1957, 63.

23   Linton, 1936, 336.

24   One of the earliest (but very brief) studies is contained in Hunter, 1936, which deals with the development of the earliest union of African workers, the Industrial and Commercial Union, see 566-570. See also Roux, 1948, Chapters 15-16.

25   The process in the Sudan was similar to that in Tanganyika. Fawzi, 1957.

26   Unions are, of course, only one type of institution that can "manage" protest. Among other types are, for example, millenarian movements, organized churches, and cooperatives. Cf. Kerr, Dunlop, Harbison, and Myers, 1960, *passim.*

27   For example, Ashby, 1964, Chapter I.

28   The distinction between formal and informal organization has been the subject of some controversy among behavioral scientists. I have attempted a reformulation in terms of the differences between formal and nonformal behavior in which the informal is a form of nonformal behavior within formally delimited social units. See Friedland, 1969.

29   Referring to the "constitutions" (the written forms) and the "conventions" (the normative understandings), Ashby writes of the importance of the conventions in supporting university autonomy even when the universities are supported by the state. "What is sometimes overlooked in Africa is that . . . it is the conventions, not the constitutions, of university government which provide the real safeguard for academic freedom . . . When universities are exported, these conventions are unlikely to be exported with them . . . " Ashby, 1964, 71.

30   Consider, for example, the different meanings of the term "freedom." For most Westerners, freedom is concerned with the ability of the individual not to be restrained or constrained by others and, most particularly, by the state. For most African nationalists, freedom is concerned with the ability of a colonial and underdeveloped people no longer to be constrained economically and politically by another people; freedom is explicitly denied as having a connotation of individual freedom. See Bidney, 1963.

CHAPTER II

1   Moffett, 1955.

2   For greater detail see Bates, 1962; Taylor, 1963; Friedland, 1966.

3   Moffett, 1958, 306. According to the 1952 census, 270,782 people lived in the gazetted townships of Tanganyika.

4   The lack of precision of the term "tribe" is illustrated in Tanganyika by the inability to determine accurately the number of existing tribes. For an excellent example of the difficulties confronted by the social scientist see Gulliver, 1959. The problem is that many of the groups designated as tribes have no sense of group integrity. Among the group designated as the Luguru, for example, there is no recognition that they constitute a tribe. Cultural variation within the tribe can be as great as variations between the tribes. See Young and Fosbrooke, 1960, 39-41. Many Tanganyikan tribes are acephalous and have no coherent political structure or cohesion. The significant social unit is, in many cases, the lineage: cohesion beyond the lineage is practically nonexistent except for some particularized social obligations between different corporate groups mainly for purposes of burial and protection while traveling. A number of lineages may share the same language and some cultural forms. Because of this, British administrators have been somewhat justified in using the term tribe. The term is useful in an imprecise way to refer to people living in the rural areas following traditional styles of life.

5   For a general discussion see Balandier, 1965, 36-57.

6   Mboya, 1963, 21.

7   Goffman, 1959, 151-152.

8   de Blij, 1963, 18-20, 31-43.

9   This is a slightly oversimplified picture of the situation since there were some British with little wealth and some Asians and Greeks with a great deal of money. Unlike Brazilian society where money "whitens," in Tanganyika money did not whiten until the past few years. During the period of the field research, Asians and Africans could not belong to the Dar es Salaam Club, the Yacht Club, the Gymkhana Club, and others, even if they could afford to pay dues.

10   Molohan, 1957.

11   Moffett, 1958, 82.

12   Wood, 1950; Frankel, 1953, 141-153.

13   ARLD, 1947-1962.

14   A discussion of early protest will be found in Friedland, 1961.

15   Thurnwald, 1935, 128.

16   Tanganyika Territory, 1940.

17   Friedland, 1967.

CHAPTER III

1   For bibliographical references see Brown, 1959, 380-391; and Flanders, 1957, 167-170. For a history of British trade unionism see Citrine, 1960.

2   Quoted by Flanders, 1957, 24, from W. Milne Bailey, *Trade Union Documents,* (London: Bell, 1929), 1.

3   Flanders, 1957, Chapter II; Bell, 1954, 131-153.

4   *Ibid.,* 143.

5   *Ibid.,* 137.

6   Goldstein, 1952, Part III, presents a good case study of the branch.

7   Roberts, 1956, Chapter VI-XI, discusses the functions and powers of executive councils, delegate conferences, general secretaries, and officials, respectively. Allen, 1954, is also concerned with the structure of power within unions as is Bell, 1954, who refers to a "trinity of delegate conference, executive committee and full-time officials which form the basis of the constitutions of most British trade unions," 154.

8   Roberts, 1956, 162.

9   Quoted in Allen, 1954, 190, from J. R. Clynes, *Memoirs,* 1869-1936, 256.

10 *Ibid.,* 225.

11 Roberts, 1956, 289.

12 Allen, 1954, 192 ff., discusses the social conscience of trade union leaders. This description does not imply that many unionists are not careerists and socially mobile.

13 Roberts, 1958, discusses early TUC history from 1868-1921; Flanders, 1957, Chapter IV, focuses on more recent history. Events from the point of view of a trade union leader can be found in Bryan Roberts, 1961.

14 Great Britain, Ministry of Labour, 1961, 146.

15 Clegg and Chester, 1954, 326. Unless otherwise noted, all material describing joint consultation is based on Clegg and Chester, 1954, 323-364.

16 Flanders, 1957, 157.

17 For example, in 1955, the trade unions paid affiliation fees to the Labour Party of £140,935 out of a total party income of £162,408. *Ibid.* 144.

18 In 1950, 68 percent of the membership of the National Union of Printing, Bookbinding and Paperworkers contracted out; only one percent of the Mineworkers and one percent of the Transport and General Workers contracted out. See Roberts, 1956, 370.

19 Flanders, 1957, 157.

CHAPTER IV

1   International Labour Office, 1958, 469.

2   Letter of the Governor of Tanganyika to the Secretary of State for the Colonies, 24 February 1926. Quoted in Orde Browne, 1926, 15.

3   In 1947, of the twelve senior staff officers of the department for whom information is available, only two had any prior experience in matters relating to labor. Of the rest, four had come from provincial administration, five had military experience, and one had been a sleeping sickness surveyor. Experience with provincial administration was supposed to provide an understanding of the African mind, while military service was thought to be useful in developing abilities to handle men. The experience of two of the Labour Commissioners is somewhat typical.

One came from provincial administration and left to become chief official of the Tanganyika Sisal Growers Association; the second came from
provincial administration and returned there. Of those department
officers encountered by the writer, only one had had prior personal
experience with industrial relations. Roberts, 1964, 214, notes similar
inexperience among labor officers in other British colonies.

4   Roberts, 1964, 215.

5   For an excellent description of European life in Tanganyika see Tanner,
     1964.

6   Concerns about the deleterious effects of urbanization, modernization,
     industrialization, westernization, and the spread of literacy are wide-
     spread in British colonial administrative literature. It was this concern
     that gave rise to an inquiry in Tanganyika as to how problems of "detrib-
     alization" should be handled. See Molohan, 1957.

7   Roberts, 1964, 261.

8   ARLD, 1958, 11; ARLD, 1960, 10; ARLD, 1961, 12.

9   ARLD, 1957, 16.

10   Roberts, 1964, 179-180, 188.

11   *Ibid.*, 229-231.

12   Cf. Jones, 1954.

13   ARLD, 1949, 27-28.

14   ARLD, 1950, 18.

15   ARLD, 1951, 20.

16   ARLD, 1951, 21-22.

17   ARLD, 1953, Appendix V, 109-110.

18   ARLD, 1957, 15.

19   ARLD, 1954, 14.

20   ARLD, 1957, 16. The Model Constitution was never published; it circu-
     lated only in mimeographed form. A copy is possessed by the writer.

21   Methodologically, these models were elucidated in interviews with labor
     officers and trade unionists. It is not clear whether the department for-
     malized policy in the form of written internal directives to its officers.

22   ARLD, 1953, 21.

23   *Ibid.*

24   N. Pearson, 1947; G. G. Hamilton, 1947-1951; A. Armet, 1951-1961.

CHAPTER V

1   The relations between the central federation and its affiliates is dis-
     cussed in Chapter VI.

2   The quotation is from the Minutes, TFL Annual Conference, Dar es
     Salaam, October 5-7, 1956. Unless otherwise specified, minutes of all
     TFL bodies were written in Swahili. These were translated into English
     by Mathew Kashindye who worked with the writer during 1960.

3   "Summary of the resolutions adopted at the TFL Annual Conference,
     November 25-27, 1957."

4   Minutes, TFL Emergency Committee, Sept. 30, 1958.

5   *Ibid.*

6   Minutes, TFL Annual Conference, November 23-26, 1958.

7   The railways were controlled by the East African Railways and Harbours Administration, an interterritorial High Commission service. This administration employed all workers on the railways and those operating cranes in the ports. Stevedores and longshoremen, however, were employed by a number of port employers, the most significant of which was the East African Landing and Shipping Company, and interterritorial private company owned by the Railways Administration. Control was not, however, direct and immediate. The Landing and Shipping Company controlled handling of cargo on shore; stevedoring (handling of cargo on the ships) was handled by private concerns.

8   A list of registered African unions, 1950-1963 is given in Appendix II.

9   The reason for the shift from "association" to "union" is not completely clear. On the face of it, this may have represented a recognition that the organizations that were being created were militant organizations rather than associations—which may have been associated with the idea of social control functions. During 1954, the Tanganyika African Association changed its name to the Tanganyika African National Union. The shift from what was, essentially, an African cultural organization to a militant African nationalist political movement was associated with the change in name. As TANU gathered strength, the term "union" took on increased significance in Tanganyika. A host of new organizations that were created in the following period used the term.

10 In the text, the following discussion is summarized from the Minutes, TFL Annual Conference, November 23-26, 1958.

11 Kawawa had spoken to various audiences and had proposed that amalgamation of the various unions take place. The nature of the membership and the vagueness of the ratification procedures, however, meant that decisions were not taken in a manner that provided definite instructions to officers. See Chapter VIII.

12 Jack, 1959, 2-3.

13 See Table II.3, p. 19.

14 At the TFL Annual Conference in 1956 one delegate suggested that it might be advisable if the unions adopt the structure of political parties, that is, have a single union for the entire country. Minutes, TFL Annual Conference, 1956.

15 Lipset, 1962, 99.

16 *Tanganyika Trade Unions, Chapter 381 of the Laws, Annual Supplement, 1956* (Dar es Salaam: The Government Printer, 1957) Part 4, paragraph 29, p. 15.

17 *Tanganyika Trade Unions, Chapter 381 of the Laws (Subsidiary Legislation of 1957).* Para. 12 and forms J, K, L, M, N, O.

18 While change was occurring on a large scale within the unions, it was also manifested through change in formal instrumentalities of the unions. An examination of formal change in the case of one union's constitution is contained in Appendix IV.

19 Deutscher, 1952, 505.

CHAPTER VI

1   According to interviews with the TFL leaders.

2   Millen, 1963; Klenner, 1956, 111.

3   Minutes, TFL Annual Conference, 5-7 October 1956.

4   ARLD, 1954, 14.

5   In the text, the following discussion is based on Minutes, TFL Annual Conference, 5-7 October 1956, confirmed by interviews.

6   Over five pages of minutes (in translation) out of a total number of 29 were devoted to the discussion of structure.

7   In his address to the first congress of the National Union of Tanganyika Workers (NUTA) in March 1965, NUTA General Secretary M. M. Kamaliza made reference to the old idea: "The desire to establish one strong national union for the workers did not start last year only, but had existed in the hearts and minds of trade union leaders from the time the now defunct Tanganyika Federation of Labour was formed in October 1955. Unfortunately, the Colonial Government, at that time, did not wish to see strong unions emerging and it was, therefore, extremely difficult to form one trade union which would be for all the workers of the country and run union affairs from one central office." From a speech by the Hon. M. M. Kamaliza, M. P., General Secretary of NUTA, given at NUTA's Annual Congress, March 1965. (Mimeographed copy in possession of the writer.)

8   In the text, the following account is taken from the minutes of the various meetings mentioned.

9   The 1956 general council received a report from Kawawa and Ohanga which stated that the Labour Department advised against the formation of trades councils at the time. At the recommendation of Kawawa, a resolution was adopted to create councils in towns where three union branches existed.

10   At a conference of one of the better-led and more efficient unions attended by the author in 1960, for example, a decision was made which led immediately afterward to a conflict of interpretation between my translator-assistant and myself, because of a difference in our conception of the meaning. Seeking clarification, we checked with various people and discovered, five minutes after the decision was made, that there was no agreement on what had been agreed upon.

CHAPTER VII

1   Roberts, 1956, 277-287. In Great Britain, there is a significant variation in the extent of detail included in the constitutions.

2   See Allen, 1957, 110; Political and Economic Planning, 1955, 35-37.

3   The methodology and the limitations of the data are discussed in Appendix I. Appendix III presents the date in tabular form. All figures are rounded off to the nearest full percentage point. Data originating from the survey must be used with considerable caution because of methodological limitations.

4   Kennedy, 1955; Ghosh, 1960, 132-142.

5   The basis for these estimates is in Appendix V.

6   *Sunday News* (Dar es Salaam), June 11, 1961.

7   For a discussion of membership apathy in Britain see Goldstein, 1952, and Allen, 1954, introduction to Part I.

8   Of the full-time unionists interviewed, I would estimate that 75 percent operated as entrepreneurs. Ringrose, 1951, notes a similar type of trade unionism which he calls "fictitious." Self-designated secretaries of unions make themselves available to any worker to write letters to employers for a fee (the dues). Ringrose cites cases where secretaries of such unions disappear after making a little money.

9   *Officers of the Tanganyika Federation of Labour 1955-1959**

Post	1955	1956	1957	1958 (until Nov. 1959)
President	J. B. Ohanga	J. B. Ohanga	M. Kamaliza	M. Kamaliza
Senior Vice-President	F. B. Jumbe	F. B. Jumbe	F. E. Mngodo	K. H. M. S. Kungulilo
Junior Vice-President	Shaba	Barwani	E. N. N. Kanyama	M. M. Songambele
General Secretary	R. M. Kawawa	R. M. Kawawa	R. M. Kawawa	R. M. Kawawa
Assistant General Secretary	M. M. Mpangala	M. M. Mpangala	M. M. Mpangala	M. M. Mpangala
General Treasurer	M. Kamaliza	M. Kamaliza	Mpina	B. S. Kajunjumele
Assistant General Treasurer	A. Odoro	Abdullahman	E. A. Akena	Mpina

*Only those with names underlined were still active in the Tanganyika unions in 1960.

10   For presidents and general secretaries of Tanganyikan unions in 1957, see U. S. Dept. of Labor, 1958, 35.4-35.7.

11   Because of the constant shortage of funds, some ad hoc adaptation occurred. The Tanganyikans found that short intensive drives were sustained better by the lower leaders than were regular dues collections.

12   The East Africa High Commission was an interterritorial agency set up in 1948 to administer common services in the British-controlled territories of Kenya, Uganda, and Tanganyika.

13   Tanganyika, *Trade Unions, Chapter 381 of the Laws, Annual Supplement, 1956,* Part V, Para 25, p. 14.

14   Gluckman, 1960, 55-70; Mitchell, 1956; Epstein, 1958.

15   It was a peculiarity of British colonial administration that there was acceptance of the role of voicer-of-discontent in politics and economics. They were very firm, however, in insisting on a distinction between the two. Thus, nationalist movements and trade unions were tolerated as long as the connection between them was not close.

16   Weber, 1956, 59-60.

17 Weber, 1946, 296; see also Bendix, 1956, 34-46 for similarities in Britain.

18 The union leaders were not necessarily lazy, but they preferred to channel their activities along other lines than money collection. There were, it is true, low levels of motivation which produced relatively low levels of activity. Unionists were capable of high levels of activity at various times, however.

19 The closed shop and union shop have limited the voluntary character of membership organizations such as trade unions. To the extent that unionism becomes compulsory, the arguments about voluntarism are not valid.

20 Parsons and Shils, 1954, 82-83.

21 G. T. Bell, provincial commissioner, Eastern Province, *ARPC, 1958*. The same contradiction between membership and the payment of dues has been noted also in political parties in Nigeria:

> It is certain that the subscriptions collected from paid-up members represents only a small proportion of expenditure, especially as (even in election time) it has become the common practice in British West Africa not to pay one's subscription to the party which one supports unless one has to be a *fully paid-up member* (or, as it is locally termed, a *"financial" member*) in order to be eligible for office. Price, 1960, 141. (Emphasis added W.H.F.)

22 Mwewa, n.d., 7. (Emphasis added W.H.F.)

23 I am grateful to Messrs. A. Armet and N. Bull, then of the Tanganyika Labour Department, for calling my attention to their idea of the concept of adherents.

CHAPTER VIII

1 Simon, 1957, 1-11, 45-78; March and Simon, 1958, 121-135; Chandler, 1964, 257-305; Dubin, 1961, 318-347.

2 For discussion of standing orders see Roberts, 1956, 180-184; ICFTU, 1960, 9-10. British systematic guides to meetings procedures tend to be individualized for each union. A specific example of such a guide is published in the form of a *Member's Handbook* by Britain's Transport and General Workers Union. In the United States, in contrast, most unions depend upon a manual of procedure such as *Robert's Rules of Order.*

3 In the text, the following discussion is based on Roberts, 1956; ICFTU, 1960; and Transport and General Workers, 1959; unless otherwise noted.

4 Inexperienced parliamentarians often identify the motion and the resolution as the same thing. This was the case in Tanganyika.

5 As I have discovered since joining a university faculty, consensus is utilized far more frequently than is formal voting in making decisions in a department meeting.

6 Speakers rigidly adhered to the practice of addressing the chair and never addressed the meeting or replied directly to another speaker. In the many conferences and meetings I attended only once did I see a speaker address someone directly, ignoring the chair. Another index of the respect for the chair was found in the practice of bowing to the chair before leaving the hall and on returning. At the first general council meeting of the TFL in March 1956, the failure of a council member

to request permission of the chairman prior to leaving the room led to considerable discussion among a number of delegates convinced that the delegate was "guilty." Minutes, TFL General Council, 28-31 March 1956. The practice of bowing to the chairman and receiving a nod of the head in return was used in the Tanganyika Legislative Council and it was probably from this source that the practice was imported by the unions. To my knowledge, bowing to the chair is not practiced in British unions. Thus the diffusion of the practice was British Parliament to Tanganyika Legislative Council to the unions.

7   Excerpted from one of three agendas used by the Plantation Workers Union at their first annual conference in October 1959.

8   Roberts, 1956, 175.

9   The difference between procedures in Tanganyika and in executive councils of unions in Britain should be emphasized. There are British unions where formal votes are not taken but where the chairman sums up the "sense of the meeting." It is not clear from the available reports whether a search for consensus actually takes place; this may rather represent a situation in which the chairman "estimates" what sentiments are and if his estimate is not unsatisfactory it is accepted by the council. Although this may resemble a search for consensus, there are distinct differences. In Tanganyika, the chairman does not sum up the sense of the meeting; rather, he must estimate when a motion has been proposed which sums up the sense of the meeting. Council members are prepared to disagree with him should he estimate that a motion represents consensus when they feel that it has still not been adequately discussed.

10   Fortes and Evans-Pritchard, 1955; Middleton and Tait, 1958.

11   Schapera, 1955, 60; Read, 1956, 90-91.

12   Schapera, 1955, 72; Hunter, 1936, 395-396, 416; Gluckman, 1955, 33.

13   Wilson, 1954, Chapter 2. See also the heavy emphasis placed on the need for village peace among the Lele discussed by Douglas, 1954, 13-15, and the Lovedu by Krige, 1954, 75-81.

14   Mason, 1958, 78-80.

15   Fallers, n.d., 184.

16   Holleman, 1958, 88-93. The search for consensus in cases of conflict is illustrated among the Ngoni, by Read, 1956, 92; and similarly, among the Chiga of Western Uganda, by Edel, 1957, 117. In the Southern Sudan, the role of the *mar* in crystallizing public opinion is discussed by Buxton, 1958, 80-81; and a similar procedure is discussed among the Swazi by Kuper, 1947, 64. See also, for the Amba, Winter, n.d., 154.

17   Wagner, 1955, 220.

18   One reference was encountered for a non-Bantu tribal grouping in Nigeria. "The trial is commonly a public matter, and the public present in court are frequently (e.g., among the Yoruba and Igara) called on to express their opinion before the final decision, going either to the right or to the left side of the court, according as they believe the evidence to be true or false." Meek, 1925, Vol. I, 263.

19   Chapple and Coon, 1942, 682.

20 Friedland, 1964.

21 "In primitive African society this question of the limits of responsibility as between the individual and the society in which he lives was not very clearly defined. The traditional African community was a small one, and the African could not think of himself apart from that community in which he lived. He was an individual: he had his wife, or wives, and children, so he belonged to a family. But the family merged into a larger 'blood' family, which itself merged into a clan or tribe. Thus he saw himself all the time as a member of a community, but he saw no struggle in that traditional community—he saw no struggle between his own interests and those of his community, for his community to him was an extension of his family. He might have seen a conflict between himself and another individual member of the community, but with the community itself, he saw no struggle." Nyerere, 1960, 157.

22 TFL Emergency Committee, Minutes, November 3, 1958. To establish whether the translation I have provided is accurate, I asked Tanganyikans studying in the United States to translate the key sentence independently. All translated the key term as "misunderstanding."

23 Cf. Hodgkin, 1961, 33.

24 For a description of a branch meeting of a British trade union see Goldstein, 1952, Chapter 14.

25 In this respect there are resemblances to early British trade unionism: "The early trade club was thus a democracy of the most rudimentary type, free alike from permanently differentiated officials, executive council, or representative assembly." The reasons for this in Britain appear to be different from those in Tanganyika, however. "The general meeting strove itself to transact all the business and grudgingly delegated any of its functions either to officers or committees." Webb, 1920, 8.

26 This is characteristic not only of Tanganyika, but also of other parts of Africa. Northern Rhodesian African unionists interviewed, for example, never referred to "branch meetings" but always to "mass meetings."

27 See, for example, Appendix VII, Case 4.

28 At one annual conference that I attended, it appeared obvious to me that the overwhelming majority of delegates supported the incumbent general secretary against his opposition. Nevertheless, none of the leaders would attempt to estimate what new officers would be elected. At first, I thought that this represented a form of modesty or coyness, which is a cultural expectation at times and in certain situations in African society. See Fraenkel, 1959, 37, 61. Evidence collected later indicated conclusively that the officers were in fact not able to judge the feelings of the delegate body.

29 Organizational inexperience was not restricted to the membership. Cases 5-8 of Appendix VII are intended to provide a graphic indication of some of the problems of internal operations of the unions.

CHAPTER IX

1 Brown, 1959, Chapter III.

2 An expression common among Europeans even in 1960.

3   For some descriptions of the character of industrial relations, see Appendix VII, Cases 9-12.
4   Moffett, 1955, 271.
5   Many of these strikes were spontaneous to the employer because of inadequate communications. For example, see Friedland, 1960, 87-89.
6   In this respect Tanganyikan employers were no different from those elsewhere. Cf. W. J. Ashley, *The Adjustment of Wages*, 1903, 22-25, quoted in Flanders, 1954, 261-262.
7   Tanganyika, Labour Department, "Collective Bargaining and Consultative Machinery in Plantation Industries," typescript in possession of author.
8   ARLD, 1962. 7.
9   ARLD, 1958, 13-14. This was the first public mention of such a policy, and the *Report* did not make clear where it originated.
10   ARLD, 1959, 13.
11   ARLD, 1960, 14.
12   Whitson, 1960.
13   ARLD, 1961, 14.
14   ARLD, 1962, 7.
15   African Commercial Employees Association, "First Annual Report for the Year ending 31 December 1953," Typescript.
16   Interview with author, October 9, 1959.

CHAPTER X

1   Threats were made on several occasions. For example, *Tanganyika Standard,* December 30, 1960.
2   Kambona mentioned this visit in an address to the Tanganyika African Postal Union, July 1960.
3   Most writers assume that unions in underdeveloped countries are politically oriented. See Sufrin, 1964; Millen, 1963a; Lodge, 1962; Ghosh, 1960; Roberts, 1964; and Wright, 1962. Berg and Butler, 1964, have questioned this assumption.
4   Perlman, 1928.
5   Nkrumah, 1959.
6   Scott, 1964, 24.
7   Nyerere, 1961. See also *Tanganyika Standard,* December 30, 1960.
8   Berg and Butler, 1964.
9   Minutes, TFL Annual Conference, October 5-7, 1956.
10   Minutes, TFL General Council, July 4-6, 1957.
11   *Tanganyika Standard,* August 12, 1957.
12   *Ibid.,* August 20, 1957.
13   The exact nature of TFL representation in TANU remains unclear because of contradictory evidence. According to the Minutes, TFL Emergency Committee, Nov. 28, 1958, a letter was received from TANU asking TFL to send a delegate to TANU meetings. General Secretary Kawawa urged that a TFL delegate be sent to all TANU Provincial Committee meetings.

This is contradicted by two sources. Kawawa, 1961, states " . . . at the end of 1958, two representatives of the TFL joined the TANU national executive, followed by members of the co-operative movement and the youth league." Bennett, 1963, is more specific: " . . . two places were provided for the TFL on TANU's National Executive by a revision of the latter's constitution in January 1958." As authority for this statement, Bennett cites the official TANU newsletter, *Sauti ya TANU*, no. 19, February 13, 1958. Bennett does not state, however, that TFL became officially represented at this time, and subsequent action in 1961 makes the accuracy of his sources questionable. In a statement to the press following a 12-day meeting of the TANU National Executive in February 1961, Organizing Secretary Kambona stated that both TANU and TFL wanted a socialist Tanganyika and that TFL, in the future, would have two representatives on the TANU National Executive. See *Tanganyika Standard*, Feb. 14, 1961. This action took place after the bitter Mwadui strike that pitted the unions against government and led to the creation of a joint committee of unionists and ministers to work out differences.

14 Cf. Kawawa, 1961. "The TFL never affiliated to TANU, though the idea was once mooted."

15 Cited by Bennett, 1963, 24. Nyerere's belief in the autonomy of the unions stands in sharp contrast to his subsequent expressions about unions and party being "legs" of the same movement. See Note 7 of this chapter.

16 The main exception is N. T. C. Msumba, an early TANU activist, who became general secretary of the Domestic and Hotel Workers Union and unintentionally played an important role in the events leading up to the 1956 general strike situation.

17 Bennett, 1963, p. 24, states that Kawawa was the leader of the Youth League. Similarly, a letter by M. R. Barwani in the *Tanganyika Standard*, August 30, 1956, notes that Kawawa is a leader of the Youth League. The Youth League, at this time, was not very well developed and its existence received little public notice. Even had Kawawa been a leader, it is doubtful that he could have been engaged in important political activities. Kawawa did not join TANU until February 1956 and subsequently spent considerable time outside Tanganyika. From July to September, for example, Kawawa was in Europe. The TFL Annual Conference on Oct. 5-7, 1956, resolved, as noted earlier, that no union leaders "should accept positions of leadership in political organizations". Kawawa notes this separation in his own article on TFL-TANU relations. See Kawawa, 1961.

18 As contended by both Kawawa, *ibid.,* and Bennett, 1963.

19 As suggested by Kawawa, 1961.

20 Minutes, Emergency Committee, September 30, 1958. It is possible, of course, that both were evading the issue. The fact that questions were addressed to them by the members of the emergency committee indicates, however, the sensitivity of the unionists during this period to being accused of being too close to TANU.

21 This figure does not include two marginal cases in which respondents worked briefly in TANU offices before finding employment elsewhere.

22   It has been contended that unions in the Tanga area conducted a "hold-
      ing operation" for TANU when the organization was based in the area.
      See Bennett, 1963, 4; and Cliff, 1965, 8. Both appear to have based
      their claim on Hughes, 1963, 65, who states: "The cooperative move-
      ment . . . and the trade unions, particularly in Tanga, carried on the
      nationalist struggle, raising funds, sustaining organizational efforts, dis-
      seminating news and ideas." That the unions were sympathetic to TANU
      is unquestionable, as is the fact that they organized and sought to collect
      dues. That this constituted a holding operation for TANU is, however,
      doubtful since it is likely that they might have met the same proscrip-
      tions as TANU.

23   In the text, the following summary of the main economic disputes in-
      volving the unions is based on interviews with participants, newspaper
      reports, ARLD for the years cited, and, in the case of the postal strike,
      direct observation.

24   For greater detail, see Friedland, 1967.

25   Nyerere, "Ujamaa," in Friedland and Rosberg, 1964, 244-245. Whether
      forced savings by workers (obtained by keeping wage levels low) is
      effective in facilitating economic growth is a subject of considerable con-
      troversy. The view expressed by Nyerere and the TANU government
      was, essentially, that higher working class wage levels would be morally
      wrong as well as bad for economic growth.

CHAPTER XI

1   Roberts, 1964, 42-69.

2   National union organizations such as the AFL-CIO and the British
      Trades Union Congress are usually referred to as "national centers."
      This practice will be followed here.

3   Lichtblau, 1963.

4   Roberts, 1964, 146-151.

5   Zack, 1964, 150-152. The value to the Tanganyikan unions of external
      educational programs has been partially assessed in a study conducted
      by the writer. In May 1960, of the nine Tanganyikans who attended the
      first two Kampala courses (November 1958 - February 1959 and June -
      September 1959), four were full-time leaders, three were peripherally
      active, one had disappeared, and one was in the process of disappearing.
      When Tanganyika was revisited in 1963, of the 13 students attending
      the first three Kampala courses, only two were still fully active in the
      unions, nine were completely out of the unions, and two could not
      be found.

6   Brown, 1959, 125-126.

7   Roberts, 1964, 214-215. There were a few genuinely sympathetic labor
      officers scattered throughout Africa but there were remarkably few. In
      addition, there were a number of sympathetic organizations and indi-
      viduals such as the Fabian Colonial Bureau and the Anti-Slavery Society.
      For the most part these organizations, while occasionally helpful, could
      not provide any significant or consistent help.

8   For French Africa see Morgenthau, 1964, 15, 22-27; for a description of
      similar contributions in a non-African area see Feuer, 1946.

CHAPTER XII

1   When the Ghana Trades Union Congress (GTUC), for example, became interested in developing a new structure, it sent a mission to Germany and Israel to study the unions in those countries. A decision was reached to base the GTUC "new structure" on that of the Israel Histadruth. At the same time, the organization chart of the German Trade Union Federation (DGB) was taken over almost intact. Compare, for example, the organization chart for Ghana shown in Tettegah, 1958, with that of the DGB in *Bericht des Deutschen Gewerkschaftsbundes Ortsausschuss Hamburg, 1950-1952,* DGB, n.d.

2   Charles, 1952, 437-438.

3   Beaglehole, 1954, 420.

4   Mitchell, 1956.

5   Epstein, 1956.

6   Gluckman, 1960, 349, 360.

7   Turnbull, 1962. This has also formed a theme for many perceptive novelists such as Joyce Cary and Chinua Achebe.

EPILOGUE

1   I am indebted in this epilogue to a considerable degree to Nikos Georgulas, whose paper "Post-1964 Trends in the Tanzania Unions: A Brief Commentary," was read at the 1967 meeting of the African Studies Association. The interpretation and assessment contained here are solely the responsibility of the writer and not of Dr. Georgulas.

2   The demands of the mutineers were concerned primarily with higher wages and Africanization, two major demands of the unions in the post-independence period. Contact with the unionists was logical, therefore, but I have no evidence that such contact was made or was of any significance in the formation of the mutiny.

3   Friedland, 1968.

4   Tordoff, 1966, 426.

5   Republic of Tanzania, *Report of the Presidential Commission on the National Union of Tanganyika Workers,* Dar es Salaam: Government Printer, 1967.

6   From a speech to the TANU bi-annual National Conference, October 17, 1967. Quoted in *Africa Report,* January 1968, 24.

APPENDIX II

1   Sources of data: ARLD, 1950-1958; 1950, p. 50; 1951, p. 75; 1952, p. 78; 1953, Appendix III, Table 5; 1954, p. 71; 1955, p. 71; 1956, p. 77; 1957, p. 76; 1958, p. 71; 1959, p. 69; 1960, p. 66; 1961, p. 66; 1962, p. 56; 1963, p. 47. The listings do not include the Tanganyika Federation of Labour, which was registered as a trade union in 1955. Many membership figures were estimates made by the Labour Department and all figures must be treated with great care.

     Note that no European and Asian groups have been included here although there were a number of such associations registered as trade unions. Also omitted are those organizations known as staff associations unless they were registered as trade unions.

2   I have no information as to whether this organization consisted of African or Asian members but the name would tend to indicate an African constituency.

3   All membership figures from 1958-1963 were estimated in the ARLD.

APPENDIX IV

1   To distinguish between the general models developed by the Labour Department and the department's formal document—the Model Constitution—wherever reference is made to the latter, capital letters will be used. All citations and quotations in this chapter are taken from the Model Constitution prepared by the Labour Department and the constitution of the Transport and General Workers Union. Wherever citations are made, they will be included within parentheses, with numbers and letters referring to rules, sections, and subsections. Both constitutions are mimeographed documents; copies are possessed by the writer.

2   For example, both the Dockworkers and Stevedores Union and the Tanganyika African Postal Workers Union reproduced the following misspellings in their own constitution (misspellings underlined here): "No person shall be elegible . . . who is a member, consistant supporter, or . . . " TAPU even reproduced a trivial typing error so that Rule 3 perpetuates "tradeor."

3   "Permanent and full-time officers" would refer to the officers other than those elected by the annual conference. Note, however, that the general executive council was given power of dismissal over *all* officers.

4   The predecessor organization of the Commercial and Industrial Workers Union was the African Commercial Employees Association.

5   The nonracial character of the unions became an important internal question for the unions in 1960 when the TFL began to encourage its affiliates to remove the word "African" from their names and specifically to open the unions to all races. The move was generally resisted by delegates to annual conferences, but a number of unions complied at this time or subsequently as pressure increased.

APPENDIX VI

1   ARLD, 1952, 29.

2   Guillebaud, 1959, 102.

3   Jack, 1959, 3.

4   Epstein, 1956, 1956a, 1958; Lewin, 1941, 11-14; International Labour Office, 1936; North Rhodesia, 1940.

5   These affinities were discussed by Jerrard, 1937, 19.

APPENDIX VII

1   The public session, although actually the first meeting of the annual conference, was open to the public, and 40 to 50 people in addition to the delegates and officers attended.

2   The government bench consisted of all full-time secretaries of the union present at the conference. They and the officers were considered to be "the government" and had to account for their stewardship to the annual conference.

3   An examination of the constitution reveals that the election of full-time

officials as delegates was technically not unconstitutional, although the general secretary was correct that the spirit of the constitution implied that it was, because full-time officials were explicitly precluded by the constitution from serving on union bodies (such as conferences) which reviewed their work.

4   This section is based on extensive interviews supplemented by data collected from a variety of sources including Guillebaud, 1959, particularly Chapter IV, "Labour and Employment"; and Jack, 1959. Minutes of the first six meetings of the Central Joint Council of the sisal industry were also made available by the Tanganyika Sisal Growers Association, and the Plantation Workers Union supplied a copy of the constitution of the Central Joint Council as well as other documentary information. The *Tanganyika Standard* was particularly useful in providing dates for events.

5   *Tanganyika Standard,* February 15 and 19, 1957.

6   Jack, 1959, 3.

7   *Ibid.*

8   See Central Joint Council of the Sisal Industry, *Constitution of the Council and its Dependent Consultative Machinery,* Articles 2, 3, 18 and 19, for description and formal functions.

9   Area committees were actually organized only in the Tanga and Central Line regions. Estate committees in the Northern and Southern regions elected representatives directly to the regional committees.

10 Thus the employers were, with the support of the Labour Department, doing exactly what the unions were condemned for: building from the top down. A major criticism of the Tanganyika Federation of Labour was that it created a central body before the constituent elements were developed.

11 See the *Tanganyika Standard* for that period.

12 The reluctance of the union to change its name was only partly based on principle. A practical reason was that it had already printed and dispersed membership cards and stationery with the name "National Plantation Workers Union" and these would all have to be recalled and redone. Not only was the cost substantial but the problems of recalling the old materials were almost overwhelming. A mailed request to branch secretaries to return the old membership cards would be unreliable; membership cards were "sold" and it was a major problem trying to keep track of one set of membership cards, let alone two, with the new possibilities for peculation.

13 *Tanganyika Standard,* July 16, 1958.

14 Interview, M. M. Mpangala.

15 *ARLD,* 1958, 12.

16 Jack, 1959, 13.

17 *Ibid.,* 14.

18 *Ibid.,* 23.

19 *Ibid.,* 6.

20 Central Joint Council of the Tanganyika Sisal Industry, *Election Rules for Estate Consultative Committees.*

21   The cumbersomeness of the CJC can be seen by taking, as a crude index, the degree of participation in discussion on substantive issues. The table below shows the number of speakers from each side that participated substantively in discussions (substantive participation does not include simply making or seconding a motion; speakers had to make some comment before they were considered to have contributed substantively):

Meeting	Number of Employers' Representatives Speaking	Number of Employees' Representatives Speaking
First	5	1
Second	2	2
Third	5	6*
Fourth	7	9
Fifth	7	12
Sixth	5	5**

*At this meeting the chairman deliberately sought to draw out speakers, especially from the employees' side.

**At the sixth meeting, there was actually a sixth speaker but he spoke only after the other employee representatives had withdrawn since he was being "boycotted" by them.

22   Minutes of the sixth meeting of the Central Joint Council, 14.

23   This study of the railway strike is based almost entirely on personal observation. A short description of the strike will be found in Millard, 1960.

24   Now called the East African Common Services Organization.

25   East African Railways and Harbours Administration, "Consultation and Negotiations between Management and Staff," (pamphlet, August 1957).

26   *Ibid.* For Britain see Great Britain, Ministry of Labor, 1961, 84.

27   Friedland, 1960, 87-89.

28   *Tanganyika Standard,* December 3, 1960.

29   Grade C included most of the manual positions and consisted almost entirely of African workers. Grade B represented a higher level, which was also mainly African.

30   The timing of this notice confirmed suspicions that the general secretaries of the three unions had set a date in February for the systemwide strike.

31   *Tanganyika Standard,* February 14, 1960.

32   Names and minor details are changed to preserve anonymity. While most of the proceedings were in Swahili, occasional summaries were made formally for me by people sitting at the front table; in addition, I obtained additional summaries from Bwana DO, Pallani, and was able to follow parts of the proceedings myself.

Bibliography

Allen, V. L. 1954. *Power in Trade Unions,* London: Longmans, Green.
_____. 1957. *Trade Union Leadership,* London: Longmans, Green.
Almond, Gabriel A. and James S. Coleman, (eds.). 1960. *The Politics of Developing Areas,* Princeton: Princeton University Press.
Apter, David. 1963. *Ghana in Transition,* New York: Atheneum.
Ashby, Eric. 1964. *African Universities and Western Tradition,* The Godkin Lectures, 1964, Cambridge: Harvard University Press.
Balandier, Georges. 1965. "The Colonial Situation," in Pierre L. van den Berghe, *Africa: Social Problems of Change and Conflict,* San Francisco: Chandler.
Bates, Margaret L. 1962. "Tanganyika," in Gwendolen M. Carter (ed.), *African One-Party States,* Ithaca: Cornell University Press.
Beaglehole, E. 1954. "Cultural Factors in Economic and Social Change," *International Labor Review, 69.*
_____. 1957. *Social Change in the South Pacific,* New York: Macmillan.
Bell, J. D. M. 1954. "Trade Unions," in Allan Flanders and H. A. Clegg (eds.), *The System of Industrial Relations in Great Britain,* Oxford: Basil Blackwell, Chapter III, 128-196.
Bendix, Reinhard. 1956. *Work and Authority in Industry,* New York: John Wiley.
_____. 1960. *Max Weber: An Intellectual Portrait,* Garden City: Doubleday and Co.
Bennett, George. 1963. "An Outline History of TANU," *Makerere Journal,* 7, 15-32.
Berg, Eliot and Jeffrey Butler. 1964. "Trade Unions," in J. Coleman and C. G. Rosberg (eds.), *Political Parties and National Integration in Tropical Africa,* Berkeley: University of California Press, 340-381.
Bidney, David (ed.). 1963. *The Concept of Freedom in Anthropology,* The Hague: Mouton.
de Blij, Harm J. 1963. *Dar es Salaam,* Evanston: Northwestern University Press.
Boskoff, Alvin. 1957. "Social Change: Major Problems in the Emergence of Theoretical and Research Foci," in Howard Becker and Alvin Boskoff (eds.), *Modern Sociological Theory,* New York: Dryden Press, 260-302.

Brown, E. H. Phelps. 1959. *The Growth of British Industrial Relations*, London: Macmillan.

Buxton, Jean. 1958. "The Mandari of the Southern Sudan," in John Middleton and David Tait (eds.), *Tribes Without Rulers*, London: Routledge and Kegan Paul, 67-96.

Chandler, Margaret K. 1964. *Management Rights and Union Interests*, New York: McGraw-Hill.

Chapple, E. D. and C. S. Coon. 1942. *Principles of Anthropology*, New York: Henry Holt.

Charles, Rev. Pierre. 1952. "Tribal Society and Legislation," *International Labor Review*, 65.

Citrine, Norman A. 1960. *Trade Union Law*, 2nd. ed., London: Stevens & Sons.

Clegg, H. A. and T. E. Chester. 1954. "Joint Consultation," in Allan Flanders and H. A. Clegg (eds.), *The System of Industrial Relations in Great Britain*, Oxford: Basil Blackwell, Chapter VI, 323-364.

Cliffe, Lionel. 1965. "Nationalism and the Reaction to Enforced Agricultural Improvement in Tanganyika During the Colonial Period," East African Institute of Social Research, *Conference Papers*.

Crozier, Michael. 1964. *The Bureaucratic Phenomenon*, Chicago: University of Chicago Press.

Deutscher, Isaac. 1952. "Russia," in Walter Galenson (ed.), *Comparative Labor Movements*, Englewood Cliffs, N. J.: Prentice Hall.

Douglas, Mary. 1954. "The Lele of Kasai," in International African Institute, *African Worlds*, London: Oxford University Press, 1-26.

Dubin, Robert (ed.). 1961. *Human Relations in Administration*, Englewood Cliffs: Prentice-Hall.

Durkheim, Emile. 1947. *The Division of Labor in Society*, Glencoe: The Free Press.

Edel, May Mandelbaum. 1957. *The Chiga of Western Uganda*, New York: Oxford University Press for the International African Institute.

Epstein, A. L. 1956. "African Leadership on the Copperbelt," *The Listener*, 56, 1437, October 11, 540-541.

——————— . 1956a. "An Outline of the Political Structure of an African Urban Community on the Copperbelt of Northern Rhodesia," *Social Implications of Industrialization and Urbanization in Africa South of the Sahara*, UNESCO, 711-724.

——————— . 1958. *Politics in an Urban African Community*, Manchester: Manchester University Press for the Rhodes-Livingstone Institute.

Ericksen, Ephraime G. 1964. *Africa Company Town*, Dubuque: W. C. Brown.

Etzioni, Amitai. 1964. *Modern Organizations*, Englewood Cliffs: Prentice Hall.

Fallers, Lloyd. n.d. *Bantu Bureaucracy*, Cambridge: W. Heffer.

Fawzi, Saad ed din. 1957. *The Labour Movement in the Sudan, 1946-1955*, London: Oxford University Press.

Feuer, Lewis. 1946. "End of Coolie Labor in New Caledonia," *Far Eastern Survey*, 15, 17, August 28, 264-267.

Flanders, Allan. 1954. "Collective Bargaining, " in Allan Flanders and H. A.

Clegg (eds.), *The System of Industrial Relations in Great Britain,*
Oxford: Basil Blackwell, Chapter V, 252-322.

—————— . 1957. *Trade Unions,* Scotland: National Council of Labour.

Fortes, Meyer, and E. E. Evans-Pritchard (eds.). 1955. *African Political Systems,*
London: Oxford University Press for the International African Institute.

Fraenkel, Peter. 1959. *Wayaleshi,* London: Weidenfeld and Nicholson.

Frankel, S. Herbert. 1953. *The Economic Impact on Underdeveloped Societies,*
Cambridge: Harvard University Press.

Friedland, William H. 1960. "Some Urban Myths in East Africa," in Rhodes-
Livingstone Institute, *Myth in Modern Africa,* Proceedings of the Four-
teenth Conference. Lusaka: Rhodes-Livingstone Institute.

—————— . 1961. "The Institutionalization of Labor Protest," *Sociologus*
*11,*133-148.

—————— . 1964. "Basic Social Trends," in William H. Friedland and Carl
G. Rosberg, Jr. (eds.), *African Socialism,* Stanford: Stanford University
Press, 15-34.

—————— . 1966. "The Evolution of Tanganyika's Political System," in
Stanley Diamond and Fred Burke, (eds.), *The Transformation of East*
Africa, New York: Basic Books.

—————— . 1967. "Cooperation, Conflict, and Conscription: TANU-TFL
Relations, 1955-1964," in Jeffrey Butler and A. A. Castagno (eds.),
Boston University Papers in African Politics, New York: Praeger, 67-103.

—————— . 1968. "Labor's Role in Emerging African Socialist States," in
Willard Beling (ed.), *The Role of Labor in Nation Building,* New York:
Praeger.

—————— . 1969. "A Sociological Approach to Modernization," in
Chandler Morse (ed.), *Modernization by Design,* Ithaca: Cornell University Press.

—————— and C. G. Rosberg, (eds.). 1964. *African Socialism,* Stanford:
Stanford University Press.

Georgulas, Nick. 1967. "Post-1964 Trends in the Tanzania Unions: A Brief
Commentary," presented at the African Studies Association Meeting,
November 1967. (Mimeograph)

Ghosh, Subratesh. 1960. *Trade Unionism in the Underdeveloped Countries,*
Calcutta: Bookland Private.

Gluckman, Max. 1955. *Custom and Conflict in Africa,* Oxford: Basil Blackwell.

—————— . 1960. "Tribalism in Modern British Central Africa," *Cahiers*
d'Etudes Africaines, 1, Paris: Mouton

Goffman, Erving. 1959. *The Presentation of Self in Everyday Life,* Garden
City: Doubleday Anchor.

Goldstein, Joseph. 1952. *The Government of a British Trade Union,* Glencoe:
The Free Press.

Gouldner, Alvin.W. 1959. "Organizational Analysis," in Robert K. Merton,
Leonard Broom, and Leonard S. Cottrell, Jr., (eds.), *Sociology Today,*
New York: Basic Books.

Great Britain, Ministry of Labour. 1961. *Industrial Relations Handbook,*
London: Her Majesty's Stationery Office.

Guillebaud, C. W. 1959. *Economic Survey of the Sisal Industry of Tanganyika,* Arusha, Tanganyika: Beauchamp Printing Co.

Gulliver, Phillip H. 1959. "A Tribal Map of Tanganyika," *Tanganyika Notes and Records,* No. 52, March, 61-74

Hamilton, William B. (ed.) 1964. *The Transfer of Institutions,* Durham: Duke University Press.

Hanson, Robert C. 1958. "Institutions," in Joseph S. Roucek (ed.). *Contemporary Sociology,* New York: Philosophical Library, 64-86.

Herskovits, Melville J. 1958. *Acculturation,* Glouchester: Peter Smith.

Hodgkin, Thomas. 1961. "A Note on the Language of African Nationalism," in K. Kirkwood (ed.), *African Affairs, Number One,* St. Anthony's Papers, No. 10, London: Chatto and Windus, 22-40.

Hoebel, E. Adamson. 1949. *Man in the Primitive World,* New York: McGraw-Hill.

Holleman, J. F. 1958. *African Interlude,* Capetown: Nasionale Boekhandel BPK.

Hoselitz, Bert F. 1960. *Sociological Aspects of Economic Growth,* Glencoe: Free Press.

Hughes, J. A. 1963. *East Africa: The Search for Unity,* Baltimore: Penguin Books.

Hunter, Monica. 1936. *Reaction to Conquest,* London: Oxford University Press.

International Confederation of Free Trade Unions. 1960. *How to Conduct a Union Meeting.* "You and Your Union, No. 3," Brussels: International Confederation of Free Trade Unions (study outline).

International Institute of African Languages and Cultures. 1938. *Methods of Study of Culture Contact in Africa,* Memorandum XV, London: Oxford University Press for the International Institute of African Languages and Cultures.

International Labour Office. 1936. "Mining Labour in Northern Rhodesia," *International Labour Review, 33,* 5, May, 721-726.

_____ . 1958. *African Labour Survey,* Geneva: International Labour Office.

Jack, D. T. 1959. *Report on the State of Industrial Relations in the Sisal Industry,* Dar es Salaam: Government Printer.

Jerrard, R. C. 1937. *Hints on the Care and Management of African Labour,* Tanganyika (mimeograph).

Jones, H. Wynn. 1954. "Trade Unions on Trial in Africa," *Time and Tide, 35,* 13, March, London.

Kawawa, Rashidi. 1961. "TFL, TANU and Unity," *Spearhead, 1,* 2, December, 14-16.

Kennedy, Van Dusen. 1955. *Problems of Indian Trade Unionism and Labour Relations,* Institute of Industrial Relations, Reprint No. 77, Berkeley.

Kerr, Clark, John T. Dunlop, Frederick Harbison and Charles A. Myers. 1960. *Industrialism and Industrial Man,* Cambridge: Harvard University Press.

Klenner, Fritz, 1956. *The Austrian Trade Union Movement,* Brussels: ICFTU.

Krige, J. D. and E. J. Krige. 1954. "The Lovedu of the Transvaal," in International African Institute, *African Worlds,* London: Oxford University Press, 55-82.

Kuper, Hilda. 1947. *An African Aristocracy, Rank among the Swazi,* London: Oxford University Press.

Lewin, Julius. 1941. *The Colour Bar in the Copper Belt,* Johannesburg: South Africa Institute for Race Relations.

Lichtblau, George. 1963. "Communist Labor Tactics in the Colonial and Former Colonial Countries," in E. Kassalow (ed.). *National Labor Movements in the Postwar World,* Evanston: Northwestern University Press.

Linton, Ralph. 1936. *The Study of Man,* New York: Appleton-Century.

Lipset, Seymour M. 1962. "Trade Unions and Social Structure: II," *Industrial Relations, 1,* 2, February, 75-110.

Lodge, George C. 1962. *Spearheads of Democracy,* New York: Harper and Row.

Lowie, Robert H. 1937. *The History of Ethnological Theory,* New York: Farrar & Rinehart.

MacIver, Robert. 1942. *Social Causation,* Boston: Ginn and Co.

Malinowski, Bronislaw. 1922. *Argonauts of the Western Pacific,* London: G. Routledge.

——————— . 1945. *The Dynamics of Culture Change,* New Haven: Yale University Press.

March, James G. 1965. *Handbook of Organizations,* Chicago: Rand McNally.

——————— and Herbert A. Simon. 1958. *Organizations,* New York: John Wiley.

Mason, Philip. 1958. *The Birth of a Dilemma,* London: Oxford University Press.

Mboya, Tom. 1963. *Freedom and After,* Boston: Little Brown.

Meek, C. K. 1925. *The Northern Tribes of Nigeria,* London: Oxford University Press.

Merton, Robert. 1957. *Social Theory and Social Structure,* Glencoe: Free Press.

Middleton, John, and David Tait (eds.). 1958. *Tribes Without Rulers,* London: Routledge and Kegan Paul.

Millard, Charles H. 1960. "History in the Making," *Free Labour World,* June, 229-232.

Millen, Bruce. 1963. "The Relationship of the Norwegian Labor Party to the Trade Unions," in Everett M. Kassalow, (ed.), *National Labor Movements in the Postwar World,* Evanston: Northwestern University Press, 119-141.

——————— . 1963a. *The Political Role of Labor in Developing Countries,* Washington, D. C.: Brookings Institution.

Mitchell, J. Clyde. 1956. *The Kalela Dance,* The Rhodes-Livingstone Papers, No. 27, Manchester: Manchester University Press for the Rhodes-Livingstone Institute.

Moffett, J. P. (ed.). 1955. *Tanganyika: A Review of its Resources and Their Development,* Dar es Salaam: Government Printer.

——————— . (ed.). 1958. *Handbook of Tanganyika,* Dar es Salaam: Government Printer.

263

Molohan, M. J. B. 1957. *Detribalization,* Dar es Salaam: Government Printer.

Moore, Wilbert, 1951. *Industrialization and Labor,* Ithaca: Cornell University Press.

—————— . 1964. *Social Change,* Englewood Cliffs: Prentice Hall

Morgenthau, Ruth Schachter. 1964. *Political Parties in French-Speaking West Africa,* London: Oxford University Press.

Mwewa, Parkinson B. n.d. *The African Railway Workers Union,* Rhodes-Livingstone Communication No. 10, Lusaka: Rhodes-Livingstone Institute.

Northern Rhodesia. 1940. *Report of the Commission Appointed to Inquire into the Disturbances on the Copperbelt,* Lusaka: Government Printer.

Nkrumah, Kwame. 1959. "Speech to the 10th Annual Delegates Conference of the CPP," *Ghanaian Worker,* August 8, 1959.

Nyerere, Julius. 1960. "Africa's Place in the World," in *Symposium on Africa,* Wellesley, Massachusetts: Wellesley College.

—————— . 1961. "The Task Ahead of Our African Trade Unions," *Labour* (Ghana Trades Union Congress), June 1961.

Orde Brown, G. St. J. 1926. *Labour in the Tanganyika Territory,* London: His Majesty's Stationery Office, Colonial No. 19.

—————— . 1946. *Labour Conditions in East Africa,* London: His Majesty's Stationery Office, Colonial No. 193.

Parsons, Talcott, 1960. *Structure and Process in Modern Societies,* Part II, "Social Structure and Economic Development." Glencoe: Free Press.

—————— . 1964. "Evolutionary Universals in Society." *American Sociological Review, 29,* 3, June, 339-357.

—————— and E. A. Shils. 1954. "Values, Motives and Systems of Action," in Parsons and Shils (eds.), *Toward a General Theory of Action,* Cambridge: Harvard University Press.

Perlman, Selig. 1928. *A Theory of the Labor Movement,* New York: Augustus M. Kelley.

Political and Economic Planning. 1955. *British Trade Unionism,* London: Political and Economic Planning.

Price, J. H. 1960. "The Eastern Region of Nigeria, March 1957," in W. J. M. Mackenzie and Kenneth Robinson (eds.), *Five Elections in Africa,* Oxford: The Clarendon Press.

Read, Margaret. 1956. *The Ngoni of Nyasaland,* London: Oxford University Press for the International African Institute.

Redfield, R., R. Linton, and M. J. Herskovits. 1936. "A Memorandum for the Study of Acculturation," *American Anthropologist, 38,* 149-152.

Redwar, H. W. Hayes. 1909. *Comments on Some Ordinances of the Gold Coast Colony,* London: Sweet and Maxwell.

Ringrose, H. G. 1951. *Trade Unions in Natal,* Natal Regional Survey, Volume 4: Capetown: Oxford University Press.

Roberts, B. C. 1956. *Trade Union Government and Administration in Great Britain,* Cambridge: Harvard University Press.

_____ . 1958. *The Trades Union Congress, 1868-1921,* Cambridge: Harvard University Press.

_____ . 1964. *Labour in the Tropical Territories of the Commonwealth,* London: G. Bell.

Roberts, Bryan, 1961. *The Price of TUC Leadership,* London: George Allen and Unwin.

Rose, Arnold M. 1958. "The Comparative Study of Institutions," in Arnold M. Rose (ed.), *The Institutions of Advanced Societies,* Minneapolis: University of Minnesota Press.

Roux, Edward. 1948. *Time Longer Than Rope,* London: Victor Gollancz.

Schapera, I. 1955. "The Political Organization of the Ngwato of Bechuanaland," in M. Fortes and E. E. Evans-Pritchard (eds.), *African Political Systems,* London: Oxford University Press for the International African Institute, 56-82.

Scott, R. D. 1964. "Labour Legislation and the Federation Issue," *East African Journal,* November, 23-28.

Simon, Herbert A. 1957. *Administrative Behavior,* New York: Macmillan.

Smelser, Neil J. 1959. *Social Change in the Industrial Revolution,* London: Routledge & Kegan Paul.

_____ . 1964. "Toward a Theory of Modernization," in Amitai and Eva Etzioni (eds.), *Social Change,* New York: Basic Books, 258-274.

Smith, Harold E. 1964. "Toward a Clarification of Social Institution," *Sociology and Social Research, 48,* 2, January, 197-206.

Social Science Research Council Summer Seminar on Acculturation. 1954. "Acculturation: An Exploratory Formulation," *American Anthropologist, 56,* 973-1002.

Sorokin, Pitrim. 1957. *Social and Cultural Dynamics,* Boston: Porter Sargent (one volume abridgement).

Spencer, Herbert. 1958. *First Principles,* New York: DeWitt Revolving Fund.

Steward, Julian H. 1955. *Theory of Culture Change: The Method of Multilinear Evolution,* Urbana: University of Illinois Press.

Sufrin, Sidney. 1964. *Unions in Emerging Societies,* Syracuse: Syracuse University Press.

Tanganyika Labour Department, *Annual Report,* 1947-1963, Dar es Salaam: Government Printer.

Tanganyika Ministry of Commerce and Industry. 1961. *Commerce and Industry in Tanganyika,* Dar es Salaam: Government Printer.

Tanganyika Territory. 1940. *The Report of the Commission to Enquire Into Disturbances in the Port of Tanga, August 1939,* Dar es Salaam: Government Printer.

Tanner, R. E. S. 1964. "Conflict within Small European Communities in Tanganyika," *Human Organization, 24,* 4, Winter.

Tanzania. 1967. *Report of the Presidential Commission on the National Union of Tanganyika Workers,* Dar es Salaam: Government Printer.

Tanzania. 1967. *Proposals of the Tanzania Government on the Recommendations of the Presidential Commission of Enquiry into the National Union of Tanganyika Workers,* Dar es Salaam: Government Printer.

Taylor, J. Claggett. 1963. *The Political Development of Tanganyika,* Stanford University Press.

Teggart, F. J. 1918. *The Process of History,* New Haven: Yale University Press.

Tettegah, John, 1958. *A New Chapter for Ghana Labour,* Accra, TUC (pamphlet).

Thurnwald, Richard C. 1935. *Black and White in East Africa,* London: George Routledge.

Toennies, Ferdinand. 1955. *Community and Association,* London: Routledge & Kegan Paul.

Tordoff, William. 1966. "Trade Unionism in Tanzania," *Journal of Development Studies, 2,* 4, July.

Toynbee, Arnold. 1947. *A Study of History,* abridged version by D. C. Somervell, London: Oxford University Press.

Transport and General Workers Union. 1959. *The Union, Its Work and Problems,* London: Transport and General Workers Union (study outline).

Turnbull, Colin M. 1962. *The Lonely African,* New York: Anchor Books.

U. S. Dept. of Labor. 1958. *Directory of Labor Organizations - Africa,* Washington, D.C.: Government Printing Office.

Wagner, Gunter. "The Political Organization of the Bantu of the Kavirondo," in Meyer Fortes and E. E. Evans-Pritchard (eds.), *African Political Systems,* London: Oxford University Press for the International African Institute, 197-236.

Wallace, A. F. C. 1956. "Revitalization Movements," *American Anthropologist, 58,* 2, 264-281.

Webb, Sidney and Beatrice. 1920. *Industrial Democracy,* London: Longmans, Green.

Weber, Max. 1946. *Essays in Sociology,* H. H. Gerth and C. Wright Mills (eds.), New York: Oxford University Press.

_____ . 1947. *The Theory of Economic and Social Organization,* New York: Oxford University Press.

_____ . 1956. *The Protestant Ethic and the Spirit of Capitalism,* New York: Charles Scribner & Sons.

White, Leslie A. 1949. *The Science of Culture,* New York: Farrar, Strauss.

Whitson, H. A. 1960. *Report on the State of Industrial Relations in the East African Railways and Harbours Administration,* Nairobi.

Wilson, Godfrey and Monica Wilson. 1954. *The Analysis of Social Change,* Cambridge: The University Press.

Winter, Edward H. n.d. *Bwamba.* Cambridge: W. Heffer.

Wood, Allan. 1950. *The Groundnut Affair,* London: The Bodley Head.

Wright, Giles R., II. 1962. *Pan Africanism and the Ghana Trades Union Congress,* Howard University M. A. Thesis (microfilm).

Young, Roland and Henry A. Fosbrooke. 1960. *Smoke in the Hills,* Evanston: Northwestern University Press.

Zack, Arnold, 1964. *Labor Training in Developing Countries,* New York: Praeger.

Znaniecki, Florian. 1954. "Social Organization and Institutions," in G. Gurvitch and W. E. Moore (eds.), *Twentieth Century Sociology,* New York: Philosophical Library, 172-217.

Index

Kambona, Oscar, 117; mentioned, 126

Kanyama, E.N.N., 121, 122

Kashindye, Matthew, 245*n*

Kawawa, Rashidi: expels Building and Construction Workers Union from TFL, 63, 64; reputation for dependability, 67; trip to Europe, 135; as leader of TFL, 20, 198; skills as mediator, 68; calls for end to sisal workers strike, 220; speech to 1956 TFL Annual Conference, 46; formulates TFL's basic position, 119; trial and conviction, 125; mentioned, 47, 50, 120, 121, 123, 137

Kenya, 12, 13, 35, 227

Kenya Federation of Labour, 21

Kibaura (Worker), 69

Kigoma-Ujiji, 48

Kilimanjaro, 48

Kilimanjaro Native Cooperative Union, 18

Kinship structure, 13, 14

Labor: dissatisfaction, 34; statistics, 18, 19; problems, 35, 36; wages, 6. *See also* Wages

Labour Commissioners of the East and Central African Territories, 34

Labour Department: problems and policies, 43; Annual Report, 103-106; discouraging of union amalgamations, 49; inability to adapt to changed circumstances, 114; inexperience of, 101; encourages joint consultation 109; formulates joint consultation model, 142; model constitution of, 72-74; organizes union, 40; overwhelmed by change, 48; mentioned, 15

Labour Department model of unions, 49, 117, 143

Labour Tribunal, 152

"Ladyclerks," 187

Lead, David, 220

Leadership, 21. *See also* Unions

League of Nations, 12

Legislation. *See* Workmen's compensation legislation

Legislative Council, 20

Living standard. *See* Standard of living

Local Department Committees (LDC), 105

Local Government Workers Union, 49, 107, 110

Local Workers dispute, 124, 125

Lugard, Sir Frederick, 13

MacIver, Robert, 21

Mahari (bride wealth), 76

Maji Maji rebellion, 12

Malinowski, Bronislaw, 3, 145

Mandawa, Patrick, 123

Salaries, 78

Salehe, Mr. (union official), 220

Sanders, Kenneth, 229

Savings plans, 149

Scandinavian construction unions, 67

Scholarships, 133

School teachers, 55

Scott, R.D., 122

"Scramble for Africa," 12

Security of Employment Act, 150

Self-government. *See* Government

Services, 68

Shinyanga-Mwadui, 156

Sisal industry: center in Tanga, 218; conflict in, 106; establishment of joint consultative machinery, 39; joint consultative arrangements in, 103; production in Tanganyika, 16, 18; seeks to evade confrontation with unions, 104; strike of Plantation Workers Union, 105; mentioned, 53, 150, 188, 189, 196, 216, 220. *See also* Tanganyika Sisal Growers Association; United Tanganyika Party

"Slot machine" theory, 89, 90

Smelser, Neil J., 1

Social activities, 16

Social control, 6, 7

Social forces, 178

Socialist-egalitarian work ethic, 74

Socialists, 27

Sociologists, 1-3

Sorokin, Pitrim, 2

South Africa, 215

Southern Rhodesia, 13

Soviet bloc, 137, 138

Soviet trade unions, 152

Soviet Union, 149

Spearhead, 149

Spencer, Herbert, 1

Staff committees, 104

Standard of living, 84

Strikes: Brewery (1958), 125-26; on the Copperbelt (1935), 190; description of, 224-32; DMT (1957), 125-26; dockworkers at Tanga (1938), 21; East African railwaymen, 228; in Kenya and Uganda, 227, 228; postal (1959-60), 125-26; of postal workers, 228; railway, 224-32; railway workers (1960), 55; sisal workers, (1957), 216; near Tanga, 220; of 1950, 37; mentioned, 102, 103. *See also* Plantation Workers Union; Railway strike; Sisal industry; Sympathy strikes

Structural parallelism, 54
Sultan of Zanzibar, 12
Swahili, 14; mentioned, 197, 198, 238
Swedish trade unions, 152
Sympathy strikes, 60, 110

Tabora, 48, 156
Tailors, Shoemakers, and Garment Workers Union, 51, 52
Tanga, 14, 21
Tanga Dockworkers Union, 57
Tanga Motor Drivers Union, 49
Tanganyika, 11-14, 21, 36
Tanganyika African Association, 20
Tanganyika African Government Servants Association (TAGSA), 69; mentioned, 109
Tanganyika African Government Workers Union, 52
Tanganyika African National Union (TANU): conflict with, 120, 139; foundation and growth of, 20, 21; felt to be monolithic and authoritarian, 182; takes over government, 22, 23, 116; as nationalist party, 53, 54; mentioned, 60, 63, 116-31 *passim*, 144, 209. *See also* Tanganyika Federation of Labour
Tanganyika Federation of Labour (TFL): abolishment of, 23, 139; difficulties with affiliates, 59; opposes retention of word "African," 203; and reconciliation of African Commercial Employees Association, 68; annual conferences, 46, 119, 121; boycott of Mazinde estate, 221; compared to foreign systems, 65; dissolution under National Union of Tanganyika Workers (Establishment) Act, 148; establishes contact with entrepreneurs, 218; experimentation with American type of structure, 74; formation of, 21, 22; falls under government control, 128; internal weakness and financial problems, 22, 59, 62, 70, 71; opposed by Labour Department, 49; launching in 1955, 59; leadership expertise, 69, 70; first limitations on, 60, 61; merging activities, 50; officers of, 1955-59, 248n; serious split in, 63; as spokesman in foreign affairs of unions, 65; involvement in strike activities, 61; and general strike call of 1956, 35; supports sympathy strikes, 60; causes of conflict with TANU, 126; representation in TANU, 127, 252n; mentioned, 20, 38, 40, 43, 209, 230. *See also* United Tanganyika Party
Tanganyika Labour Department, 32; mentioned, 45
Tanganyika Sisal Growers Association, 196, 216, 217, 218. *See also* Plantation Workers Union.
Tanganyika Standard, 120, 124, 219
Tanganyika Union of Public Employees, 52
Tanganyika Workers Development Corporation, 149
Tanganyikan Army. *See* Army mutiny
Tanganyikan Railway African Union (TRAU), 57; mentioned, 105
Tanganyikan unionists, 40

278

Taxation, 101
Tea Growers Association, 106
Technical assistance, 137, 138
Teggart, F.J., 2
Tettegah, John, 149
Thurnwald, Richard C., 21
Toennies, Ferdinand, 1
Towns, 14, 15
Toynbee, Arnold, 2
Trade councils, 65
Trade Union Ordinance, 35, 56, 83
Trade unionism, 6, 21, 39, 48, 146. *See also* Unionism
Trade unionists, 6, 22, 46, 128. *See also* Unionists
Trade unions, 4, 6, 14, 155. *See also* Unions
Traditionalism, 85
Transfer, 6
Transfer agents, 8-9
Transfer institutions, 143, 144
Transfer model, 7-10, 32, 143, 144
Transfer process, 5
Transport and Allied Workers Union (TAWU), 178, 179
Transport and General Workers Union (TGWU), 51, 52, 179-83; mentioned, 27, 56, 107, 178
Tribal "elders," 146
"Tribe," 243*n*
Tribes, 13, 14. *See also* African tribes
Trusteeship agreement, 13
Tumbo, C.S.K., 57, 226; mentioned, 227, 229-31

Uganda, 227. *See also* Railway strike
Union, 45, 49, 61, 62
Union collectors, 186, 187
Union demands, 90. *See also* Demands, union
Union entrepreneur, 77, 78. *See also* Entrepreneurs
Union leaders, 105, 106, 187; mentioned, 249*n*
Union leadership, 75, 76, 79-83, 84, 125. *See also* Union leaders
Union membership, 86, 88-90
Union officers, 68, 78, 213-16
Union offices, 40, 41
Unionism, 118, 140, 141. *See also* Trade unionism
Unionists, 45, 46, 74, 117. *See also* Trade unionists

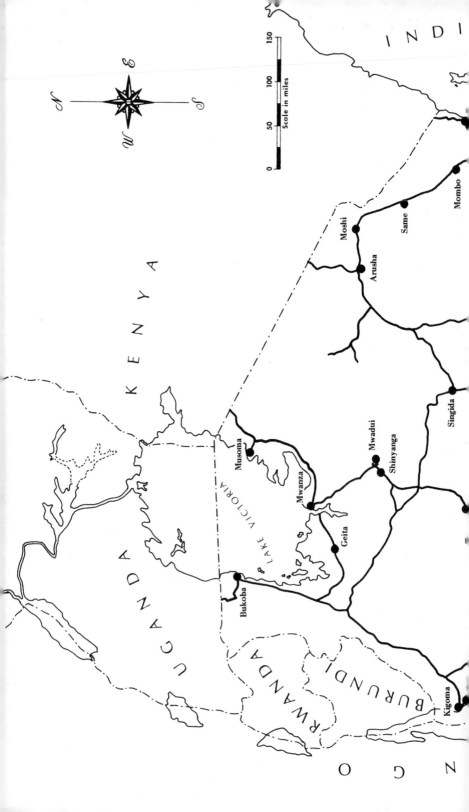